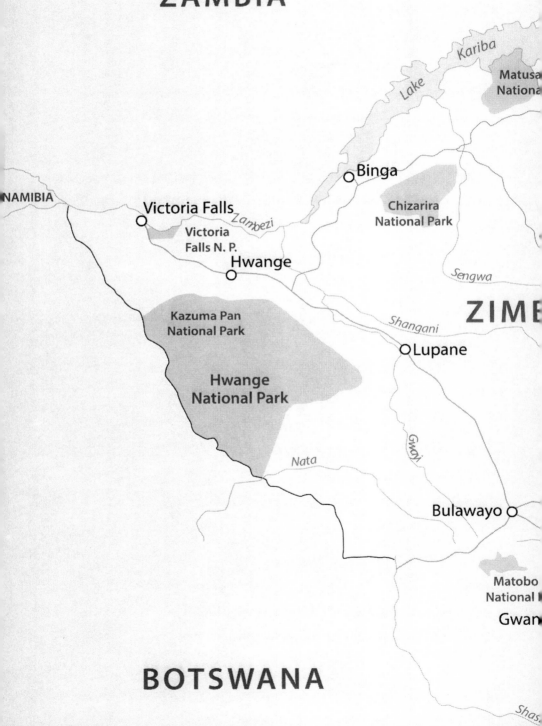

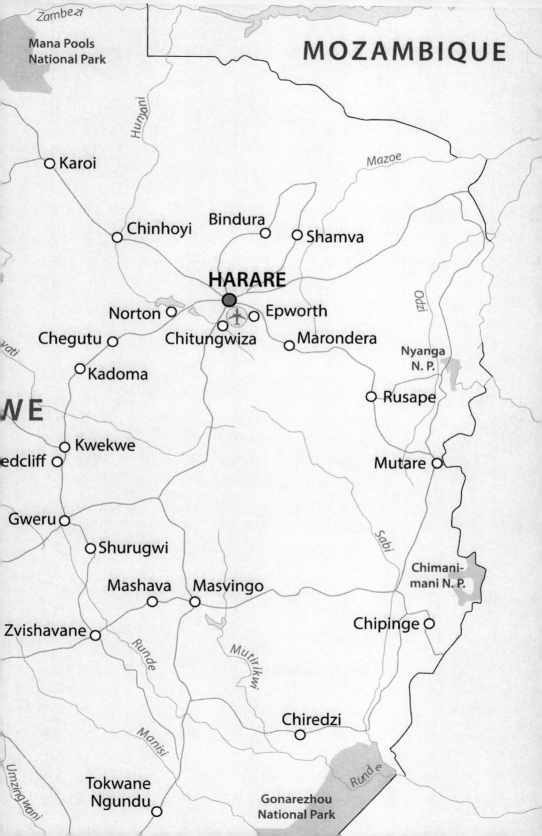

To
Live
in
Paradise

A Memoir of Dreams Found and
Dreams Lost in the Heart of Africa

To Live in Paradise

A Memoir of Dreams Found and
Dreams Lost in the Heart of Africa

Cindi McVey

HOMEBOUND
PUBLICATIONS
Independent Publisher of Contemplative Titles

PUBLISHED BY HOMEBOUND PUBLICATIONS

This book is based on actual events. Some names have been changed for privacy purposes.

For bulk ordering information or permissions write:
Homebound Publications, PO Box 1442
Pawcatuck, Connecticut 06379 United States of America
Visit us at: www.homeboundpublications.com

FIRST EDITION
ISBN: 978-1-938846-25-0 (pbk)

BOOK DESIGN
Front Cover Images
© Crossed Giraffes with Elephants by Pearl Media (shutterstock.com)
© Cheetah by Richard Whinston (shutterstock.com)
© African Bush Viper by Willie Davis (shutterstock.com)
© An African sunset in Hwange National Park by Villiers Steyn (shutterstock.com)
© Close up African Elephant by Donovan van Staden (shutterstock.com)
© Interior Map by Rainer Lesniewski (shutterstock.com)
Cover and Interior Design: Leslie M. Browning

Library of Congress Cataloging-in-Publication Data

McVey, Cindi.
  To live in paradise / by Cindi McVey. —First edition.
    pages cm
  ISBN 978-1-938846-25-0 (paperback)
  1. McVey, Cindi. 2. McVey, Cindi—Travel—Zimbabwe. 3. Americans—Zimbabwe--Biography. 4. Businesswomen—Zimbabwe—Biography. 5. Young women—Zimbabwe—Biography. 6. Zimbabwe—History—1980- 7. Social conflict—Zimbabwe—History--20th century. 8. Social change—Zimbabwe—History—20th century. 9. Zimbabwe—Social conditions—1980- 10. Zimbabwe--Description and travel. I. Title.
  DT2999.M35A3 2014
  968.9105'1—dc23
  [B]
                                                                            2013049414

10 9 8 7 6 5 4 3 2 1

Homebound Publications holds a fervor for environmental conservation. We are ever-mindful of our "carbon footprint". Our books are printed on paper with chain of custody certification from the Forest Stewardship Council, Sustainable Forestry Initiative, and the Programme for the Endorsement of Forest Certification. This ensures that, in every step of the process, from the tree to the reader's hands, that the paper our books are printed on has come from sustainably managed forests. Furthermore, each year Homebound Publications donates 1% of our annual income to an ecological or humanitarian charity. To learn more about this year's charity visit www.homeboundpublications.com.

For My Mother

Part One

Chapter One

W ith bags packed, I made my way to the airport for a midnight flight out of Anchorage. I felt an eerie excitement as I drove in pitch-black darkness along deserted lanes. The streetlights stood muted behind a veil of falling snow, giving a surreal quality to the hushed night. I still carried my guilt and felt like a thief sneaking away from the responsible path, slipping off for adventure.

As I sat back in my plane seat and felt the jet pulling away from Earth, my mind was calmer than I could ever remember. I had done it. I had blasted out of the orbit I was stuck in, and jetting off into a boundless unknown. I looked out the window down into the vast darkness, filled with satisfaction at flying over that chasm which had held me back.

* * * * *

Surely I must be crazy. Really I could say I had it all, and here I wanted to leave. I was blessed with a terrific job, the perfect apartment, my family nearby and a close circle of friends. And for someone whose passion was nature, how could anything be more spectacular than a home in the Last Frontier. As a private pilot, I took flight over Alaska's sprawl of wilderness, soaring above rugged mountains, feeling lighter than air as I cruised amongst the clouds. In awe, I gazed down into the splintered depths of ice-blue glaciers, feeding rivers like molten steel that rolled out to shimmering inlets. With my mother or a friend next to me, we'd eagerly peer into the deep green below for glimpses of wide-antlered moose, or scan the inlet's waters for the pearly humps of beluga whales. All the while, noble bald eagles glided with easy freedom off the plane's wingtips.

So why then exactly, did I have such an urge to flee? Actually, I felt guilty about it. I should be more appreciative, I told myself, for the good fortune of being born in one of the most inspiring places on Earth. After all, I had been raised by parents who celebrated Alaska as their Shangri La.

Certainly I'd run out of patience with the never-ending trial of being snowed under for six months of the year. Now at thirty, I wryly calculated I'd spent half my life trudging through winter's icy clutches. It seemed a cruelty of nature to have so few months when a cushion of grass lay under foot, and windows could be thrown open to fresh air.

And that was a big part of it. I hated spending so much time closeted indoors. I envied other accountants who thrived in their desk jobs, wishing it could be me. Meanwhile, sitting at my desk, I longed to feel the brush of a warm breeze against my cheek, and to hear the lilting echoes of songbirds. One consolation was that my office had a large window, letting in a sprinkle of sunlight, and through which I looked upon a lushly leafed tree growing from a square in the pavement. This tree had been brought from another place where the climate was different, and when the more Spartan native trees all turned yellow and lost their leaves in autumn, it carried on being lush and green. When winter's flurries arrived, the snow clung heavily to its leaves, while next to it the austere branches of the native trees rested unburdened. Gazing out my office window, with the Arctic afternoon already drowsy in winter twilight, I often thought how I, too, seemed out of sync.

But more than just feeling as though planted in the wrong spot, something in the back of my mind needled me. I couldn't stop thinking I'd tumbled into a rut that wasn't my groove, and felt a growing panic that I needed to find a way out. As time passed, with both excitement and a little apprehension, I realized my only cure would be to set sail for distant parts, and leave behind the place where I'd spent every year of my life.

* * * * *

Like an oilskin chart to a pirate's treasure, sprawled on the wall above my desk hung a colorful map of the world. Glinting in a dapple of light, during stolen hours at work my friend Mary and I would study it and amuse ourselves by discussing the endless places for adventure. Certainly the vastness of the United States itself held intrigue, with its own grand fusion of pined mountains, sunbaked deserts, whispered forests and beckoning plains. Yet something pulled me farther away. The wandering blood that had spurred my ancestors over the ocean to America also pulsed in my veins like an urge that couldn't be subdued. Only in a foreign land could I find my cure.

As the months went by, with Mary's help I narrowed the options. Having had my fill of wintry weather, I flatly ruled out northern destinations. And not wanting to make things too difficult, I decided to set out for somewhere that spoke English. I'd once spent a few weeks hiking the evergreen hills of New Zealand, and found myself enchanted. Or instead, what about the wide plains of sunny Australia? But no, I knew this voyage must take me to a place with unusual possibilities, even perhaps some measure of risk. It should be a place where people's lives were lived differently from anything I'd ever known.

One enticing option was southern Africa, which I'd already visited twice, the first time six years earlier. On this trip I'd been subtly captivated by the friendly country of Zimbabwe, drawn to her rich landscape of bold African bush, breezy woodlands, and fields of wild grass where buck browsed untroubled. Although her charm was blemished by the towns' ramshackle colonial buildings, their faded paint peeling and fronted by littered sidewalks, she was still an alluring prospect and I began to be swayed.

As a wildlife enthusiast, Mary also awarded Zimbabwe high marks on our list. She too had visited this Eden-like country with its enviable climate, easygoing folk and low crime, which made an appealing spot for adventure. So after months of entertaining debates, we reached the conclusion of our game and all that was left was for me to put the plan into action.

* * * * *

Actually, Zimbabwe was an ironic choice. Because while I'd been thrilled by my first trek into southern Africa in 1992, during the few weeks I'd spent in Zimbabwe she didn't strike me as a place to call home. To begin with, even though a decade had passed since the end of her civil war, in this land of opportunity I found a country still hobbled and suppressed. Catching my attention the most were all the ready-for-the-junkyard cars and old buses clattering about, unbelievably not a new one to be seen. This circumstance was the natural outcome of a bizarre law that banned the importation of vehicles, plus a lack of assembly plants in the country. Also puzzling to find were bare store shelves, kept empty in part by extortionate customs duties and surely an unnecessary deprivation. Zimbabweans struggled to buy such basics as toothpaste and ink pens, not to mention the unavailable "luxuries" of magazines, spices, and anything other than rudimentary clothing.

On my first wanderings into this beautiful domain I was also astonished, in a tourist's amused way, by Zim's antiquated phones still used in 1992, which resembled those in the U.S. during the 1930s. A caller had to shout over crackling party lines, while his neighbors might be listening in. Television and radio amounted to a couple of mundane government stations. A washing machine was a rare find, with most laundry being laboriously scrubbed by hand. My Zimbabwean peers had their own eccentric style of dress, with men wearing shorts that barely covered their buttocks in 1970s style, along with rough-cut locally made shoes of brushed animal hide. Women's wear was meager, especially footwear, the ladies' battered heels looking like Depression Era dustbowl fashion. And while Coca-Cola had reached into this forgotten corner of the globe, it came only in recyclable glass bottles, the same as an early 1900s collectible.

It seemed I'd stumbled back several decades in time, landing in a place with a dose of dilapidation laid upon it, its people deprived of much outside news so their point of view could be skewed, then mixed with a measure of simplicity from having only the very basics in life. Topped off with some odd laws such as taxing working wives at 90% in order to keep them at home, I confidently commented at the time, "I'd never live here!"

Four years passed before I next ventured to southern Africa in 1996, on this trip allotting *The Country That Time Forgot* only a few days. Once again I was astounded on my visit to Zimbabwe—yet this time in a completely opposite way. Wide-eyed and speechless, I looked upon a bounty of shiny new vehicles whizzing about. Next to the old masonry buildings peeling in dirty pastels, soared modern highrises of glinting glass. In my friends' homes were now computers and fax machines, satellite dishes and VCRs, CD players and cell phones, plus just-out-of-the-box washing machines and microwaves. With amazement I looked upon magazine racks full of foreign newspapers, store shelves full of everything, photo shops, video stores, and even a trendy clothing outlet or two. I discovered Zimbabweans could now buy contact lenses and sunglasses, and they even had the Internet! Plus, as a mark of progressive thinking, I was told wives were now taxed the same as men. I could hardly believe that in only a few years, and as an outcome of an economic plan put in motion with encouragement from the International Monetary Fund, the country could change so drastically.

With this momentum of a revved up economic engine, one sector to benefit was wildlife. A now thriving tourism industry meant a breeding herd of game had become a valuable asset, and particularly in arid parts of the country, private ranch land was turned into wildlife sanctuaries. Intrinsically, this also meant the protection of birds, reptiles, amphibians, rabbits and rodents, beetles and butterflies. Zimbabwe was exactly my kind of paradise, this vigorous land abundant with the world's most intriguing fauna.

And when I scouted the map for a destination to launch myself, above all it had to be a place where nature dominated. There weren't many spots on the globe that could outdo Zimbabwe on this account, and now combined with her economic renaissance, this flourishing country became the obvious choice.

* * * * *

Yet the next step of my plot took me into reality, and I suddenly found myself intimidated. Although my scheming with Mary had sounded practical enough, it now dawned on me that a real life-changing journey would mean quitting my comfortable job, giving up my hard-to-come-by apartment, selling my Bronco, packing my things, and jetting off to a land as far as I could go from home. A pesky whisper in the back of my mind said might it not be better to keep to the safe path, buying a nice little house and filling it with my favorite things. Certainly the idea of spending the years ahead in my secure little circle also had its appeal. Perhaps I wouldn't like it in another place, or couldn't get a job. What if I ended up lonely, and found myself unhappy on that far-off foreign soil.

Yet this intriguing thought of a faraway land was exactly what kept me yearning, and when another friend made an interesting—if not entirely practical—suggestion of simply trying it out for a few months, I was conspiring once more. Yes, that's right, I thought to myself, if I could wrangle three months off from my good-natured boss, then I'd have my job and home waiting for me, if things didn't work out on the other side of the world. While I wasn't convinced I could make it happen, I still pressed myself to think of a way to persuade him to grant me several months of leave.

Unexpectedly, an opportunity soon appeared while he and I attended a Medicaid conference in Baltimore, put on jointly by the National Healthcare Lawyers Association and the American Association of Healthcare Attorneys. No surprise, the conference was as exciting as the name suggests, a week of tedium spent in sterile rooms of subdued lighting and grey decor. The atmosphere could make adventurous pursuits appealing to anyone, and my plea for three months to traipse off to Africa seem downright reasonable.

As conference guests, one evening my boss and I were invited to a reception at the aquarium, where our hosts generously plied us with alcohol. After snagging a couple of meatballs on toothpicks we went off on a stroll, casually looking at tanks filled with creatures from the deep, sipping our drinks all the while. At the indoor pool we relaxed on bleachers and sipped plenty more, watching the lively dolphins put on a show. After a few hours we walked back to the hotel, making our way along the waterfront in the mystic darkness of late evening. A tantalizing smell of sea air whispered round us, mixing with lapping waves that sparkled with moonlight, and when mingled with the pleasantness of the wine, drew us into talk of adventure and the freedom to pursue our dreams. Sensing my chance, I took a deep breath and asked for a few months off to head out to Africa. While I was prepared to beg, make concessions, or at least give a long justification, instead to my surprise he simply said yes.

Next week back in the reality of the office I fully expected him to renege. But he didn't, so I wasted no time in making my plans before either he, or I, could change our minds. Mary helpfully gave me the name of a friend, Georgie, with whom I could stay in Zimbabwe, and I swiftly completed my plans. I'd leave Alaska's winter at its coldest and darkest, and fly off into the southern hemisphere's summer sunshine.

Chapter Two

|||||||||||||||||||||||||||||||||||||||||||||||||||||||||||||||||||||||||||||||||||||

S prightly and fiftyish, Georgie had close cropped hair and a swirl about her like a blustery breeze. She'd come to meet me at the Harare airport, and I'd be staying with her for these few months. Scuttling me into her old Mercedes of faded green, like a mother hen scooping me under her wing, she whisked me off on a route through the center of the city, Zimbabwe's largest and its capital.

"I've got a lovely room set aside for you, with windows looking onto the garden. And I can find out who you need to talk to about accounting jobs if you like. Is there anything in particular you prefer for breakfast?" Georgie chatted on in her open and direct way, with that lyrical Zimbabwean accent.

"Oh, I'm happy with most anything. Whatever's easiest," I replied, my thoughts wandering as we pushed through the buzz of downtown. Thinking back to my first visit six years earlier, Harare (Huh-rar-ee) had been sleepy then, but now I was surprised to see tides of pedestrians flowing alongside feverish boulevards. Although the city was even dirtier, with grime in every crack and trash pounded into sidewalks, at least now an array of glinting skyscrapers was shooting upward. People in business suits clipped along with purpose, mixing with poorer folk who streamed in and out of older shops. Its rhythm gave a stronger beat to my own enthusiasm, and reawakened a familiar connection with the place.

The hum of the city carried us along with it, and soon we were gliding through Georgie's tidy neighborhood. I leaned close to the window, and peering out thought how this could be a friendly suburb in the States from the 1950s, with one added attraction. It looked nestled amidst a botanical garden, where an azure sky competed with the trees' lushness to command space overhead. Fuchsia-blossomed hedges looked barely contained, ready to burst out in unruly exuberance. Splashes of budding yellow, pink, red and orange were in dizzying abundance. Even Georgie's small garden was a palate of perkiness, a jumble of plants and flowers in every shape and rainbow hue. So marvelously opposite from the frozen and colorless Arctic, and I thought to myself, "Now this is my groove!!"

That evening Georgie had friends round for dinner and her living room filled with a celebratory mood. Their cheerfulness was contagious. I leaned back in an overstuffed chair, my head feeling light and every nerve tingling, partly from the long flights, but even more from sensing adventures were soon to begin.

I sipped at my wine and let the flurry in my mind settle, my feet starting to touch the ground. As the velvet blackness of evening descended, Georgie's son Darren showed up unexpectedly. His mother lit up with joy, when out of nowhere he let himself in through the front door. He'd just driven three hours from the town of Kwekwe, where he supervised the drilling operations of a gold mine. Having come direct from a drill site, still in work shorts and with sleeves rolled up, his wavy brown hair was tousled, and he was smudged with dirt and grease. But I saw a confident spring in his step, and his blue eyes sparked with all the vitality of someone living the adventures and risks of a frontier. His tanned face hinted of laughter and he brought an irresistible energy to the room. From that first moment I felt a flicker of comradeship between us. Yet the furthest thing from my mind was a romantic entanglement. Little did I realize, however, at that instant my destiny had taken a sharp turn down an unmarked path, with the accelerator stuck to the floor.

Over the next few days Darren and I spent hardly a moment apart. He willingly took on the role of attentive and chivalrous guardian, helping me get settled by arranging such details as a car and post box. Every minute spent with him lured me in more. His optimism and zest for life was an elixir from which I couldn't pull away. Our friendship quickly flourished amidst an Africa now awash in fortifying summer rains.

One sunny afternoon our shared passion for flying had us venturing out to the small plane airport for a look around. While we strolled along the taxiway under a bright sun, admiring the finer points of each plane, it was already too late when we noticed the sky in the distance had completely disappeared, a mass of dark clouds blanketing to the ground. With disbelief we saw the horizon being swallowed up, and for a moment watched as the engulfing blackness boiled towards us, the earth vanishing before our eyes.

"We'd better run!" Darren shouted over the rumble of the storm, grabbing my hand. As we sprinted for the car, a curtain of rain charged down the airstrip towards us. Within seconds we were enveloped in an ocean of downpour, instantly soaked to the skin. So we simply stopped running, out of breath and laughing, the deluge pouring over us. Darren swept me up in his arms, the vigor of the elements echoed in his embrace. My eyes closed softly as I realized I'd found that first missing piece of the puzzle. The energy here and this world of new possibilities giving me the courage to try anything. From my core to my fingertips, I felt life soaking through me.

* * * * *

My spirit soared as beneath us the narrow highway rushed away. For me nothing was more irresistible than streaking along an infinite road toward parts unknown. Added to the excitement was entrusting myself to Darren, whom I'd met only the week before. Still, I had every confidence in this enterprising man, now at the wheel of the ten-ton truck we cruised in. At thirty-one he'd been working in the rough business of exploration drilling for several years, and these interludes from the loneliness of a bush-life put him on a high. He chatted away with enthusiasm now, setting spark to a cigarette with elbows precariously holding the wheel.

As a sun-flooded countryside swept by, I sat relaxed in the passenger seat; still as snow-white as the Arctic landscape I'd just fled.

With the window open wide, it felt exhilarating to have left behind my snow-swept existence, and those endless days in an office toiling over computer and ledgers. Now, as a plush breeze tossed my hair and stroked my skin with a silky caress, I had that enviable sense of being exactly where I should be.

Gazing out the truck window I watched as a potent land glided past, its mix of airy woodlands, hardy grasses, and open African skies ringing with possibility. I glanced over at Darren and was sure he also felt the energy of it all. He was animated as he leaned forward in his seat, not leaving any detail unexplained of the places and things we'd encounter.

Our destination was the town of Victoria Falls, where Darren needed to collect a piece of machinery. We had split the drive by spending the previous night in Kwekwe. At dawn our plan had been to cover the last four hundred miles that day. Yet maddeningly, a delay had kept us at anchor until noon. Spending the morning killing time, with each minute dragging torturously by, had made us all the more edgy to get on the road. Now breezing along the open highway, our frustrations dissolved into the billowy warmth of summer.

Having just begun to feel the wind in our sails, we approached the outskirts of Gweru—a medium-sized town in African terms— where the highway widened from two to four lanes. My attention was fully on Darren, listening close as he talked over the hum of the truck engine, and when he hesitated I automatically glanced out and also noticed something seemed odd. For one thing, we saw no cars streaming along what should have been a busy thoroughfare. And curiously in the distance, pedestrians darted furtively across the roadway. Then, just as a few red tiled roofs began to peek above the treetops, we were startled to see a car motoring towards us in our lane.

"What's going on up there?" Darren casually called out his window to the driver, as we pulled up alongside.

"There are riots in town and they've blocked the road," was his firm reply. "No one is being allowed through. You'll have to turn around and go back."

Darren and I both shifted in our seats at this unsettling news, although it was not entirely a surprise. During my first few days in the capital of Harare there'd also been rumors of workers demonstrating there, protesting the skyrocketing costs of staples such as bread, sugar and cornmeal. However, neither of us had witnessed a march, nor was anyone we knew affected in the slightest way, so it seemed only a minor drama.

And now, to have to go back! Surely it couldn't be that bad. Darren and I were still feeling triumphant at finally making it on our way, such that the thought of turning around was out of the question. We hardly had to discuss it—with a glance at each other, we knew we would press on. Meanwhile, as we drifted steadily closer to town, before us was the disquieting sight of even more people hurrying on foot and scattering off. Many dodged across the treed meadows, while in our lane up ahead the few cars were turning away from town. Ominously, I noticed that on the other side of the median all lanes coming out were empty. As Darren and I began to wonder about our next step, we spied several vehicles peeling off on a track into the trees.

For my part, I was only mildly nervous. I had always felt at ease among good-natured Zimbabweans. I sensed no hostility in the air even now, and as we discussed what to do Darren was also calm. We'd been on the road for less than a half hour and determinedly wanted to continue.

"Well, since you're the one venturing into foreign territory," Darren said casually, "I'll leave the final decision to you."

I didn't have to consider for long. "Really, the situation doesn't feel all that threatening," I replied matter-of-factly. I also took comfort in being seated up in a sturdy truck. "Why don't we go a little further and see how things look?" I suggested. Then too, I couldn't resist the lure of that mysterious trail nearby, watching cars disappear into its shady wood.

"Alright then," Darren pronounced, steering in that direction.

Soon we were bumping over a rutted path that wound through scrubby trees, invitingly open at first, then gradually closing in. Obviously only small pickups sometimes ventured through here, while recent rains had turned parts of the track into soft mud. There'd be no way to turn around, but just as we began to think we'd made a mistake, we popped out behind a building on the light-industrial side of town.

Edging the truck onto a paved road, as we crept along Darren studied the low masonry buildings, trying to find his bearings. The two-lane streets lay thick with people milling in every direction, yet eerily hushed. While the atmosphere felt charged, these folks weren't rioting and surprisingly took little notice of us, despite no other cars being about. Shop doors were all locked tight, and I was only a little unnerved when now and then we stalled for a minute as Darren struggled with the truck's unfamiliar gears. All the while, the quiet crowds shifted past us, occasionally glancing up with curiosity at the only white people to be seen. They were the workers of this little town, going home early since businesses had quickly closed at the first hint of trouble. With buses being privately owned and their drivers also staying away from possible danger, everyone was left to find their way home on foot.

Darren and I could only guess that the rumored riots must be in some other part of town. From the happenings in Harare, I knew the discontent was in response to the latest spike in inflation, part of a dangerous cycle of economic stresses recently set in motion. The first blow had come six weeks earlier when Zimbabwe's president had promised hefty payouts to war veterans, to be paid from the country's already debt-burdened coffers. At the same time, he demanded that holders of foreign currency suddenly convert their funds into untradeable local dollars. Then doing the final damage, at his heed the government issued an expropriation wish list comprising three-quarters of private farmland. With agriculture being the country's premier industry, even announcing such desires dealt a deadly right-hook to Zimbabwe's economy. The immediate fallout had been a plummet in the value of its currency, and now six weeks on, the economic domino effect of inflation had hit.

As I studied the scene out the truck window, I expected these African workers to be in faded, threadbare castoffs. Instead, I was heartened to see them all tidily dressed in clothes that looked new, some in workshop overalls, although most wearing shirts and trousers, and ladies in dresses. Their clothes were neat and in good repair, and the only clue they were actually poor folk—that is, not by their standards but by my own First World notions—was that sometimes an outfit was ill-fitting or of last decade's style. This was because much of what they wore was Salvation Army leftovers. One fellow walked by in a t-shirt commemorating the Boston Marathon, while another sported a Dallas Cowboys cap. I found myself smiling at the thought that home wasn't really so far away. Then I even had a little laugh, seeing a fellow whose shirt front showed Austin Powers in that mischievous sideways grin, while on the back was written, "Shall we shag now or later?"

Amongst this subdued flooding to the streets of these ordinary citizens, I felt only slightly uneasy, instead mostly drawn to the excitement, while also supportive of their rally against the government's mismanagement of affairs. I knew that when a Zimbabwean had a complaint, a letter to his parliamentarian or other means of voicing descent had no real effect. Taking to the streets en masse was one of their few options. And besides, when it came to my own safety, I sensed no ill will towards Darren and myself, and knew that on the whole Zimbabweans would rather avoid a scuffle.

Just when it seemed time was dragging on and we wondered if we'd ever get back on the road to Victoria Falls, Darren recognized where we were and had the truck rolling along slightly faster than the crowds. Now with assurance, he steered a beeline toward the intersection where the highway eased south out of town. Yet scarcely had we sighed with relief when the road became increasingly crowded, some of the people now waving us back and raising their voices to, "You can't go there, you must turn around!"

Undeterred, Darren simply ignored them and kept pushing on to the intersection, now in sight and only a few blocks away.

"Stop! Stop! You must go back!"

Reluctantly Darren slowed, then leaned out the truck window to coolly ask, "What's the problem?"

"There are riots in the center of town. They are smashing windows, and taking people's bicycles and destroying them. They will break your truck!"

"We're just going up to the highway turnoff," Darren calmly explained, knowing it wouldn't help to become annoyed. With exasperation, I also thought it unnecessary to wheel around, when a clear path within a minute's distance lay before us.

Darren didn't wait for a reply and pushed forward again. However, others further along became more insistent, confident they had *de facto* authority in the situation. A few stubbornly stood in the path of our truck, hands on hips. An edge of tension crept into the air. Yet to see the turnoff only yards ahead when we'd made it this far, just to turn back, was unthinkable. A few in the crowd, however, became more belligerent, planting themselves in front of us and with a frown pointing that we must go back. It now seemed to continue might only provoke them, so Darren began to ask out his window if anyone knew a different route to the highway. A few worrisome minutes passed with only headshakes no, before a grubby, thin ruffian-type stepped forward from the crowd. With eyes darting furtively down, in what I took as humility but could have easily alluded to more dubious motives, he quietly said, "I know another way."

Mostly it was his bushy, unkempt hair and hint of a swagger that gave him the look of a down-and-out hoodlum. Plus his baggy clothes needed a good washing, making it unlikely he went to a job each day. Yet he wasn't in rags and his face had a gentleness, and something about his demeanor put me at ease. He came over to my side of the truck, and as he reached up to pull himself onto the passenger seat I scooted to the middle onto the engine cover. Our shoulders were nearly touching and I tried not to bristle at his griminess, while for his part he tried not to be embarrassed by it.

Darren and I put our trust in him as he took us off the town's main routes, and wasted no time in directing us through a labyrinth of motionless neighborhood streets, where the middle-class folk had already tucked themselves safely inside their homes. He said little and brushed off our small talk, as we eventually eased onto winding back roads, leaving swirls of red dust behind us.

While our instincts told us he was an honest chap, there was always a chance that Darren and I were being lead into some kind of ambush. Unfamiliar territory can loom suspicious, and the increasingly shabbier outskirts of town were looking skeptical to us, making Darren raise an eyebrow and ask often of our un-talkative guide, "Are you sure you know the way?" With no change in expression, he'd softly reply, "Yes…, I think so." We hadn't needed to worry though, as finally in the distance we saw the highway stretching before us, just as a bus zoomed in our direction back towards town. To this our guide suddenly leapt from the truck before Darren could fully stop, grabbing the bus fare I quickly handed down. In his haste he never once glanced back, while Darren and I gratefully called out our thanks. In the next instant he vanished into the bus and was gone.

This helpful stranger seemed to me a microcosm of Africa herself. With a rough exterior that can put a person on guard, an outside appearance that reminds of hardships endured. Yet underneath is a goodness and honesty. This was the Africa I wanted to have as a friend. Like our peculiar guide I trusted her, and sensed she had much to teach me.

And never did it occur to me that these rumblings might be a warning, an early sign that paradise could be in peril.

* * * * *

As Darren and I pressed on through a sun-soaked afternoon and then into amber evening, the highway cut through an endless expanse of robust bushland, sometimes more scrubby, sometimes closely packed with rugged trees, and occasionally rolling with low hills. I found the breadth to the earth here inspiring, with an uncomplicated tranquility that gave a sense of abandon. The few unhurried small towns, whose stout buildings were mainly whitewashed masonry squares, took only a minute or two to pass through. In this country not shackled with heavy industrialization, the land resonated with a restful freedom. The countryside we traveled through was especially undisturbed, since few cleared expanses lay in this district unsuited to farming. Now the middle of the rainy season, the trees and grass were a healthy green. Immersed amongst it all, I felt as unrestrained as Africa herself.

As darkness settled in we reached the halfway milepost between Bulawayo and Victoria Falls, where one of the few places to stay was an inviting roadside inn. Its mood fit the landscape, exuding old country charm in a common Zimbabwean style, with sturdy white masonry walls and a steep thatched roof. Inside, the towering interior of the roof was crisscrossed by wooden poles painted black with tar to discourage borer beetles from devouring them. From the beams hung fans beating out a subtle rhythm, and keeping a freshness to the air inside.

The evening had turned late by the time Darren and I stepped into the main room for dinner, where only a few guests still talked quietly at tables. The room's satin light cast a candlelight feel, while a black night pressed at the windows. The warm evening was soft and sensual, so different from the crisp coolness of the Alaska I'd just left. Such a polar change made a new energy spark within me, and an enlivening sense of anything being possible. The two of us edged close as we settled into chairs. In the hushed night, with the power of Africa resting in the shadows, I looked over to Darren, his face lit with excitement.

"I'm going to open my own drilling company," he said leaning in, determined. "I'm telling you, there are opportunities out there. All I need to get started is one rig, and I know of a used one for sale," Darren's eyes glinted while I eagerly listened, completely drawn into his magic.

"I've got it all planned out," he rushed on. "I know the perfect guys to hire for a crew, and I've got a few ideas for business prospects." He flashed a smile as he paused.

Caught up in his passionate schemes, I also wanted to be a part of whatever intrigues lay ahead. Without hesitation, I would let the whim of fate sweep me along to wherever it might take me.

Chapter Three

||||||||||||||||||||||||||||||||||||||||||||||||||||||||||||||||||||||||||||||||||||||||||||||||||||||||

E verywhere around me nature tumbled out in vibrant flour-
ish. For an Alaskan, such warmth and bloom was nothing
less than addictive. After my decision to stay in Zimbabwe
for a while, Darren and I had rented a cottage on the outskirts of Harare. Now, to simply sit on its veranda was marvelous,
drawing in lungfuls of fresh air, while the saturating rays of the African sun thawed bones chilled by thirty years in the Arctic. All my
senses were indulged, as a seductive scent of wild jasmine floated
about me, and overhead a symphony of songbirds filled the trees
with harmonies. Later at that hushed hour between afternoon and
evening when the earth softens to a whisper, only to be heard was
the cooing of doves, its delicate music echoing over the golden
fields, and through the woodland's growing shadows.

Drawn into the heart of this irresistible new world, my habit
soon became to set out on horseback in late afternoon. As a mellowing sun cast the land in amber, I could catch glimpses of russet-colored bushbuck, dainty-hoofed and diminutive duiker, and
spiral-horned kudu bounding among the bushes and tall grass. At
the sight of them I'd lean forward and urge my mount to gallop
in pursuit, attempting to follow a darting antelope and capture a
breath of its freedom.

Often I ambled through the reeds of a nearby marsh, where a
peacefulness drifted out in the mingled calls of its birdlife, placidly

making ground nests and fishing in the dam's mirrored water. As my horse pushed through tall grass, sometimes I'd disturb a hidden flock of sleeping marsh owls. To my enjoyment a dozen or more would suddenly rise gently around me, then drowsily circle above my head, waiting for me and my mount to pass before settling back to their grassy beds.

As a welcoming gift Georgie presented me with a little mutt, a fluffy ball of black and white patches that, at six weeks old, easily fit in my hand. This concoction of several breeds of terrier with a splash of dachshund thrown in, when all cleaned up looked the perfect little lap dog, and certainly wasn't my first choice for a companion. Yet I soon discovered she was a go-for-it scraper with all the toughness of a Rottweiler, whose fluffy coat was more often-tangled in brambles and mud. I named her Scruff, and from the start she shared my passion for horse rides, chasing along behind and refusing to catch a lift upon my mount even through the rough stuff. As my horse gingerly stepped through vines on a waterlogged path, I watched as Scruff stubbornly struggled behind, battling her way by half swimming, half climbing, through the murky entanglement. Upon reaching a swiftly moving creek, I looked on nervously as pint-size Scruff got carried off downstream. But with a terrier's determination, she'd always find a way to claw herself up the other side.

I was living my dream in perfection, while enticingly, something about the place made it exist just outside the bounds of reality. People's lives had a specter of the fairytale, and like a cat drawn to a flickering sunbeam I wanted to capture some of this essence for myself. Each passing week brought new enchantments. Even driving the quiet highway south from Harare, on our way to visit Darren's sister and brother-in-law, cast me under a spell. Tracing through miles of peaceful countryside, the scene of hardy grasslands scattered with thorn trees and scrub, a proud antelope here and there amongst it, was an exotic new world to me.

Several hours of driving eased us from the capital's higher altitude of five thousand feet, down to the Lowveld where summer temperatures were often a hundred degrees. The vigor of the heat only added to its alchemy, where every deep-rooted tree, every thorny bush, and every blade of tough grass stood with that stoic strength needed to survive in this part of the world. While I couldn't call it lush nor was the land sparse, and I knew there weren't many places on Earth where the wildlife was more abundant.

Eventually we turned onto a dirt shortcut and for a half hour passed through the healthy scrub of several cattle ranches. Another twenty minutes on a gravel road took us nearly to his sister's home, as we cut through a vastness of sugar cane farms. Closer to her place we drove through miles of vigorous cane, looking like bright green reeds on steroids, soaring up high as a house and a truly unbelievable sight to my Arctic eye.

Rounding a bend, we motored past several baboons sitting relaxed on their haunches beside the road, a green wall of cane towering behind them. Although considered by many to be vermin, I found them intriguing, these haughty gremlins like something out of Oz. These fellows barely gave us a glance as we whisked by, too occupied with the succulent cane stalks they held in nimble fingers, and crunched with sharp, pearly white teeth. Further along a stout lady warthog—cousin to the wild pig, yet more dignified with ivory tusks and athletic build—trotted across in front of us. As she darted out of the long grass, her six little hogs jogged in a tidy line after her. Everyone, including mom, perked their thin piggy tails with bouncing tuft on the end, in antenna fashion skyward.

The midday sun was beating down when we pulled into Darren's sister's drive, her home resting on the banks of an offshoot of the Mtilikwe River. We piled out of the hot car and then Darren led me round to her award-winning "garden", as Zimbabweans called their yards, where for a moment I stared in awe. Spread before me was an acre of emerald lawn, flanked by boldly flowering bushes, hanging baskets of exotic plants, tumbling vines, and thick swathes of flowerbeds in pink, orange and yellow. Mahoganies lay a cool blanket of shadow here and there, while a curved stone stairway swept invitingly down to the river's edge.

"Jane?" Darren called as he stepped briefly into the house. "Jane, are you here?"

"Wow, this heat is intense," he said, as he walked back out. Even the air conditioner couldn't keep up. "Let's wait on the veranda, where it's coolest."

We settled into wicker chairs and gazed down to the placid flow of the river.

"I feel refreshed already," I sighed as I leaned back. "The tranquility here is hypnotic."

In this hot, dry climate, rivers and lakes seemed poured from the carafes of gods, and a sun-soaked afternoon spent by the water's edge in the Lowveld, was to go to the next level above earthliness.

"Oh hello, you've arrived!" Jane exclaimed with a warm smile as she glided out from the house, a cheerful sight in the swish of a bright skirt and painted red toenails. "Welcome, it's wonderful to finally meet you."

She gave me a friendly kiss on the cheek and Darren a hug, her shiny black hair framing a soft and beautiful face, her eyes a magical mix of greens and hazels. When passing through the house earlier, I noticed her signed paintings on the walls, proving her gift as an artist.

A few minutes later her husband Vic showed up as well, his hair bleached white-blond by the sun, and arriving upon us with all the vitality of someone built trim and athletic. In their wildlife translocation business, the gutsy Vic had to fly his helicopter at a bare skim above the treetops, to swiftly steer darting buck towards capture pens. Next on the ground, on foot he and his crew herded the sharp-horned antelope into a succession of paddocks, by holding up black drapes to encourage the animals forward. Vic's fleet-footedness had many times saved him, when an intrepid beast suddenly plunged towards the blackness with daggered horns sweeping furiously down, Vic missing being impaled by millimeters.

"Nathan and Shawna will be home from school soon," Jane commented as she brought out the tea tray.

"Shawna is just the sweetest girl," Darren said of his seven-year-old niece. "I can't wait for you to meet the two of them. Cinz, do you remember me telling you about our enterprising Nathaniel?"

Nathan was only nine, yet already a conservationist in his own right. Six years earlier during The Great Drought of 1992, when half the country's wildlife perished, Zimbabweans launched a collective effort to save the desperate animals. Wells were drilled deep into parched ground to keep watering points trickling, while hay and feed were painstakingly laid out upon the dusty earth. Many antelope, zebra, warthog, and giraffe were moved to areas that fared slightly better, with some so near to breathing their last, that people could simply walk up and lead them off to trucks. Young Nathan had done his part by collecting dying tortoises, which he'd then looked after, bred up, and now six years on, was releasing back into the wild.

By late afternoon the saturating heat had begun to mellow, Nathan and Shawna luring us out of the shade to bat a ball around in a backyard game of cricket, the British version of baseball. Next to us, the gray-blue river eased soothingly by, and as the bright yellow of afternoon slipped to evening's peach glow, the crickets' trills built to a pulsing whir. For someone who'd just fled the Arctic, such an atmosphere was a potent elixir.

"Hey everyone, here's your cool drinks," Jane called out from the veranda, setting down cold cokes and beers.

As we got comfortable in our chairs, Vic began their usual evening ritual of, "Who can spot the sneaky crocodiles?" A clandestine trio lay in stealth under the calm surface of the river below. Near them, a half dozen yawning hippos began to waken as the day cooled, rising in the water like expanding gray balloons. Their baritone grunts and spray mixed with our laughing chatter, its harmony blending into the fading amber of a setting sun. Sitting there soaking it all up, I couldn't believe people lived such a charmed existence, and that even more, it might be within my grasp.

The next morning, before the lazy dawn had a chance to turn into hot day, Darren and I were out with Vic to help with his day's chores. First on the list was to vaccinate and deworm twenty wild sable antelope held for resale. Before we got underway, I snuck a peek at them through a slit in their enclosure, as high as a house to keep them from leaping out, made of rough-cut posts lined up tight to form a wall, like a Middle Ages fortress. Even in this confined space they looked majestic, and took my breath away. Their black scimitar horns were honed to a sharp tip, which they could agilely wield at any foe, whether a natural predator, or more likely, a poacher and his pack of snarling dogs. Their coats were a sleek luxuriousness of the deepest brown, with clean white undersides and bold blazes. Steadfastly territorial, the proud sable were known for fighting fearlessly to the end rather than fleeing to safety elsewhere. Unfortunately, this tenaciousness at standing their ground meant their numbers had suffered greatly from poaching and loss of habitat.

The first step was to move the sable into a holding pen, then one at a time, let each through to a padded crush. In an instant, a handler swiftly gripped the base of each horn, while another placed a cloth over its eyes. During this moment of stillness, before the sable began to fight against the blindness, Darren and I quickly helped Vic, squirting deworming paste in its mouth, giving it a vaccine injection, and pouring a line of tick repellant along its back. We tried to work fast with each nervous animal, while being vigilant of a thrash from a daggered horn. I did my part in wordless awe, thinking how they seemed a myth's creation, this exotic buck who looked kin to the fabled unicorn.

With the sable done and back safely in their pens, our next task was to load a dozen young kudu and zebra onto a truck, to be released on ranches of new owners. All went smoothly and soon Vic led us off to check on the orphaned elephants, being trained for elephant-back safaris near tourist spots. If a pachyderm could be called graceful these surely were, as we amusingly joined them in kicking a soccer ball around. Imposing beasts though they were, they made me feel perfectly at ease as I stroked the rock-hard roughness of their hides, while with agile trunk tips they gingerly took feed from my hand. Such an "ordinary" day spent with Vic certainly didn't fit with my notion of a job in the real world, and once again, I felt I'd stumbled into a curious place down the road from Alice's Wonderland.

"Thank you for the most amazing visit," I said the next morning as I hugged Jane good-bye, holding tight for a moment. I didn't want to leave their little corner of paradise. Darren, however, was looking forward to seeing his Uncle Sam and Aunt Janet.

"They're not really my aunt and uncle, you know," Darren explained, as he looked over to me from the driver's seat. "They're actually friends of my mum, but I spent a lot of time with them growing up. Their cattle ranch was a great place for a boy to spend school holidays. I have many enjoyable—not to mention, suspenseful—memories of my times with them."

His visits had been in the 1970s during Zimbabwe's tumultuous civil war, when Sam and Janet sometimes had to defend their home against attacks from bush fighters. During these shootouts, as they ducked under windows to return fire, Janet's hands were often burned raw from reloading the searing hot cartridge holders of Sam's guns. These Wild West tales were made all the more real, when later Janet pointed out the bullet holes still showing in the walls of their farmhouse.

Their arid ranch lay several hours southwest of Darren's sister, in the Beitbridge district. Here the heat can be of the cruelest intensity, and the ground merely coarse sand. With scant rain the thorny vegetation is sparse and brittle, yet still the land feels powerful in its severity. And having come from the Arctic, to me theirs was yet another life to envy. We swam in the warm pool with the Labradors, traipsed about the unbridled acres where their finely bred Brahman cattle shared the land with the African game, and checked in on three orphaned giraffe raised by Sam and Janet who had now grown up to towering heights. I'd always thought of giraffes as mild characters, since from a distance their leggy swagger looked deceptively slow and docile. Yet now standing next to one, I knew I was in the presence of a true giant with all his strength, as he arced his long neck down to look at me with curiosity, standing somewhere about his knobby knees. Even with his head stretched low I couldn't quite touch his stubs of horns, perched above long-lashed eyes, and had to settle for stroking the rich blondness of a lean muscled shoulder. When they eventually grew bored of us they simply turned away, and I watched still captivated as they wandered off in those lanky, smooth strides.

On the last evening of our marvelous few days, the four of us decided quiet time together watching TV would be a relaxing end to our visit. As usual, Sam was the first to head off to bed. Darren, Janet and I drowsily called out goodnight from the living room, as he sauntered off with heavy feet down the hall. But not a minute later he bolted back to us, suddenly wide-eyed and alert.

"There's a snake in the bedroom!!" he burst out to our looks of surprise. "Now I know why the cats were acting so strange earlier."

We all jumped up in a flurry, with Darren grabbing a cricket bat and handing Sam his walking stick for a weapon. We rushed off toward the bedroom, which was really no more than a screened porch, having cinderblock walls on only two sides.

"It's critical we catch the snake before it slithers off and finds itself a nice hiding spot," Darren declared.

I could imagine it liking the attractively dark pantry, or maybe the snug clothes closet.

"Where is it? Where is it?" the three of us demanded of Sam. I hung near the back, like everyone leery of where to step.

"I think it might have gone under the bed," he replied with a nervous edge to his voice.

At this Darren, Sam and Janet all leapt onto the mattress, thinking it a safer vantage point, while I manned my video camera from a cautious distance near the door. I still wanted to catch a glimpse of him though. This was a golden opportunity for an Arctic refugee, the chance to see a snake, or any interesting reptile for that matter.

So much for our "relaxing" evening, I thought with a smile. As I looked on, the three of them stood uneasily peering down from the bed, scanning round for the shy intruder. With his stick, Sam gingerly edged the nightstand away from the bed.

"It's here! Hit it!" he suddenly shouted.

With a lunge Darren tried to get a whack at it, but in a glistening black streak the snake ducked behind the stand again, the two men bouncing atop the bed and awkwardly swinging their "weapons" like a well-practiced comedy team.

"Your sticks are too short. Here, use these," Janet ordered, passing a mop and broom as she hopped back onto the mattress alongside them. As the creature blasted out from behind the nightstand once again, I watched with amusement, as the trio vaulted in unison to the opposite edge of the bed like acrobats on a trampoline.

Pressing itself against the wall, the elegant reptile hissed menacingly in desperation. I did feel sorry for our sneaky visitor, although it was out of the question he'd be left to sleep in the same house as us. Finally, Sam was able to pin it and Darren quickly smacked it on the head. Sam then carefully lifted its limp body with the mop handle, and we all nervously admired the steely gray beauty, adrenaline still pumping in our veins.

"Just as I thought," Janet proclaimed, "a Mozambican Spitting Cobra!" One of Africa's most lethal, with pinpoint accuracy at shooting venom up to eight feet.

Feeling excitement rather than fear, each little adventure confirmed to me that this was where I needed to be. While I might not know exactly what I was searching for, I knew for certain that Africa was the path to find it.

* * * * *

For me, life had definitely taken a turn for the better. I had unquestionably found the place, the people, the groove for me. Yet for Darren, life was more about practical matters, and his plans weren't going well at all. Although he'd poured his energy into trying to get one business scheme or another off the ground, by the time I'd been in the country for six months none of his deals had come off. He'd mainly been searching out drilling opportunities, and when none of these came to pass we started tossing ideas about for something to do together, since I also needed to earn a living.

In the evening we'd wander out to the veranda with frosty beers, and in the drowsy warmth of day's end, settle into chairs and sound out ideas. Our cottage sat on the outskirts of town, and we looked past a swathe of lawn where thoroughbreds grazed, to a gentle rise of countryside. The scene lay brushed in watercolor softness, as the setting sun eased from golden to amber then mauve, a collage of quiet meadows, strips of scrub, and distant lines of timber. I felt a potency to this land which gave me confidence that any venture could succeed.

Darren and I weighed up the options within our reach, given our limited capital. We did have one thing working in our favor, being that all our savings were in US currency. This meant that in Zimbabwe dollar terms our money was growing. When I'd first arrived in January the exchange rate stood at sixteen Zim dollars to the greenback. However, by midyear it'd climbed through the twenties, and now August, the rate was closing in on thirty-to-one.

So what could Darren and I do? Somehow we couldn't get excited about restaurants or retail shops. We discussed opening an oil and lube franchise, but couldn't muster up enthusiasm for that either. How about buying rundown houses, fixing them up and reselling them? Yet the real estate market was in the doldrums. There was the possibility of transport, although that business was a whole other story in itself. We learned that the price for goat meat was good, and for the short term thought about driving around the countryside and buying goats in the communal areas, then selling them to the butchery. But that too had its downsides. Certainly there must be something both practical and profitable that interested us.

Expectantly, we flipped through the paper to look in the classifieds under *Business Opportunities*. Reading down the column, we came across an ad that listed various farming enterprises for sale. Now there was something that sounded appealing, and after all, agriculture was the premier industry in Zimbabwe. Even more persuasive was the many success stories of those who'd earned an enviable living—as good or better than what I'd made as a well paid professional—in farming here over the years.

Buying a farm soon seemed like a terrific idea. When Darren and I added up how much we'd need to start a business in town, plus buy a house, it seemed an even better plan to combine those funds for a farm. And for me I'd be living a childhood dream. While growing up in the Arctic I'd desired only to be a cattle rancher, imagining the feel of a warm wind as I loped my steed over rolling, wide acres. Farming was certainly an appealing lifestyle: making a living in open spaces, along with the satisfaction of contributing to the cycle of life by planting, growing and harvesting. Not to mention other perks like having as many dogs and horses as we could want. And while in the U.S. farming had become an almost forgotten industry, in Zimbabwe it reigned as the predominate sector of society, with much expertise at hand, and an infrastructure that ran like a well-oiled machine.

In the past Darren and I couldn't have hoped to own a farm, since the expensive price tags had made it out of our reach. But real estate hadn't caught up with the Zim dollar's devaluation. As each month in 1998 went by, our US dollars were giving us more purchasing power. Also, the market for farms was depressed, keeping prices low. This was mostly due to the troubling announcement at the end of 1997 by Zimbabwe's president Robert Mugabe, declaring that the government would acquire, with payment uncertain, thousands of farms on which to settle peasants. Added to this, many agricultural commodity prices were down. Yet we knew it was this volatile mix of factors that made buying a farm within our reach.

There is the old saying that the more risk involved, the higher the potential for gain. What gave us confidence more than anything, were the many farmers who'd earned a good living in Zimbabwe over the years. Like Darren's friend Jean in Raffingora, Sam and Janet's daughter, an extraordinary character who'd accomplished much with hard work and determination.

Slim and energetic, Jean was a chartered accountant who'd packed it all in, trading her office and urban existence for the earthy life on a tobacco farm. Always composed and with an obvious confidence, I knew she had to be a special kind of woman to run a farm in Zimbabwe by herself. Jean had earned the respect of workers who were mostly men with scant education, and from a society in which women were expected to take orders, not give them.

"Here we are!" Darren announced, as we pulled up in front of Jean's farmhouse. Tumbling out to meet us in the sunshine was the usual Zimbabwean welcomers—a crowd of exuberant dogs.

"As I'm sure you've discovered, anyone living in, or even just visiting Zimbabwe, must have some fondness for mutts," Darren commented as we stepped out of the car and into chaos.

"Yes, I've noticed few homes are without this canine flurry," I replied with a laugh. On farms, a jostling gang of a half dozen may be bumping underfoot in a melee of fur and wagging tongues, the first to pour out the front gate in a boisterous greeting.

"Nzeve! Basil! All of you, get out of the way," Jean was soon there attempting to impart order. "You'll just have to push your way through," she advised, waving us towards the veranda. "Tendai, please bring out the tea tray," Jean called back into the house as we settled into comfortable chairs. "So what is this I hear, that you want to go farming?"

"Well, it seems to be the best opportunity for us," Darren started to explain, amid a swirl of thumping tails and wet noses.

As always, Jean could be counted upon to be unhesitatingly frank. "Yes, I can certainly understand the draw of owning a farm. And it's true you are in a unique position at the moment because of the currency devaluation. But you'd better act fast," she warned, "because even though farms are at their cheapest ever, it won't take long before prices catch up."

By the time we'd poured out with all of our news, late afternoon had eased upon us and the activities of the farm were winding down for the day.

With a glance at her watch, Jean summarily stood up and insisted, "Come along with me to check on things. I'll show you around the place."

After piling onto two motorbikes—Darren and I, Jean and her young daughter—we buzzed off towards the green fields. Jean's long-legged weimaraners sprinted to catch up then loped easily alongside, smooth muscles rippling under the gloss of pewter coats, long ears and tongues flapping in time with reaching strides.

Streaming through the summer air, it was just as I'd imagined as a child, so long ago. We glided past rows of pert tobacco seedlings, the broad sweep of these fertile fields calling out to me. As we passed through endless acres of young plants straining skyward, drawing in energy from the sun and converting it into the cycle of life, I knew I had a friend in this inspiring land.

We continued to coast along the dirt farm tracks, Jean proudly taking us past her herd of fat cattle, then through wide acres of cornstalks reaching high above our heads. We toured her chicken houses from which she sold hundreds of eggs every day, and gazed upon her flock of wooly sheep that would end up in Jean's butchery, where she manned the high-powered band saw herself. As the sun began to mellow and sink low in the sky, we looked out across the sparkling waters of the dam she'd built, to feed the irrigation systems she had designed. Erewhon Farm was a thriving business employing hundreds, and certainly an inspiration to Darren and me. Jean had created her own idyllic corner in paradise, and we silently hoped fortune would shine upon us, too, and we'd find such a future for ourselves.

Chapter Four

||||||||||||||||||||||||||||||||||||||||||||||||||||||||||||||||||||||||||||||||||||||||||||||||||||

I magine a continent of such expanse that upon it rests no less than fifty-four nations. From islands forgotten and windswept as Cape Verde, to the sprawling Congo, Algeria, and Sudan, each a million square miles. Woven into the fabric of Africa's vastness, are dense jungles dripping with humidity in which thousands of creatures thrive, yet also unbounded barren waves of scorched sand. The mighty rivers of the Nile and Congo flow long and wide, not to be outdone by several lakes as big as seas. There are people whose lives follow the rhythm of the salty ocean, while others live in languid villages nestled into lush mountain slopes. Along with metropolises of modern high-rises, are still unexplored corners where a white-skinned person has never been seen.

Tucked in the southeast of the continent sits landlocked Zimbabwe. She possesses few natural lakes and perennial rivers, and is further hindered by erratic, seasonal rains. Even so, she manages to be lush enough to nurture an abundance of wildlife and humanity. At 150,000 square miles, just smaller than California and larger than Montana, she's been a country of amazingly diverse industry, fostering vast mining, manufacturing, unrivaled agriculture, fishing, timber and tourism. Twelve million Zimbabweans called her home, seventy percent hailing from the Shona tribe, and Ndebele making up much of the rest. As far as Indians, whites and Asians, when I arrived in the country they numbered no more than eighty thousand, or not even a scant one percent.

Eager to learn about this beautiful nation that captivated me, I hunted out more about her past. I discovered that ancestors of today's Shona settled in this region over a thousand years ago, and because they are Bantu-speaking like tribes of central and east Africa, historians guess the early Shona may have migrated down from these places. Yet it can't be known for sure, since they had no written language until the twentieth century, leaving many blank pages in the story of their past.

I also learned that the early Shona, like most still today, were tillers of the soil. In centuries long ago they first planted grains of north African origin, such as sorghum and millet. Several hundred years later rice from Asia found its way to Africa. In the 1600s, however, arrival of corn from the Americas brought about a most favored staple. Four centuries on, this American import of corn, or maize, is still the mainstay of the Zimbabwean diet.

I soon realized that meat, on the other hand, was a rarer treat to the supper pot. Although for generations the Shona have kept goats and cattle, this was often meant not so much as foodstuff, but as a form of asset accumulation. While in centuries past Europeans laid claim to land, gold and gems as their "financial" security, most Africans were instead using livestock as their wealth. For many this habit of the ages hasn't changed, and with limited options for preserving wealth, is practiced still today.

Cattle hadn't always been their only form of capital, however, and hundreds of years ago the Shona collected the prized gold and ivory, using it to barter with Arab and Portuguese traders in exchange for cloth, beads and tools. As far back as 1667, European merchants recorded that the Shona traded an astonishing 3,300 pounds of gold that year. Unfortunately for their grandchildren, by the middle of the next century less than 1,000 pounds per year could be gleaned from the land. Only a few decades on in the late 1700s, their take was down to a meager 100 pounds a year. By the mid nineteenth century, all the gold that could be tapped without modern mining techniques was spent. Doubling the calamity, by this time elephants were a fraction of their former glory in areas dominated by human settlement. This steady loss of gold and ivory shriveled up much of the ancient Shona's wealth before the twentieth century dawned.

I knew the Shona to be deeply spiritual, feeling strong ties to their ancestors and other mystical forces, considered to play a weighty hand in steering society and daily life. At times a Shona may feel the need to contact those departed, and it isn't uncommon for a witchdoctor to be called upon to help bridge the divide to the afterlife. Another practice, familiar to me because it's also found among Alaskan tribes, is the tradition of having a clan totem. Often symbolized by an animal, even in modern times a Zimbabwean's surname might be Nzou, meaning elephant, or the frequently heard Moyo, the word for heart. In days long ago the clan symbol had practical uses, such as announcing prerogative over land, when clan motifs in carved stone were used to mark out claimed territory.

While Zimbabwe's other large group of people, the Ndebele, also feel strong ties to their ancestral spirits, their history reads unlike any other tribe. They are, in fact, related to the Zulus of South Africa. During tumultuous times there in 1837, in a flight from these troubles, the Ndebele migrated up to what later became southwestern Zimbabwe. They found a harsh territory, dry and stony, but at least uninhabited. While agriculturists like their Shona neighbors, they were also admired for their thriving herds of cattle. The bounty of their herds may have owed in part to their most distinctive, and potent, cultural difference to the Shona. A militaristic tradition existed within their society, the prowess of young Ndebele warriors renowned. Also better equipped in weaponry and shields than the more pastoral Shona lads, the Ndebele often used this to their advantage to raid Shona settlements nearest their territory. On these incursions they demanded tribute from terrified villagers, extorting the cream of their cattle, along with stores of grain, tools and other livestock, plus whatever else took their fancy.

It was already the dawn of the modern era, in the 1890s, when whites began to settle in Zimbabwe and put down roots in this untamed bushland. Most interesting to me was discovering a similar tale to my home of Alaska, which before becoming a U.S. possession in 1867, for decades saw a scattering of Russian traders and missionaries tramping about its fringes. It wasn't until the last days of the nineteenth century, that whites finally ventured in greater numbers up to the mountains and tundra of the Arctic. Rumors of gold abounded, and virtually overnight thousands of adventurous Americans flooded northward. The ships steaming out of Seattle took them to the shores of southeastern Alaska, where makeshift towns and commerce sprung up within days. These rustic settlements were abuzz with the excitement of untold possibilities and dreams of fortune, as spirited characters set out to make their riches in this uncharted corner of the world.

Zimbabwe, too, felt the early boot steps of foreign traders. Mainly Arabs, Indians and Portuguese, who made forays into Zimbabwe's wilderness for hundreds of years before white pioneers packed their wagons and headed out in search of a better life there. Like Alaska, it was the prospect of gold at the end of the nineteenth century, that lured a stream of white-skinned folk to this other frontier land. Also a northern trek, most of these trailblazers started their journey in South Africa, where the roads and railways began. Some of these adventurers were from Europe, but many had been born in South Africa, like their parents and grandparents before them. Making them as through and through African as my ancestors were American.

With hundreds of "gold miners" pushing north into Zimbabwe, dusty outposts quickly evolved to sell supplies and a warm bath to weary travelers. As in Alaska's Gold Rush era, these recently established "towns" were mainly a collection of tents, where men vastly outnumbered women, and where everyone needed an unflinching will, in what could be a merciless land.

Both Alaska's and Zimbabwe's much heralded gold rushes fizzled before a decade could pass. And in the end, shopkeepers and hotel owners made their fortunes, rather than those who sifted through tons of dirt, one bucketful at a time. Decades later, corporate gold mines using modern methods would find success in both places. However, it was the tenacious resolve of those who had forged into undeveloped territory, establishing the first roads and supply lines, that enabled today's cities and industry to spring forth.

Despite the failed gold rush, the years before and after World War I saw more white settlers carrying their hopes along the trail to Zimbabwe. She was known as Rhodesia then, now a British colony such that many of her settlers came from England. Cattle ranching was one venture widely tried, in spite of heavy losses to predators and disease. But at least this was slightly more profitable than the experiments of the early farmers, searching out which crops might grow best in this country of varied climates and soils.

The hopeful years after World War II attracted many more immigrants, both black and white. Each black Zimbabwean I've chatted with about his family, had a parent or grandparent who trekked from Zambia, Mozambique or Malawi. The 1950s were boom years in Zim, still called Rhodesia, and blacks from neighboring countries were also drawn to the opportunities in this prospering nation. Within a few decades, the population of Zimbabwe rapidly swelled from several hundred thousand, to millions.

In the early 1960s, with a sweep of the hand, Britain changed the status of most of its colonies into independent nations. Zimbabwe's colonial neighbors of Zambia and Malawi were now, quite abruptly, self-ruled. Yet Zimbabwe, with her growing web of roads, electricity and telephone networks, numerous schools and hospitals, along with burgeoning industry, was much more developed than these other former colonies. A great deal was at stake for the people of this rapidly evolving nation. Amid this blossoming modernity, the two societies that existed there—the modern and the tribal—both wanted to be rulers of their destiny. Was there a smooth way forward for this disparate country, where cities and industry with Western-style legal and political systems, co-existed next to still primitive tribal villages?

For more than a decade, bitter civil war raged. And while Britain and others tried to ease Zimbabwe into a democratic government, communist countries provided arms and military training to rebels. Throughout the late 1960s and '70s these communist-backed militants waged brutal guerilla warfare, often aimed at civilians. So it was with immense relief for all the country's citizens when the conflict, which had left its scars on Zimbabweans from every walk of life, finally ended. On April 18, 1980 a new nation was born, melding its Western-style legal and civil systems with its new communist influences, along with its age-old tribal laws and customs. Modern power stations, communication systems, the stock exchange, banking and other industry, would be under the same umbrella as villages where water was still fetched by bucket on a woman's head, transportation mostly by foot, and cooking done over a simple fire.

By the 1990s when I came to know her, Zimbabwe, the stunning land trumpeted as Africa's Paradise, was applauded as the continent's success story. A hopeful model for all of Africa. The country was peaceful and economically prosperous, with a middle class enjoying a First World standard, her citizens among the best educated in Africa, and rural peasants living well compared to others in the world. Plus, a diverse industrial base and seemingly broad-minded government meant infinite opportunity for an even better life. Everywhere she was cheered because, without a doubt, the future could only be bright.

Chapter Five

||||||||||||||||||||||||||||||||||||||||||||||||||||||||||||||||||||||||||||||||||||||||||||||||||

T ucked at the southern end of Zimbabwe's rugged Eastern Highlands lay the peaceful community of Chipinge. The area's claim to fame was its burgeoning coffee and tea plantations, and as Darren and I wound along a narrow highway hugging mountain slopes, I found a comforting feel to the quiet valleys below, patterned in deep green rows of coffee trees and fields of leafy tea.

Helping us in our continuing quest for a farm were Darren's friends Karen and Trevor, who lived on a remote farm in Chipinge. Trevor's father was the first to settle on his farm's virgin hills, in the not-so-distant past of the 1960s. The nation was still evolving from frontier into modern state, back then when he made a living raising cattle on his mountainous acres bordering Mozambique. By the mid '70s, however, it had become a perilous place to have a home, since guerillas fighting in Zimbabwe's civil war camped out just across the border.

It takes only one tragic moment to change destiny, as it did for Trevor's family. Early one morning, Trevor's father unsuspectingly opened the door of his workshop, and surprised a band of jittery guerillas hiding there. Instantly, he was shot at point blank range. Trevor was just nine. His mother, still stunned with grief, had no choice but to pack a suitcase and abandon her home, moving with her children into town and leaving the farm vacant, their livestock in the care of family farming nearby.

More than ten years passed before Trevor managed to return to his father's empty farm, determined to make it a success once again. He found little awaiting him there. The cattle were now few in number, the buildings falling down, the scraps of equipment remaining in musty sheds nearly rusted away. It didn't help that Trevor's property was literally where the road ended, at the very edge of the district. In his first years back he didn't own a car, and instead hiked to neighbors to catch rides into Chipinge town.

With title deeds to the land as his only real asset, Trevor borrowed what he could to revive his father's farm. Cattle wasn't the booming industry it'd been in his father's day, and coffee looked to be the crop best suited to the place. For a couple of seasons Trevor also tried to grow burley tobacco, although the rainfall on his farm proved too much for this crop. Despite his setbacks he'd made phenomenal achievements, having built up a prospering business from a start of very little capital. His compelling story gave Darren and me all the more determination. It showed that in Zimbabwe a person truly could make something for himself through sheer hard work. This was a land that would reward our efforts with dividends.

"So you managed to find us alright," Trevor said with a smile as he strode towards our car. "We're a bit off the beaten track out here."

We stepped out into summer sunshine, the air fresh from an afternoon rain.

"Trevor, my friend—it's good to see you," Darren said as they shook hands. "I'd like you to meet Cindi."

"It's wonderful out here," I gushed. "You're lucky to live in such a beautiful place."

"Yes, you're right. And it's great being back on the family farm, making a go of it. Come, let's have tea on the veranda."

Karen, pretty and blond, her face always lit with an easy smile, joined us in the comforting shade of their veranda.

"Now, what you need to know about coffee farming is . . ." For the next couple of hours Trevor, in his contemplative way, caught us up on the latest in farming trends and prices. He was a fountain of knowledge, and like all Zimbabweans, generous in helping us.

By late afternoon the day had softened to gold, and with our news caught up and teapot empty, Trevor said enticingly, "Would you like to go explore?" Two motorbikes stood on the front lawn just asking to be revved up, and soon Darren and I were streaking after Trevor and Karen, down their curved drive and out the front gate. We first zipped past the many brick outbuildings Trevor had built, then for a few minutes slowly motored alongside the hum of activity in the workers' village. Next, I held on tight to Darren as we charged up near vertical hills between rows of robust coffee trees. At the top we bumped along a rough track only that day cleared by a backhoe, Trevor proudly showing us the roads he was putting in. Further along we paused at a ridge where a breathtaking view swept out across the rolling farm, its quilted squares of coffee fields laid out amongst the vast bushland. This little corner of Earth looked healthy and strong, and as we scanned the broad scape before us, I felt the blood pump stronger in my veins. Being amidst this vibrant land made me want to experience so much more.

Just gazing upon so much possibility kept us enthralled, and by the time we cruised off again the sun had shifted low in the sky. Not wanting to go back yet, we decided to follow a track to the edge of Trevor's farm, where a small "border post" guarded a dirt path slipping into Mozambique. Puttering on up to a rounded ridge, I was surprised to find the hilltop border station to simply be a grass roofed hut. Next to it, a flimsy pole balanced upon two feeble stumps served as a boom across the walking path. From out of the hut's low door appeared the humble Mozambican border guard, who quietly greeted us in bare feet, wearing a dingy shirt and ragged calf-length pants. Although he was affable, in a detached sort of way, I saw a weariness to his spirit that was unsettling. Probably because the buoyant nature of Zimbabweans, along with their good fortune in African terms, kept the debilitated side of the continent more dis-tant. With a slight wave of his hand, he authorized our little jaunt into his country and we motored off down the track.

Immediately upon gliding over the ridge top, I sensed a dis-tinctly different mood than Zimbabwe. To begin with, this side of the mountain had captured and held back the fog, keeping it from creeping over the ridge into Zim, and here leaving misty slopes in a shifting languidness. Even more noticeable was the lack of development, giving an atmosphere of a place left behind by the march of time. It was almost eerie, as though we meandered through the fleeting image of a troubled dream. We saw few people and only scant signs of activity, as we carefully kept to the narrow path. Unspent land mines lurked off the beaten track, lethal leftovers from the '70s civil war when used to deter guerillas from making border raids. When now and then we did come across a family's homestead, I saw virtually nothing modern about it. Just a couple of mud huts with patches of corn and veggies, a few sleepy cattle and lean chickens. We didn't linger long in the disheartening mood of this other world, and soon stole back across the border to the cheerfulness of Zimbabwe. I was glad to return, wanting to think of my new companion Africa only in terms of prosperity, strength and hope.

The next morning Darren and I were eager to get to the main reason for our visit. We had learned of several farms for sale in the area, and with coffee being one of the more profitable crops, were excited to look at opportunities here. Trevor volunteered as our guide, and the three of us set out from his place. A half hour of driving first took us to the hamlet of Chipinge, where we then eased southwest out of town.

We continued to trace through gently hilled country, abundantly lush and green, the Eastern Highlands having the most reliable rainfall in the country. The appeal of this blooming landscape as a home had me crossing fingers even more.

After another half hour, Darren and I realized just how generous Trevor was to give of his time. Eventually the paved road narrowed to a single lane, our curiosity growing with each passing mile. While driving along, throughout the district I'd seen forest tucked amongst the neat orchards and fields. Now as we traveled further, the countryside took on less of the look of rolling farmland, and more of a backwoods flavor. After an hour since passing through Chipinge town, Trevor finally turned us off the paved strip road and onto a barely visible track, overgrown with high grass.

Pausing, he said to Darren and me, "I think this is the place, but I'm not sure." The unused track looked doubtful as a road to a once successful enterprise. Then Darren exclaimed, "Wait, what's that?" He pointed to a weathered sign, mostly hidden by tall grass, with *Elizabethville* barely readable. We had, indeed, arrived at the right place.

Still skeptical, Trevor let the car roll forward along two nearly invisible tire tracks, a woodland of eucalyptus growing high on each side. We eased into its dimmer light, where in contrast to the sun-baked heat of the paved road we'd just left, the air was invitingly cool. Soft sunlight twinkled around us, filtering down through lofty trees. As we crept along in curious silence, I felt the place called Elizabethville whispering to us.

The first thing we came across was a burley tobacco barn, towering several stories high. Burley tobacco is cured by air and such a barn is really just a roof protecting a labyrinth of beams, from which the tobacco leaves are hung to dry. The sides of the barn were made of removable reed panels that could be adjusted for prevailing breeze and temperature. Nearby stood other structures: tobacco grading sheds, a workshop with a jumble of broken equipment, a network of concrete troughs making up the coffee "factory" to process beans. Like everything else, the farmhouse was a dingy shell, hinting of what must have once been a thriving business. But Darren and I hardly noticed. The prospect of bringing it all to life again had us inspired. We reckoned that such a place was probably the best our bit of capital could buy.

A caretaker crisscrossed us over Elizabethville's steep hills, a feature not usually desirable for a farm. Yet to us the deep green slopes of bush, plus a shadowy ravine with a crystal creek and small waterfall, were alluringly picturesque. The old coffee fields were overgrown, the roads needed work, and the buildings had fallen down, but the challenge of resuscitating this neglected piece of land only fueled our enthusiasm.

Driving to the next property, in a rush of zeal Darren and I thrashed out a ten-year plan for Elizabethville. In our excitement we couldn't imagine any place winning our affection like she had, and even considered not looking at the other two. A shred of rational thinking, however, kept us steered in their direction.

As the steep hills mellowed and we approached Chambonyi Estate, I had to admit that its nearness to Chipinge town was certainly an advantage. And as we eased closer, I noticed how this part of the district had less of a hillbilly quality and more the feel of a prosperous community. While I was drawn to the wilder side of Elizabethville, at the same time I began to feel a reassuring comfort in the stability around Chambonyi.

The farm's entrance led to a well-kept lane, invitingly lined with sturdy oaks swaying to the breeze, our path cutting through tidy rows of young coffee trees. We took the turn that led to the farm buildings rather than the house, not wanting to be too intrusive on the owner. The real estate agent had said that after some bad years financially, the bank had taken the place.

Even so, upon seeing us drive in, the owner walked down from his house and offered to take us around. I noticed a resigned sadness at having to let the place go, as unquestionably the farm was impressive. The buildings, roads, and other improvements were in near perfect condition. And while Elizabethville had no water development, Chambonyi included boreholes and irrigation systems already set up. The farm was gently sloped, perfect for aiding water and airflow, yet not so steep to make cultivating and harvesting difficult. An added bonus was a small guava orchard, and a stand of pines that could be sold for timber in the future. The purchase price was not much different, yet Chambonyi came with a few tractors that actually worked, plus ploughs and other tools, everything in impeccable order.

With our heads still churning over the possibilities for Chambonyi, Darren and I next went to visit the mountaintop farm of Smithfield. My heart skipped a beat as we drove up. Having a home here would be like out of a storybook. She was a beautifully designed place; obviously in her past someone had taken pride in her. Each rectangular field was rimmed with tall oaks, and evenly spaced sprinklers sprouted from underground pipes in uniform grids. While the farm was well planned for its business purpose, it had a personal touch that gave it charm. Although used for cattle grazing at the moment, with no operable equipment, buildings falling down and fields overgrown, Darren and I were still drawn to its peacefulness. Gazing upon the fat cattle meandering through shifting highland mist, the tall grass and surrounding bush in healthy greenness, strong oaks looking protectively down on it all.

The day had been more than I could have imagined. Did dreams really come true? It seemed so, because I was on the verge of exactly that.

In the evening back at Trevor and Karen's, added to all the possibilities of the day, their enthusiasm was contagious. Trevor was full of plans to boost his coffee operations and put in areas of timber, his most ambitious project to build a dam so he could irrigate his plantations. At the same time Karen's farm store was expanding, her customers mostly Mozambicans who didn't have shops nearby. She was in the midst of buying freezers so she could sell meat, something difficult for the locals to find.

With our choice of opportunities and the inspiration of friends, Darren and I were riding a wave of optimism. We decided our best strategy would be to limit our debt, although finding an affordable enterprise where the numbers also worked could be tricky. But the currency exchange rate was still slipping. By the end of September '98 it had fallen to thirty-five Zim dollars to one US, and like everyone we assumed it'd be fifty-to-one by year-end. Although this slide in the currency's value wasn't good for the nation, it gave the two of us with our savings in US dollars more buying power, at least in the short term. We seemed to have fortune on our side, and every confidence that, one way or another, we could make something happen. I felt like I'd won the lottery, with the chance to make a future in this bountiful land.

* * * * *

Before heading north back to Harare, Darren and I decided to steer a course to his sister's for a few days in the Lowveld. After winding our way down through the lush Highland hills, Darren turned our car onto the narrow highway curving southeast through the country. Cruising through lands I'd never before traveled, I watched with curiosity as the shrubbery became steadily sparser and more

parched, until semi-desert. We passed only a lone car or two, and
with this road being the main artery in these parts, it gave the place
a sense of abandonment. Eventually our chatter even faded out,
and our mood became subdued. The lonely aura was all the more
strange because these were communal lands, and in fact, we were
passing through a sprawl of mud hut hamlets.

To me the most unbelievable thing about it, was that these folk
were even trying to live in this withering locale. This land could
never be anything other than a merciless environment for settlement. Ever afterwards, a shroud of sadness came upon me when
journeying through these parts, where the cracking earth had become so very tired, its last drop of energy bled out.

As we slipped on through the brown stillness, amongst this now
scantily treed terrain I saw only small huts, listless goats, and an
occasional thin peasant trudging along. I spied scarcely a blade of
grass, the place laid bare from a manmade epidemic of livestock
overgrazing. The banks of the few stream beds, where once a year
the rains muddied through, had become barren, jagged ravines,
the cruel scarring of erosion leaving the sides falling off in rough
chunks like the flesh of a leper.

With its ruthless climate of trickling rainfall and searing temperatures, I knew this austere corner of Zimbabwe would sprout
sparse vegetation at the best of times. Suitable only for the migrat-
ing herds of elephant and other wildlife that, decades ago, roamed
this flat scrubland. Before people settled here, it was predictable this
harsh place could fall desolate under the constant strain of subsistence living. Only with restraint, resisting the temptation to over-
graze this land of meager bounty, plus frugalness when downing
trees for the nightly fire, might there have been a sustainable future.

Alas, even if change came now, I knew it was too late for this
land. Its plague of nibbling goats meant the more nutritious plants
had been decimated, replaced by the hardier weeds and thorn bushes during brief days of rain. And because the nutrients in the repeatedly cultivated soil had all been drained, the ground could no
longer sustain the large families trying to survive here. Then too,
soil conservation is a low priority for those crushed under poverty,

so each year a bit more of this resource was carried away as dust in the wind.

The scene was an unnerving contrast to the thriving private land around Chipinge we'd just left; a disturbing side to my new friend Africa from which I tried to turn away. Too depressing to face in anything more than hurried glimpses. And I didn't want to consider what might happen if ever the consumed and still fertile should collide.

Chapter Six

IIIIIIIIIIIIIIIIIIIIIIIIIIIIIIIIIIIIIIIIIIIIIIIIIIIIIIIIIIIIIIIIIIIIIIIIIIIIIIIIIIIIIIIII

L uck wasn't going our way with the coffee farms. Before we could tie up a deal, the worldwide price of coffee soared. Any opportunity for Darren and me quickly slipped from our grasp, as prices for properties in Chipinge went equally through the roof. I was astonished at how, in only a couple of months, this isolated and forgotten corner of the country had become "the place to be". Although disappointingly, not for Darren and me.

We couldn't dwell upon such caprices of fate, however, and knuckled down to start our search anew. I expected that making a dream become reality would have some obstacles along the way, and was ready to grind it out.

In our daily perusal of the morning paper, a listing in the classifieds first led us to a mushroom "farm", although it was really a smallholding in a growing Harare suburb. The owner had bought the property when the neighborhood was still undeveloped plots on the outskirts of town. Over the last twenty years, however, Harare's sprawl had engulfed the area and this was now a high priced locale. When Darren and I went to take a look, we drove past winding driveways that led to homes like small mansions, surrounded by manicured gardens and with the Nick Price golf course luxuriantly sprawled at the foot of the hills below. Although the house on the mushroom property was modest enough, and its steep acres of low agricultural value, the terrific view and upscale location made it pricey relative to the income potential from its mushroom sheds. It would have been great living so close to the city, but the numbers just didn't add up, and sadly Darren and I had to pass on this one.

Next we optimistically took ourselves off to Headlands, a picturesque district not far from Harare, where the main crop was tobacco. Plenty of people our age lived there, giving a youthful energy to the area, and like Chipinge many offered to help us get on our feet. Yet despite all the advice and assistance at the ready, once again our pursuits here couldn't get off the ground.

So we continued further afield, to Odzi, a more inconvenient distance from the capital that would add extra transport costs, plus had more difficult farming conditions like unreliable rain. But Darren and I knew we'd have to start from the bottom with a less desirable farm, and brimming with eagerness launched into crop projections, costings, and cash flows. When we came to the bottom line, which showed what we could pay for the property based on its income return, the real estate agent agreed we were making a good offer. However, the owner wasn't of the same opinion, to put it mildly, exploding in an angry outburst when we presented our proposal to him. And once again, that was the end of yet another prospect.

After several months of relentless searching, to our growing frustration Darren and I still hadn't found a farm. Making our quest all the more difficult, the Zimbabwe government had been gifted more funds from donor countries, for the specific reason to buy farms. By law the government had first option on any sale, so we now realized many places weren't even making it to the open market.

At this same time, the whole bizarre and disturbing farm "designations" continued. Like most people, Darren and I were perplexed by the government's actions, who although had both plenty of land to purchase and the donor money to pay for it, were still sending letters to land owners whose properties they wanted to forcibly acquire. Their tactics were another crippling hit to the economy, because banks then cut off loans for these farmers, understandably not wanting to sink money into a place threatened by expropriation.

Yet crazy as it might have sounded, without a second thought Darren and I continued to set our sights on a farm. We knew our opportunity had only come about because of these uncertainties, which had made prices low and within our reach. A convenient coincidence for the Zimbabwe government indeed, I had to think, who was purchasing farms at the same time it was destabilizing the agricultural industry.

Anyway, there were reassuring factors for us, such as the Donors' Conference on Land Reform and Resettlement, held in Harare in September 1998. A remarkable array of local and international organizations joined together for this gallant endeavor, including the Zimbabwe Commercial Farmers' Union and the International Monetary Fund. The gathering was an inspiring worldwide effort, attended by reps from European nations, the U.S., Canada, Australia, Japan, China, South Korea, Argentina, Brazil, and others. Its encouraging outcome was the "Land Reform and Resettlement Program" for Zimbabwe, meant to ease the pressures on the overused communal lands and empower more black farmers.

What's more, like most in the country, Darren and I still felt optimistic about Zimbabwe's future. The land issue was simply one of the many problems the country had tackled over the years. Farm "designations" had been in the air since I came to Zim ten months earlier, and still no properties had been forcibly taken. Not to mention, the government had been buying farms for decades, so this issue had been around for years. It didn't seem critical to our situation over the long term, and most importantly, for the farms the government wanted, it had paid fair prices.

Despite our unwavering confidence, the morale of the nation slipped ever gloomier as the economy staggered under further blows. The important tobacco industry, one of the largest exporters, had its leanest revenues in years. Other agricultural commodity prices had also dived. Added to this, the worldwide gold price hit rock bottom, bleeding another large export. Inflation had climbed to an unimaginable 50%, followed by interest rates also skyrocketing to 50%.

And it'd been a wearisome year for commercial farming. The government's desire to acquire three-quarters of private farmland was taking its toll on the nation. Understandably, farmers thought twice before sinking money and effort into improving their properties, only to lose them. Better to tuck any bit of cash away, saving it for when the farmer might find himself and his family without a home. This withdrawal of funds from development added another nail in the economy's coffin.

As it was, politics in the country hadn't changed much since the new government, headed by Robert Mugabe, had taken the helm in 1980. As the only person to have been president of Zimbabwe, Mugabe ruled with a brass-knuckled fist and snuffed out the flame of any opposition before it could spark. Yet as long as the country's crumble wasn't too glaring, there hadn't been a collective urge to make him keep up standards and be accountable. This was now starting to change.

Among his damaging maneuvers, at midyear 1998 Mugabe sent Zimbabwean troops to the Congo, embroiling the country in the civil war there. Such an expensive military undertaking was devastating to the finances of an already cash-strapped nation. While there were no benefits to the national interests of Zimbabwe, the personal gain from the Congo's diamonds and other wealth was too much for Mugabe and his inner circle to pass up.

Then along with his continuing push to snatch farms, which kept the nation fed and provided livelihoods for millions, Mugabe passed a host of stifling new laws, handcuffing business and pushing nervous investors nearer to the edge. With world commodity prices already down, as companies struggled it was a time when the president needed to support business. Instead, he added to the country's strangulation.

However, all these unfolding dramas were far in the backdrop for Darren and me. Every nation has its issues being worked out in the political sphere, and these episodes playing on the evening news seemed to have little to do with our daily life. We never thought of anything other than launching ourselves in Zimbabwe. For Darren this was his home, the place where he'd been born, like his parents and grandparents before him. It went without saying that his future lay here. All things considered, buying a farm still seemed the best choice for a business and home. When we diligently scanned our map to the destination ahead, we seemed to be on track.

And now with our futures and hopes fusing into one life together, after nearly a year since that first spark had lit between us, Darren and I became engaged. We'd set off on the path ahead together, which although troublesome in the immediate, I was sure would come together in good time.

* * * * *

Besides my future here with Darren, in Africa herself I'd found a playmate, and woke each morning in anticipation of another day in this earthy land whose rhythms moved in sync with my own. Up in the Arctic, time with nature was most often in the wet and cold. So now being turned loose in the African bushland was living life to the ultimate. A favorite way to spend a Saturday was on a paper chase, loosely styled after an English foxhunt, although without any fox or hounds. Simply put, it became a cross-country spree on horseback, of an exhilarating African kind.

Darren and I pulled out of our drive before the sun was fully awake, heading out of town and into countryside that lay sleepy in predawn. Two hours later when we arrived at Tchechenini Lodge the morning had yet to give much warmth, as we joined dozens of others also alighting from pickups and SUVs with a drowsy exuberance. The lodge sat tucked in hilly bushland, heavily wooded and with massive boulders strewn about. Scanning round, I thought how this land of hardy grasses, rocks and thorny scrub, was as far different as could be from the rolling pastures of England. For me, this rugged frontier was unquestionably the preferred choice.

"Come, let's go fortify ourselves," Darren said, taking my hand. We stepped into the lodge where others milled about with coffee and pastries, a low chatter gaining pitch in expectation. Out front sixty tethered horses, knowing something thrilling was afoot, pawed and tossed their handsome heads. The energy built as people of all ages mounted up, settling comfortably into stock saddles and pulling wide-brimmed hats down tight.

Underneath me my mount was a bundle of restlessness, as Darren and I eased into the middle of the group, everyone edging up a rocky hillside. The horde had to pack close to wedge itself onto the footpath, winding through thick bush. Our horses were fresh and stepped out in their strides, ears perked and heads held high, a mass of ready to burst vigor. Riders shared the enthusiasm and a hum of talk mixed with the clattering of horseshoes on stone.

I reveled being in the center of this sweeping energy, a potent mix of strong nature, good friends, and barely contained horsepower. Creating an exponential force like a tidal wave.

The footpath we followed soon crested a ridge, and down the steep opposite side, met with a wider track. As each high stepping stead bounded out from the bushes and onto the track below, it became spontaneous to move into an easy canter. I watched as the mob steadily poured over the ridge in front of me, before being swept along with this sea of vitality, the horses' muscles rippling under silken coats, hooves rhythmically beating the earth, and wide nostrils drawing in the clean air.

As we cantered along in intoxicating motion, the shared vigor of the ride filtered through each of us. Jean's eight-year-old son came from the back, pushing his horse past me and Darren in the middle of the pack, and I watched as he weaved his way through the crowd ahead. Women friends cantered side by side in easy tandem, while young men at the front made a game of jostling each other, and parents and children ran smoothly in tight groups.

Leaving the woodland, we followed the track as it took us onto a prairie-like plain. The pack automatically opened and spread across the expanse in a pulsing wave of equine and human energy, while I enjoyed the high of being caught in the midst of it. The day had now pleasantly warmed, and I watched mesmerized as the yellow grasses parted to my horse's reaching hooves, setting free a thousand flaxen seeds to float in the air, and dreamily mix with the streaming ebony of his mane.

Soon the group had to compress again as we approached the line of bush, everyone moving back onto the track. Now in the cooler air of a shaded wood, we trotted quietly along in filtered light from tall trees, even the horses hushed to an aura of reverence. When the trees thinned out and the shorter bushes reappeared, the sunlight became bright again, sending a ripple of laughter and low snorts through the pack. Our pace became animated, the horses' strong legs clipping along, the riders moving in time with their horses' jog.

Everyone had to rein in when we reached a slope leading down to a lazy river. Once past the tricky part, the horses took pleasure in noisily splashing through the water before bounding up the steep opposite side. Along with everyone I welcomed the spray, a refreshing blast as the heat of late morning built up.

Eventually we stopped next to a lake that lay smooth as glass, its shimmering waters a tonic to these thirsty acres. Spouses who hadn't joined the ride met us in trucks, bringing coolers and snacks, plus indulging us with grooms to unsaddle and hold our mounts. A few in the group rode bareback into the lake for a cooling swim. As I sat on yellow grass comfy as deep straw, looking out at the sunshine gleaming off the horses' strong backs while they grazed, a breeze swirling the musky scents of the outdoors around me, it was like drinking a bewitching potion. To me, this was heaven.

When time to remount, our horses knew we'd be heading for home and pranced to get underway, impatient while riders swung up in the saddles. As we moved out we had to hold our steeds tight, to which they shook their heads in protest, this profusion of tight muscles ready to burst with resistance. We couldn't contain our eagerness for long either, and soon the pack was striding out again. The pace quickened with some of the riders now galloping, grinning wide as their horses stretched their long limbs without urging. At the front horses and riders were in a mock race, while the more cautious of us kept to a slower gait at the back.

Amidst the mild chaos, I let my horse set his own pace. He eagerly moved into a steady gallop, each of his pounding hoof beats pulsing through me like a dose of moonshine. Without thinking I

left Darren behind and sprinted towards the pack ahead, lost in the
rush.

Eventually I slowed to a walk and Darren caught up, and we leisurely made our way back together. The mob was now spread over
miles, and in the winding track through the hills it was difficult to
guess how close anyone might be. Darren and I enjoyed strolling
along just the two of us, and for a moment having this amazing
wilderness to ourselves.

When we arrived back at the lodge everyone was slowly filtering in, descending upon a mouthwatering buffet and slacking their
thirst with ice-cold drinks. Balancing plates on our knees, Darren
and I sat outside chatting with Jean, who told us her farm was doing
well and she expected to have the last of her debt paid off by year's
end. In all the chatter about us was scarcely a word about the government's blunders, and other machinations like the Congolese war
a thousand miles away. To me this was paradise, the perfect place to
make my future.

Chapter Seven

I||||||||||||||||||||||||||||||||||||||||||||||||||||||||||||||||||||||||||||||||||||||||||||||||||||||||||

For my initiation into the country, I now found myself awash in the most phenomenal season of rain. In late November as usual, the heavens had first bestowed this much needed tonic upon a wilting countryside. Yet this year the skies suffered a case of absentmindedness, forgetting to turn the tap off now and then. Here it was only February, with the country already drowning in twice the norm.

With the deluge, the powdery clay track that led to our cottage was stewed into an impassable bog. On those occasions when a yawning sun did appear, Darren and I dashed out and back before the rain let loose again, dissolving the track into slick and deep, tire sucking mud. Without fail each morning, sprouted up through our cottage's concrete floor laid a fluffy field of white mold. Mirrored above our bed on the ceiling, patches of fuzzy gray mold littered spores into our hostage lungs as we slept. The clothes in our closet, and blankets on our bed, were condemned to a continual state of dampness. Of course the electricity was regularly snuffed out by the storms, and if a shower was particularly heavy a flood surged under our front door, transforming the living room into our own personal pond.

The rain also meant that a curious collection of dinosaur-like beetles and other antennaed creatures, seeking shelter from the constant downpour, found our merely moist cottage inviting. One of these critters showed up in a most unexpected spot, on a morning when I was out doing errands. Walking into an office to take care of business, I smiled down at the receptionist as she listened to her phone. I then watched with surprise as she became strangely overcome, her eyes widening while she signed frantically with her hands. Puzzled, I turned to quickly scan the room, before realizing her desperate gestures had something to do with me. Only then did I calmly notice, that upon my fleece jacket perched near the collar, sat a palm-size wall spider. These graceful beings lived on walls of homes and were perfectly harmless, causing me nothing more than a smile now. This one had obviously cuddled up in the fleecy warmth of my jacket, which hung from a hook in our living room, and for a couple of hours I must have been wearing him like a pretty brooch.

While I didn't mind sharing my home with the wall spiders, who at least kept the mosquitoes in check, I was glad that one unwelcome pest had departed after the rains began. Those devious little black ants who had managed to take up residence in our hot water tank. During the dry season, when running my bath I had to be careful to turn the hot water off before the level dropped too low. Otherwise, a revolting swarm of ants would suddenly stream out the faucet and into my bath, with me perched buck-naked in the middle of it. In the two seconds it took my hurrying fingers to shut off the flow, my bath was ruined, with only an empty echo in the hot water tank. Usually I just begrudgingly continued with my bath amid the black deluge, trying not to think of the tiny corpses becoming tangled in my wet hair. The truth was, some days the ants seemed the least inconvenience when it came to bath time.

The cottage's electricity hadn't been properly grounded, and for some reason while the hot water tank heated up, a fierce zing of current surged through the pipes and any trickle of water. When I ran my bath, the red-hot coil in the tank was triggered on, so that all running water was now "charged". If I dared to stand with one shoeless foot on the concrete floor, and one in the tub, I'd be unmercifully reminded of my carelessness with a full-body jolt. I discovered I had to, with utmost caution, either step into the tub directly out of my shoes, or make a swift leap barefoot. Because, as soon as both feet were safely in the water, I wouldn't get zapped.

The perils of the charged water didn't stop there. As even once out of my bath, the electric coil in the tank still sizzled away, waiting to pounce. Standing at the sink, to defend myself I had to brush my teeth with shoes on, since barefoot meant I'd be assaulted with a menacing shock from the faucet's electrified water.

Naturally, the hot water tank would sometimes kick on during the day to reheat. If I unwittingly strolled shoeless into the kitchen to fill a glass of water, without warning, as my fingertips brushed the faucet I'd be met with a bone-jarring electrical bolt. Even after moving from this cottage, it took some time before I got over the urge to put on a pair of shoes whenever near a water tap.

Along with the welcomed exodus of the ants, the rains brought relief from the persistent dust that settled itself upon everything—our dishes, our sweaty brows, our TV screen. Sandwiched between the swirls of our powdered driveway and a rusty dirt road, stood the clothesline. Here our wet laundry hung, attracting the chalky soil like a magnet. During the dry season, the red film clinging to our towels made them dirtier after they'd been washed, and each night I laid my head on a pillowcase "fragrant" with the parched russet earth.

But I knew this was all just part of the package, this harsh-cut world so different from the place I'd fled. It was almost like a camping vacation, where eating by candlelight during power cuts could be fun. More than making up for the inconveniences was the thunder, lightning, and rain that rushed powerfully over the land, giving a luster to life. So unlike the coastal town of my childhood where such marvelous displays were rare and mild. Here in Zimbabwe, it was like being dazzled by my first fireworks show. I stared in wonder at how the streaking bolts suddenly lit the landscape up out of deep blackness. And the thunder! Its force literally shook the house with a deafening peal. I was enrapt with this place that had so much more vibrancy than the tame grayness I'd left.

Most wondrous, I'd never felt warm rain on my skin before. As the storm exhausted itself and settled into a calm shower, I found it a sensuous pleasure to stroll outside amidst the soothing raindrops.

Feeling their gentle stroke upon my arms and cheeks, while cool grass tickled my bare feet and water squished up between my toes. Such strange and tantalizing sensations, and I thought how nature had become my playmate, and felt I'd finally joined the party.

* * * * *

Yet out there in the wider sphere, beyond the insulated circle of my life, the daily grind for most Zimbabweans wasn't such a walk in the park. For those who did have a job, many earned less than US$100 a month. For them, to have a meal with meat was a once a week luxury, and home only a rented dim room. City workers shelled out much of their pay on bus fare, leaving little to provide for their children's needs such as schooling, since even the government schools charged tuition.

Living on so little, there was no margin for any swelling in the daily cost of living. Then in November 1998 fuel prices shot up by an unheard of 67%. This was unavoidable, since all fuel was imported and had to be paid for with foreign currency at international prices. As the Zimbabwe dollar steadily devalued, the price on the gas pump had to surge upward. Transport costs then rose, increasing the price of everything. Paychecks were slow to change, so now many workers spent half their precious little wage on just getting to work. For me with my US dollars, I felt no sting in the price increases and it never occurred to me that problems might be brewing.

Shortly after the shock of the fuel increase, a shortage of maize meal also loomed, the affordable staple that every Zimbabwean depended upon for the supper table. The government had always taken it upon itself to manage the maize supplies, requiring all maize in the country to be sold to the government's Grain Marketing Board, which then set the buying and selling price. Always quick to chuck fault elsewhere like a hot potato, the government blamed transporters and millers. The real reason for the shortage was rumored to be that maize was being exported and sold by members of the regime, rather than kept for the people. Supplies eventually improved, but the rumblings of greater troubles had started to roll.

Chapter Eight

A cross the country a collective sigh of relief could be heard, as the first court rulings came out in the landowners' favor. While Darren and I impatiently waited for farm sales to pick up again after the fall harvest, many farmers "listed" for takeover had sued the government, and come out on top. While this positive news certainly lightened the outlook, we all knew that threatening cloud of land seizures still lingered.

Although unsettling, I knew these tensions over land had been around for decades. Zimbabwe had started the twentieth century as a sprawl of bushland, and the divergent evolution of her land had only become more glaring. On one hand was the commercial farmland, forever growing more modern and productive, while next door the communal lands became steadily more spent and barren. This was where most Zimbabweans scraped along, each family's loosely defined twenty acres bequeathed by a local chief, although with no formal title. The tradition had always been that a Zimbabwean grows up, gets married, and is gifted a plot of land by his chief. But now, no communal land remained without someone living on it.

Instead, thatched huts everywhere dotted a shriveling countryside. I felt for these folk whom time had raced ahead of, trying to grow a patch of maize stalks next to each little home, plus a square of stunted vegetables. Their humble herds of goats and native cattle grazed nearby, while a few chickens pecked the clean-swept dirt surrounding the huts. The more enterprising folk cultivated a small crop for sale, such as cotton, a bit of tobacco, peanuts or soybeans. Even so, this pocket money often had to be bolstered by relatives working on a commercial farm or in town, who sent extra cash home.

In stark contrast stood the still vibrant commercial farms scattered about the country. Totaling 28% of Zimbabwe, these remarkably diverse enterprises were operated as businesses, using modern agricultural methods and equipment. Products were exported to all corners of the globe—tobacco, flowers, vegetables, coffee, cotton, paprika, sugar, citrus, and other fruit. Ostrich and crocodile farms exported meat and skins. For the domestic market farmers grew wheat, maize, barley, sunflowers, soybeans and peanuts, along with beef cattle, dairy and sheep. Not to mention, the antelope, buffalo and giraffe raised to restock ranches in Zimbabwe.

Agricultural exports were critical to earning the precious foreign currency needed to purchase fuel, medical supplies, machinery and spare parts, provide electricity and telephone services, plus buy a myriad of other necessities.

Frictions over land weren't helped by the fact that commercial farming was begun by white settlers in the early 1900s, and even now few blacks had yet to establish themselves in the industry.

The well-intentioned reaction had been for the government, with the help of other nations, to buy farms over several decades and attempt to resettle peasants. Different resettlement schemes were optimistically tried, such as co-operatives. Families who came to live on the same farm joined together in agricultural ventures, in which resources were meant to be combined and revenues shared. While this might have seemed like a great idea, it turned out not so easy in practice. When the time came for everyone to pitch in for tractor fuel, or toss in their pennies to repair the well pump, even these were low priorities for a peasant already struggling to provide clothing and shelter for his family.

So other resettlement farms were instead set up simpler. The different families were each allotted a section of the property, then solely responsible for their own endeavors. Sadly, without the know-how to run a small business, nor a title deed to acquire capital, these peasant folk often ended up in the same impoverished state as before. Not made any easier by now being far from the support of extended family, and the society they had in the communal land.

Still, at the time when I arrived in Zimbabwe, these uncomplicated resettlement schemes were the most common stab at trying to ease the communal pressures. Unfortunately, converting commercial enterprise into simple subsistence only reduces a country's overall prosperity, leaving the peasant even poorer and more desperate than he was before. It was a formula inevitably headed for implosion.

* * * * *

Easter Sunday arrived as a warm late summer day, yet with a light and optimistic feel of springtime. Dieter and Joanna had invited Darren and me to their home in Marondera, an hour east of Harare. After pulling into their drive, we all headed out to the veranda where we could relax with our coffees in the morning sun. While our chatter ebbed and flowed, I skimmed through the Sunday paper, finishing as always with a glance through the *Farms for Sale* column in the classifieds. An ad by a liquidation trustee caught my eye, inviting offers on a farm in Guruve. Pronounced goo-roo-vay, almost like groovy, I thought with a name like that the spot couldn't be all bad.

"Here's a farm for sale," I said casually to Darren. "It looks interesting. Twenty-three hundred acres with good water. A liquidation sale."

"Where is it?" he asked absently, pouring himself another cup of coffee.

"Guruve. Where's that, anyway?"

"Guruve!" Darren blurted with distaste. "No, we're not going to go live in Guruve. I was there when I went to the Eureka Gold Mine, and it's not a nice place."

As I shrugged and turned the page, Dieter remarked thoughtfully, "Actually, Guruve is a great area. It's very pretty. You should go look at the property. I like it up there."

Well, Darren and I certainly had time on our hands, and it never hurt to have a look at another farm. So the next day we phoned for directions and then headed north. Guruve, Shona for "pig", sat a hundred miles from Harare and was really more of an outpost than what could be called a town. The farm was a further twenty miles beyond.

The two-lane highway edging north first took us through the packed hills of the Mazowe district, its thick bush a healthy green all year round, an area known for its bountiful manmade lake and the vast citrus plantations watered by it. Our car zipped past close to where the dam wall stood wedged into a gorge, determinedly holding back the expanse of deep blue, amid a press of forested hills. It happened to be a weekday, so only a few sailboats and kayaks skimmed peacefully over the water.

The hills began to soften as the highway enticed us on, cutting through rows of dark-green citrus trees dotted with oranges. Soon we curved past wide acres of wheat and corn, spanned by modern irrigation sprinklers. Between the cropped fields rose gently sloped grasslands, where herds of russet-colored Herefords grazed, or snoozed in the scattered shade of brawny hardwoods.

The highway kept beckoning us northward, as the countryside took on more ruggedness. Boulder outcroppings, some of the massive clusters forming themselves into knolls, became common landmarks. The bush-covered hills gradually closed in and molded into small ranges. The now steeper slopes were less suited to large cropping, and on a few farms we saw high game fencing, beyond which we could pick out modest herds of zebra, impala and eland. These were some of the many farmers who had previously "ranched game", before the government stopped issuing export permits and demand had fallen away.

Darren and I casually chatted, feeling relaxed as we continued to wind through miles of green bush, dotted with tall mahoganies and msasas, and with the occasional bit of commercial cropland tucked amongst it. Here the Earth was healthy and content, with a catching cheerfulness.

After ninety minutes we clattered over a cattle grid across the highway, a barbed wire fence stretching into the bushes on each side. This marked the spot where private farmland ended, and a communal area began. At this our chatter abruptly ceased, as we passed into an alien land.

I found the scene wholly unnerving. To have beheld on one side of the fence a lush landscape, but now on the other, a used-up Earth. Oh, how my heart sank! For as far as we could gaze, from the highway's ridge top lookout to down along the sparse rolling hills, no large trees were left. What remained of the bush couldn't really be called such, since it was little more than remnants of shrubbery here and there. Huddles of thatched huts, and the occasional one-room cinderblock home, were surrounded by small livestock pens made of roughly stacked thorn branches. Next to the huts patches of vegetables and scraggly maize stalks struggled along, while some folk also grew a square of peanuts or sunflowers, used to make cooking oil. Goats and stunted cattle grazed everywhere, searching out any bit of green that had managed to hide itself. Without realizing it I sunk low in my seat, as the baldness of the landscape changed my mood from optimistic, to withdrawn and gloomy.

I was later told by friends who grew up in the area that in the 1950s and '60s when commercial farms were developed nearby, these communal acres had been an abundant land of trees and bush just like the other side of the fence. As we drove I shifted uncomfortably in my seat, unsettled by how stark this place had become in only a few decades. A major cause of the desolation was obvious. In the early 1900s, Zimbabwe's mainly subsistence society was about five percent of what it was now. If the U.S. had similar growth its population would be 1,200 million instead of 300, and England would have nearly ten times as many people. Added to this, try to imagine us all eking out a living—Middle Ages style—on our own twenty acres. America and England would be wastelands, even if enough plots existed for everyone.

After pushing on through the communal area during which Darren and I barely spoke, both of us muted by the miles of bleak expanse, we passed the settlement of Guruve. The town offered only one fuel station, and a couple of small stores selling the basics. It had a post office but no bank, and more ox carts trundled up and down the few roads than motorcars. Thin goats and stray dogs wandered about, rummaging through the selection of garbage littering the place. Pealing storefronts faced empty dirt "parking lots". A veil of dust hung in the air, stirred up by folks wearing hardly more than rags. This was not a place to call home, and no wonder that Darren had said he wouldn't live here.

Once past the town, however, we let out sighs of relief as commercial farming began again. Darren and I had been worried driving through the communal expanse, wondering if it was "the neighborhood". We were glad to once again be looking upon green fields of crops, plantations of citrus, and fat cattle grazing peacefully in knee deep grass. And to see the tall game fences that meant wildlife had found sanctuary on private properties here. There were also the expansive center-pivots for irrigation, a sure sign that a farm is prosperous. Perhaps this district did have potential after all.

The highway shrunk to a single lane past the town, then wound through steep hills for fifteen minutes before we turned onto Gota Hill Road. As we carried on upon this even narrower strip of asphalt, we felt our skepticism creeping back, seeing that most of the farms here had been resettled. Although the countryside hadn't been stripped, there were no fields of vigorous crops or even rudimentary fencing. Native cattle and goats wandered about aimlessly, followed by young boys in scraps of cloth, carrying crude sticks for herding and with emaciated dogs tagging behind. Our enthusiasm was waning again, but since we were almost to the farm we pressed on.

As we traveled along, I looked out the window at fading reminders of the commercial farmers who had first settled here not so long ago. Most noticeable, their simple farmhouses had become graying skeletons with glassless windows. I could imagine the farmer's young family, full of hopeful plans, laughing and cheerful on their front lawn, now just a clearing of weeds. I pictured them planting neat rows of seedlings beside the road, which had grown into the majestic oaks we now passed under. Determinedly, the oaks still stood proud despite the scruffiness below them. I thought how the peasant families now living here must have dreams of their own, and wondered if they, too, would someday plant trees to help rebuild the crumbling landscape. I truly wished they'd be happy and successful here, but at the moment there wasn't much sign of prosperity.

A few minutes later we felt the washboard vibration of a cattle grid, as we crossed the fence line that was Brooklands' boundary. I always found it a strange feeling when driving onto a piece of ground that could become my home, like meeting a long lost relative. In those first moments there might be a connection, and later, a bond might develop that grows into affection over time. Or instead, maybe we never hit it off and everyone simply parts with respect, happy that curiosity has been satisfied. Whatever the outcome, that first meeting is always charged with excitement.

Darren and I peered expectantly out at the fields and woodland and, as we rambled our way over the easy slopes of Brooklands, quickly became enamored. She was a beautiful place. Hilly, almost mountainous, like all of the surrounding area. The top of each rise presented a picturesque vista, and we especially liked that most of the farm was still thick bushland. At the moment the fields weren't being cropped, instead blanketed in tall grass whispering in the breeze.

The first building we came to was the Virginia tobacco barn, where we pulled over and went to have a step inside its chambers like oversized ovens. Peering up through the empty rows of beams, I could already image them hung full with the drying russet and amber leaves, their rich, almost sweet, aroma drenching my senses. A soaring tobacco barn filled with the sight of a successfully reaped crop, the culmination of so many months of hard work and offerings to the Rain God, is surely one of the most satisfying feelings a person can experience.

The track we followed soon eased us down to Brooklands' manmade lake, sweeping out from an earthen wall and spreading itself into an expanse of blue, before narrowing to curve between two hills. On the other side of the wall, a brook's clear waters skipped over polished stones, where many exotic birds had paused to quench their thirst. Scanning the lakeshore, we waved to someone fishing with a homemade rod in a shady spot, obviously a peasant from the resettlement property next door, then trundled along the top of the dam to reach the southern part of the farm.

Near the end of our exploring, we stumbled upon a weir built on a clear creek. Tucked in a nook of rugged bush that kept the shadowed water cool, we watched as it cast peacefully over the high stone wall and down through the boulders below. With Brooklands drawing us under her spell, we made our way up to the shell of the original farmhouse, sitting atop a hill with a sweeping view. From here we gazed upon all of Brooklands' serene landscape, beckoning to us with a subtle charm. She was all the more endearing because she was like a small piece of Eden hidden away from the encroaching decay, leaving Darren and me hopelessly captivated. This was exactly the kind of place I wanted to call home.

* * * * *

Brooklands' owner rented a house on the farm next door, because instead of rebuilding the homestead, he had put his money into creating first-rate tobacco barns. In his three years on the place, he'd also built the dam, put in irrigation systems, fenced the property, cleared fields, and bought equipment. On top of all this was cropping loans, so when interest rates skyrocketed to fifty percent, he just couldn't keep afloat.

When Darren and I showed up knocking on his door, James was friendly and helpful, but said we had to negotiate with the bankruptcy trustee. So upon returning to Harare we promptly put in our bid, then it was merely a matter of waiting until the closing date when all offers had to be in. We weren't in a hurry anyway, since surely more farms would be coming on the market soon, and they couldn't keep holding the exchange rate forever.

In the meantime, Darren's longtime friend Nicky phoned to ask if he would come do some work for her. She was looking after Hammond Ranch and they had a few mechanical problems that needed sorting out. Since it meant Darren would be in the Lowveld where many of his friends and family lived, he didn't hesitate to say he'd go.

Hammond, which happened to be owned by an American family, was part of the awesome Save (saw-vey) Valley Wildlife Conservancy. Zimbabwe had an inspiring number of these privately owned conservancies, although the Save Valley was the biggest, and in fact, was the largest private reserve in the world. The conservancies were created with a simple goal in mind: to provide protected habitats in which wildlife could roam free. For this, owners of adjoining ranches had to agree to take down all internal fences, then combine resources to look after the land and reintroduce game.

The million acre Save Valley Conservancy was the impressive outcome of the efforts of twenty-two ranch owners, a vast area in which the wildlife could wander free. It provided sanctuary to thriving herds of wild buffalo, elephant and rhino, along with most species of African antelope, leopard and cheetah, jackal and wild dog, badgers, snakes, thousands of birds, and what I considered just as important, insects of every kind imaginable.

Like most ranches in conservancies, Hammond was now a tourism enterprise. Transformed from a cattle ranch where the game, considered to compete with the steers for forage, had been frowned upon, and in large measure, eliminated. However, in just a handful of years Hammond's wildlife was flourishing again, thanks to the investment and efforts of its owners.

I was excited to tag along with Darren, and when we arrived at the ranch Nicky welcomed us into the high-ceilinged, thatched lodge, with its open-air lounge and dining room, and a towering stone fireplace always glowing with embers. Beyond, past an expanse of lawn dotted with shady msasas and edging the bush, sat several thatched chalets. Then not too far away were the workshops. It was certainly an appealing place for Darren to work for a month or two. There were no tourists yet, and I was glad for the chance to simply sit in the clearing of the cozy camp, surrounded by miles of African bush and wildlife, and soak up the peacefulness. Two impala does had taken up residence in the little clearing, where they had become somewhat used to people. I found it unreal to actually walk up to these exotic ladies of delicate beauty, and as I stepped cautiously towards them I slowly reached out my hand. One allowed me to stroke her fawn coat, my fingertips tingling with the vibrant energy of her lean muscles, ready for a split second flight. Her dark eyes were watchful, while her big ears flicked quickly forward and back. To actually stroke a wild animal was pure magic, and I felt as though I'd wandered into a corner of Eden.

Darren and Nicky had known each other since before they could walk, and growing up their families had spent vacations together. So it wasn't surprising when, in their mid-twenties, the dauntless Nicky asked Darren if she could join him on one of his trips into remote Zambia, going to places where few had ventured. More than once the intrepid pair found themselves broken down on the side of the track, hundreds of miles from the nearest hamlet that might not have a fuel pump, let alone a garage. They had to sleep stranded next to the "road", until some kind of help wandered by. Their little excursion saw them running out of food, stuck in knee-deep mud in torrential downpours, desperate for a bath and risking a hurried douse in a river harboring crocodiles, and camping in hyena country rife with malaria mosquitoes.

Yet when I'd first met Nicky, she had only just landed back in Zim after several years in London. There she had worked in a glitzy high-rise and wore the suits, spent evenings at the theater and lived predictably. The first time we shook hands I met a poised young woman, dressed in sophisticated clothes of subdued colors, and with chic blond hair.

When Darren and I arrived at Hammond, it'd been several months since I last saw Nicky. She came bounding out with a smile to greet us, and for a second I stood speechless with surprise. Before me was an altogether different chick, dressed in a simple short-sleeve shirt, khaki shorts and hiking shoes, her now brunette hair in a more practical style. What hadn't changed was that air of confidence and strength, which had served her well whether in a fast-paced city of millions, or alone in the African wilds.

Nicky's dad had worked for Zimbabwe's National Parks, and had passed on to his four daughters his love of nature. But in one of life's tragic turns, in the late '70s when Nicky was ten, he was killed during Zimbabwe's civil war when his helicopter crashed. Birds had been his particular passion, and Nicky became a virtual encyclopedia of southern African species, able to recite their Latin names, plus every detail about their habitat, nesting and feeding. It wasn't long before I counted her amongst my best friends.

Co-managing Hammond was Spike, whose father had also worked for National Parks, as an ecologist. Africa's bushland had been Spike's backyard while growing up, so it wasn't unexpected that he'd always worked as a wilderness guide and naturalist. His dream had been to be a park ranger, but the dismal state of Zimbabwe's national parks, due to underfunding, poaching and neglect, made an impossible situation in which to work. A lovable character, stocky with tousled hair and vivid blue eyes, his handsome face drew me in with its warmth and hint of fun. Darren and Spike hit it off immediately, beginning a lifelong friendship.

Each day, I took endless pleasure in Spike's innate understanding of everything in nature. He could recount the life story of a blade of grass, each seemingly insignificant bug, each mammal, reptile and amphibian. He could pick up a dry leaf and tell all about the tree it came from, identify an animal that had passed by days ago from a smudge in the dirt, describe who eats whom, what lives where, and how the whole natural universe fits together.

So there were few things I enjoyed more than wandering through the bush with Spike as my guide. His finely tuned senses brought to life the astonishing wonders of nature, camouflaged amongst the quiet bushes and trees. A hidden world unfolded, as he pointed out a stately hawk sitting watchful in high branches, a diminutive duiker antelope peering at us secretively through wispy grass, and an industrious dung beetle silently rolling its eggs inside a ball of buck droppings, barely to be seen amidst the fallen leaves.

The timing of my arrival at Hammond had been most fortunate, because an exciting event had recently occurred there. The singular blessing of a pack of African Wild Dogs making their home on the ranch. As with other predators, the wild dog could create havoc on farms with livestock, so like the cheetah, lion and hyena, its numbers had dwindled along with its vanishing habitat. And while the Save Valley Conservancy had successfully increased their wild dog populations, even here they were still a rare sighting.

So one dewy cool morning I awoke before first light to venture out with Spike, in the hopes of glimpsing these uncommon beings. Spike said our best chance was during their morning activity, before they settled into the camouflage of long grass for the day. The dogs usually hunt just as dawn is breaking, then waste no time in eating their meal. When finished they return quickly to the den to feed some regurgitated breakfast to the alpha female, the only one to have pups, and the litter.

The dawn was still veiled in twilight as I sat quietly next to Spike, slowly winding his Land Rover through hushed bush, and as far as I could tell not following any visible track. In the calm of pre-dawn, Africa's presence felt like a comfortable old friend.

Just as the morning took on a misty glow, Spike stopped the truck on the edge of a grassy area. Lowering his voice, he said we would wait here by the den, to see if the dogs showed up.

"But where's the den?" I asked, scanning the openness before us and looking for something that could be shelter for a pack of dogs.

"There," Spike responded casually, and pointed into the clearing of thick grass. In the middle was a hump like a miniature hill, the only feature in the meadow, and almost concealed by the sameness of grass that blanketed it.

While we waited, on branches here and there a dove or flycatcher came sleepily out, and a subtle chirping built in the air. With the day coming to life around us I wanted to fidget, but managed to keep myself contained. Although it seemed ages, it must have only been fifteen minutes when a cautious lone female appeared. Next to me, Spike also had difficulty restraining his enthusiasm, and leaned toward me to excitedly whisper, "There's the alpha female. She stays at the den to watch over the pups, while the rest of the pack goes hunting."

I caught my breath—she was simply majestic. She held her proud head high, and her oversized round ears straight up and alert. I was surprised at her size, being larger than any dog I'd ever seen, with long slender legs and a gorgeous marbled coat of fawn, chestnut and black. We watched breathless through binoculars for a few minutes, then decided to nudge the vehicle closer.

As we crept to within yards, she warily jogged off in a feather-light gait, her padded paws noiselessly touching the ground. When she stopped to look back at us we couldn't resist moving towards her again, lured by her guarded grace. She continued several times to trot away and then pause, but upon finding herself further from her clearing and the den, began to make furtive glances towards it. We soon felt guilty at disturbing her, and although disappointed to not see the pack, knew it was time to leave this noble lady in peace. While Spike drove slowly back to the lodge, the two of us sat in awed silence. In my mind I thanked Africa for this special moment, a gift from a best friend.

* * * * *

Only forty-five minutes from Hammond, upon a wide dirt road through the bush and in the heart of the wilderness, sat Humani (hew-ma-nee) Ranch. The family that owned it had been friends with both Darren's and Nicky's families for years. The two of them had spent many enjoyable holidays on the ranch while growing up, plus Darren had worked there for a stint after high school. To put it simply, Humani was Darren's favorite place on Earth, and home to some of his very best friends.

It was in the pioneering 1920s that the family's patriarch arrived on Humani, a place two-day ox cart trek from the nearest town. He and his wife were the first people known to have settled on this piece of ground. Zimbabwe was sparsely populated then, and on early maps this uninhabited bushland was warningly labeled "Unfit for Habitation". The territory was rife with the sly malaria mosqui-toes, although worse were the tsetse flies that not only carried sleep-ing sickness, but were even more deadly to livestock. This scrubby backcountry was also perfect habitat for the lions who thrived there, and any traveler passing through was taking risk with life and limb. Stories abounded of the early cattle ranchers' unceasing battles with the lions and leopards. Yet the greatest obstacle to settlement here was the problem of so little water. This landlocked nation offered few natural lakes or perennial rivers, and for most of the year, not even a hint of rain.

So it was that the first ranchers in Zimbabwe, especially where Humani sat in the south, suffered terribly in the early years. The lions, tsetse flies and other problems made earning a living from livestock touch and go. Yet rainfall was too scarce for cropping, and inevitably, ranches changed hands often as owners went bankrupt.

By sheer perseverance, Humani's family not only managed to keep their place going through the tough times, over the decades they expanded it into a diverse enterprise. Now as part of the Save Valley Conservancy they had built up a successful tourism business, the untamed landscape being an unrivaled locale for a few snug lodges. Then as a real stroke of luck, a valuable underground stream was discovered, supplying an abundance of water for irrigation. With this they developed a thriving agricultural business, despite limited ground with soils suitable for cropping. Upon these limited acres were now corn and sugar cane, plus a citrus plantation complete with its own packaging warehouse. Among other small ventures, the ranch sawmill made timber from massive hardwoods that died during the 1992 drought, which Humani carpenters now crafted into handmade furniture. This impressive ranch, home to hundreds, had certainly come a long way since the days when sentenced "unfit" for living upon.

It was these twentieth century success stories, when Zimbabwe rushed forward to join the world stage as a modern land, that convinced me there was no better place to be. Humani's history ran a parallel path to that of the nation, evolving from an untapped backcountry into a diversified land of opportunity. And their futures, too, would be fatefully locked together.

Chapter Nine

||||||||||||||||||||||||||||||||||||||||||||||||||||||||||||||||||||||||||||||||||||

Prime time for farm sales was now upon us, but as luck would have it there was zip on the market. This put Darren and me in a very tight spot. Here it was already June, midwinter, and if we were to buy a place this season we hadn't a moment to spare. Tobacco seedbeds had to be started in July, so seedlings could be planted in the fields by October. If we didn't get a crop in by then, we'd be in the disastrous position of missing out on an entire year of revenue.

There was still Brooklands, and as it turned out, our bid had been the only offer for the place. Even so, the folks at the bank didn't appreciate the urgency of finalizing a sale. It seemed all Darren and I could do was keep pestering them. Eventually this tactic did win us some relief, when our pushiness snared us an appointment with the bank's agricultural department manager.

Since they had no other offers we felt optimistic about our chances, even with the bank being uncooperative so far. The agricultural manager was certainly affable enough, as the three of us settled around the table in his office. Darren and I were anxious to get the ball rolling, and watched with interest as he carefully pulled papers out of his file, then slowly recited details about the farm: the amount owing, the unpaid interest, and improvements made. We listened patiently, although not sure what this had to do with us, all the while waiting for him to get to the point. Had the bank accepted our offer, or did they possibly have a counter proposal?

"Have you seen our offer for Brooklands, which we submitted to the trustee?" Darren finally asked.

"Yes, I've got it right here," the bank manager quietly replied, then pulled the paper out of his file and stared thoughtfully at it.

"Well, is the bank in agreement?" Darren pressed. While I did feel the manager was trying to be helpful, there was a weariness to his efforts.

"No," he slowly stated. "I'm sorry, but the bank won't sell for less than what's owed."

Really now! I couldn't believe we had just sat through all this dragging-on, only to be informed our offer wasn't accepted. Darren and I were now thoroughly exasperated with the whole situation, which had slogged on for weeks and ended up nowhere.

"The property is simply not worth what is owed," Darren said, trying to stay calm. "Nobody will buy it for that, because it's not financially sound to pay more than we've offered. So if it's not acceptable to the bank, then I guess our business is done. Thank you for your time," he added curtly. "We're sorry we couldn't come to an agreement."

As we pushed back our chairs and headed for the door, the manager suddenly sparked up. "Wait," he called to us. "Maybe there's another way."

Darren and I gave each other a doubtful glance, and only with hesitation sat down again. We were completely surprised when the manager then laid out another plan for us to take over Brooklands, one he'd obviously thought out before we arrived. He presented us with an unusual, and certainly creative, proposal. It did involve buying Brooklands for the entire amount owing, although with twenty-five percent down, the balance paid in three annual installments without interest. This was the real hook for the deal—no interest. With rates now at fifty percent, any financing scheme was doomed from the outset. In lieu of interest he proposed we pay an annual "lease" equal to ten percent of revenue. I certainly wondered about the bank's ability to make an interest-free loan, but Darren and I figured they knew their business.

There was still the time pressure to wrap up the deal, since the deadline for planting was right around the corner. After a few more days of persistent phone calls and visits to the bank, we finally had the completed loan papers in hand. We just needed the credit manager's signature to finish things up, yet in keeping with the whole difficult process, he seemed to be avoiding us. We noticed how he'd dodge out of his office when we stopped by the bank, and would not return our calls.

Eventually our determination did land us a meeting with the regional, credit and agricultural managers, plus a few others thrown in for a full audience. Being of the notion we'd finally won the battle, Darren and I were in good spirits as we walked into a large corner office. Our brightness was quickly snuffed out, however, when cold-ly met by dour faces around a table, who gave us only curt nods. We immediately recognized the unsmiling credit manager, and also the agricultural manager who avoided our gazes.

"You are quite young!" The regional manager, Mr. de Villiars, remarked to Darren with an edge of scorn. "I was expecting some-one older. Now tell me, what is your background? What farming experience do you have?"

We tried to respond politely to the grilling that ensued, and steer the discussion toward a productive end, but our blood was rising as he continued his patronizing inquisition.

"You haven't prepared a budget to show how you can pay this loan," he reproached us, then went into a condescending lecture about it. Of course Darren and I had done plenty of budgets for Brooklands, but the bank had never asked for one. Neither had they requested resumes, bank statements, credit histories or any other documents. Yet as far as the regional manager saw it, Darren and I were the ones who didn't have our act together, not the bank and his managers.

It wasn't unexpected when he went on to inform us that the bank couldn't make a loan without interest. But to our astonish-ment, Darren and I received another scolding about how foolish we'd been to put forth such an idea. As we calmly explained that the

bank had come up with the scheme, not us, the agricultural manager just sat hunched and mute, staring at the floor and trying to
avoid the heat being fired in our direction.

The two of us decided it was time to leave, our patience having long since run out. As we stood up, the regional manager still
had the audacity to direct us to go home and work out what we
could pay for the property—which of course we already knew was
the amount of our offer—and then submit a cash flow to the credit
manager.

Darren and I could do little more than raise an eyebrow with
indifference and make our way to the door, since a rational discussion was obviously not to be found here. While I could understand
the brick walls we sometimes encountered when working with government offices, trying to persuade a private company to transact
business was a real puzzle.

Darren and I were ready to forget about Brooklands, but if we
did there'd be no time to find another property. So that afternoon
we stopped by the credit manager's office with a letter restating our
cash offer. He did not look pleased to see us. Nor did he even want
to take our paper, responding that the bank had asked for cash
flows, not a simple letter.

Once again, I was astounded. Could the manager of an entire
credit section of a large commercial bank, really think that budgets
must be submitted with a cash offer? Surely he could reason for
himself that cash flows, showing how debt repayments would be
made, didn't apply to a lump sum purchase. The whole scenario was
now verging on the ludicrous in my eyes. I felt fatefully caught up in
an illogical argument that could never be solved.

We followed up with a couple of phone calls, but true to form,
those at the bank never gave us an answer. And with that, having
done all we could do, we left them to stay lost in their own bewilder-
ing enigma.

* * * * *

"I don't know about you, but I'm immensely relieved to be done
with that bank," I said to Darren with a sigh.

"Yes, I agree, although this does put us back at square one," he reflected. "We don't have time to find another property and still get a crop in. If we bought now we'd have to carry overheads for almost two years, until next season's harvest could be sold."

The owner of Brooklands was still living on the next-door farm, Rungudzi (run-good-zee), and James and his wife had become our friends during the drawn out negotiations. At one point James asked Darren about his plans if the deal fell through with the bank, to which Darren shrugged and said he hadn't yet figured that out.

"Why don't you talk to Alan, the owner of Rungudzi?" James suggested. "He spends a lot of time away and might be interested in hiring you. We'll be moving out of the manager's house soon, and there won't be anyone to watch over things when Alan's not here."

Being at a loose end, we were glad to have something to consider. So a week later Darren and I found ourselves driving up to Rungudzi, to spend an evening with Alan. We pulled up to his house and climbed out of the car to the usual friendly swirl of dogs, as Alan walked out to greet us. With a handshake and easy smile, he showed that unassuming graciousness I'd come to know of all Zimbabweans, yet with an added distinguished air. I immediately noticed he didn't look the part of a typical farmer, as instead of well-worn shorts, workshirt and scuffed shoes, he was dressed in a crisply ironed white shirt and cotton trousers. His manner was smooth and composed, yet with an engaging warmth, making him every bit the image of a country gentleman. Tall and still strong at fifty, only later did we discover he used to have long hair and as a young man raced motorbikes. Traces of the adventurous rebel still lingered. Such as when Alan's colleagues bought vacation homes in the misty Eastern Highlands, with its quiet fishing spots and lawned golf courses, and instead Alan chose rugged and remote Rungudzi, one of the last farms before the wild Zambezi escarpment.

Although his home was middle-class size and surrounded by barely contained bush, to me it had the feel of a stately manor. A soaring staircase dominated inside, along with plenty of polished wood accents. But even more, it was because of Alan's poised and assured persona. Inside, he escorted us to his cozy den and its carved mahogany bar, the heavy wood burnished dark and glossy. The three of us settled onto stools with embroidered seat cushions, Alan quickly making us feel at ease, going about what we'd come to know as his evening ritual of serving up cokes with brandy in crystal glasses. As we sat talking, the wafts of his and Darren's cigarettes lingered in the air, adding a wistful mood to the room. Gazing out through open French doors, I was captivated by a smoldering orange and red sunset, casting a golden syrup over the bristly brush tops of strong hills.

It was an irresistible place, Alan's ridge top farm of twelve thousand rugged acres on the edge of Zimbabwe. While he seemed more interested in having us there for companionship, rather than as management, Darren and I were anxious to make a move of some kind. And at least Darren would be earning a small income. Plus there was still a possibility we might buy Brooklands on auction, and by staying on Alan's farm next door we could keep an eye on the place.

So in mid-August '99 Darren and I moved into the modest yet spacious rooms of the "manager's house", which James and his family had just left. The home rested on a slope just below Alan's tobacco barns, in a wedge of cleared bush where James's wife had sculpted a beautiful garden around it. Coming from the barren Arctic, to me it was a miniature Eden. Long-limbed shade trees sat scattered about the lawn, encircled with rainbow swathes of begonias, pansies and daffodils. On the western side of the house, a rock wall terrace topped with a row of boisterous daisies stretched to the fence line. Nearby, a bird bath nestled amongst some shrubs was a hub of activity as many feathered visitors splashed about, while clusters of ripening fruit hung from the tops of the palmed paw-paw trees.

At the back of the house, our shaded veranda sat only yards from the untamed bush. The spot drew us like a magnet, and at the end of each day Darren and I settled into chairs of woven grass and gazed out to the ridge tops beyond, bushland stretching for as far as we could see. Every evening we had front row seats to another panoramic sunset. The early evening sky began bright and open, with a symphony of the heavens lilting forth in a subtle, melodic tune. All the instruments joined in—swaying trees, whispering clouds, chirping of finches amongst rustling leaves, while from a distance came the low bay of cattle. The song would slowly build and reach a crescendo just as the bold orange sun touched the horizon, the birds singing out in their highest soprano. Then, as the glowing orb eased to crimson and slid behind the Earth, the harmony became deeper. The birdsong faded as the wind began to bellow, the hills sinking from deep green into shades of charcoal. Finally, as the last refrain rang out, the day gracefully took its bow behind the drawing curtain and darkness enveloped the stage.

Chapter Ten

||||||||||||||||||||||||||||||||||||||||||||||||||||||||||||||||||||||||||||

That dreaded time was now upon us when, every year, the peasants couldn't resist setting the countryside ablaze. While I wanted to shout that there was no reason to blister the earth in flames, I knew they viewed it as an easy way of ridding the land of the tall, dry grasses of late winter. Admittedly, I had glimpsed the succulent shoots of bright green that soon emerged from the blackened landscape, so perhaps it did make for better livestock grazing in the immediate. Yet, while this ritual might not have been so ruinous a hundred years ago when the continent was only patchily inhabited, now someone stood on every square acre wanting to set fire to the landscape around them.

And I knew there was another, more lethal, motive for the burning. It made the mostly illegal hunting down of what might remain of the wildlife easier. In the scorched countryside, now heedlessly purged of tall grass and foliage, and with only stark tree trunks amongst which to hide, even the most cunning became easy targets. Plus with much of their food razed, the antelope, warthogs, rabbits and others all conveniently collected in the tatters of bushland yet to be torched.

I tried to console myself with the fact that some of these fires would happen naturally. Alas, if only the fatal damage caused by a "hot burn" could be avoided. At the lesser extreme, a controlled "cool" bushfire will simply crackle through the undergrowth, burning dead grass and leaves, scorching trees but possibly leaving their uppermost foliage unharmed. If nature's lucky, the "cool" fire might creep along slow enough for most wildlife, including ramblers like the tortoise and chameleon, to flee its ravages.

At the deadly extreme, the more fatal "hot burn" is of such charring heat and intensity, it permanently cripples the earth, its flora, and the animal life. It was always distressing to watch my friend Africa be ravaged, as a wall of flames consumed every trace of her greenery, instantly killing the trees and shrubs. Often this "hot burn" was brought on by high winds, vigorously stirring up what the match holder had intended to be only a mild fire. The force of these gales could sweep the flames along faster than most living things can run or fly. The soil becomes so incinerated that its nutrients are wiped out, and seeds hidden in the ground reduced to ash. When this burnt land does see plant life return at some point, it is more often weeds and thorn trees that take up residence, rather than the varieties of shrubs and grasses upon which game and livestock can feed. Naturally, if the nutrients are all burned from the ground, then only less nourishing plants will spring forth from it.

The district around Rungudzi and Brooklands was particularly vulnerable to the flames, because along with the many peasants in the communal lands, was also so much resettlement. Throughout winter and into spring, I had to endure the bitter choke of black smoke, and grim sight of cindered countryside. I wished I could protect the land from this ruthless menace, always lurking and ready to pounce on defenseless Africa.

* * * * *

With spring at the door, and as the latest to hang our hats at Rungudzi's twelve thousand alluring acres, Darren and I felt the urge to explore. The moment he wrapped up work, when the scorch of the day mellowed to evening's sultriness, we'd either hop on the motorbike or into the old Mazda farm pickup. That is, if it actually still qualified as a pickup, since it had no roof, no doors, no hood, no grill, no windshield and no tailgate. Still, it was a comfortable ride with its loose-spring seat, and perfect for our wanderings over the many tracks that crisscrossed through Rungudzi's rocky bush. The best part of every drive was pausing at one of the farm's tranquil ponds, all of which had been created by Alan, to bring a bit of life-giving water to this thirsty wilderness. We'd lean back in the seat with cold beers and chocolate bars, to watch twig-legged sandpipers nod along the shore, while white-faced ducks floated peacefully beyond.

If the mood struck us for a longer drive, we'd weave our way through tight hills to an enticing spot. Tucked on a ridge was a nook sheltered by hardy bush, one side open with a drop far down to the Dande River. From our aery perch we watched unseen, as children from the communal land splashed lanky limbs in the cool ripples, their laughter a soft echo amid the rocky terrain. Beyond the river, from our mountaintop view we looked out to the unfurled valleys. I found it meditative in this small clearing, which was really the peak of a rocky outcrop, earth having built up between the boulders so now only their smooth tops showed, the cracks filled in with gray moss.

The gentle valleys we gazed upon were part of the Dande Communal area, and from our lookout the lilting tempo of its scattered homesteads drifted up to us. Cowbells tolled in a steady rhythm, like far-off church bells, mixing with what could have been tinkling choir bells, but was really the distant laughter of children. This serene spot of rock clinging to the mountainside deserved a name and I proclaimed it the Monastery.

Our little mutt Scruff couldn't get enough of our exploring either, and with her amazing stamina could sprint an incredible distance for a dog smaller than a hare. Quite to my annoyance at times, she refused to catch a lift with us, no matter how far she was soon left in the dust.

On the farm we had an unending supply of warm and lazy Saturdays, and on this particular afternoon decided our outing would be a short whiz through the tobacco fields. With the motorbike fired up, we had the usual nonsense of trying to make Scruff ride along with us, perched in front of Darren with her front feet on the fuel tank. As always though, she would have nothing of it. So we puttered along slowly for awhile, then impatiently sped ahead, before stopping to wait for her to catch up.

After an hour of touring the budding fields nearest to our house, we decided to circle back towards home. Darren and I motored on through the last field of young tobacco, openness all around and a wide blue sky above. Up ahead the track gently arced to the top of a hill, with the asphalt strip road just on the other side.

Leaning with the easy curves, enjoying the rush of warm air and with the bike's roar filling our ears, Darren and I sped onward. We popped over the hill and stopped at the paved road to wait for Scruff. Darren turned the bike off, and for a few minutes we simply took in the grand setting of strong bush, soaking up the yellow sunshine. There was certainly no reason to hurry home.

After several more minutes and with our heels now thoroughly cooled, we became a little annoyed. Scruff hadn't been that far behind, so where was she? Had she discovered an irresistible scent she just had to chase down? Perhaps she had wandered off on another track. We had only just moved here, and a cloud of concern suddenly came over me when I realized she wouldn't know her way home.

Our worry soon had us wheeling round to go look for her. As Darren steered the motorcycle back down the path between the rows of seedlings, in the distance on the edge of the track, I caught sight of what looked to be a charred stump. It stood out clearly, and I thought it odd I hadn't noticed the thing before. Then, still unsure of what I was seeing, I spied a pile of black and white fluff at the base of the "stump".

Within seconds, Darren and I were close enough to recognize—in stunned disbelief—that the black object was nothing less than a gigantic bird. It determinedly stood its ground as we zoomed up, not the least threatened by our roaring charge. In an instant my throat choked tight at the thought of my beloved Scruff's fate, my stomach twisted into a piercing knot.

Darren skidded to a halt a few feet from the bird. As we leapt off the bike, fearless Scruff was a motionless pile in the red dirt. I couldn't go close, imagining her soft underside ripped open, her insides strewn on the ground beside her. Or half eaten while she lay conscious, in pain, knowing she was dying a terrible death. I stood shaking, my hands clasped over my mouth as I gasped back cries of horror.

For a moment Darren was torn between comforting me and racing to Scruff's aid. He was also worried that if he rushed forward, the bird might suddenly take flight with Scruff in its talons, then drop her from a bone-shattering height. Thankfully, instead, the beast nonchalantly flapped its mighty wings and returned empty-handed to the skies, reluctantly leaving Scruff where she lay. At once Darren darted forward and knelt beside her. To this she half opened one eye and ever so slightly cocked a droopy ear, as if to say, "Is the coast clear?"

Now I was wracked with sobs of relief. Anxious to calm me, Darren carried Scruff over and stood her at my feet, urging her with, "Run around, Scruff, run around!" At this she bravely took a few stiff strides, and gave me as much of a tail wag as she could manage. She added a glance up that said, "Please don't be upset. See, I'm fine. No harm done," despite looking weak and a tousled mess.

As we rode off home, Scruff was like a limp rag in my arms. Totally exhausted, for once she seemed grateful for a lift on the bike. Possibly she, too, was watching as the giant bird brazenly glided on the wind overhead, obviously disappointed to have lost its lunch. With a shudder I saw that its white underside revealed it to be a Martial Eagle, which can reach up to three feet in height and with a daunting wingspan of several yards.

Back at the safety of home, on closer inspection we were startled to discover that Scruff had punctures in her chest from her attacker's beak. Dirt had been ground into her face with great force, clogging her eyes. Her mouth and nostrils were jam-packed with red clay, her teeth hardly visible. We guessed that the eagle must have dived into the little fluffball at lightning speed from behind, creaming her face into the hard-packed road, and sending her flying head over heel.

That night Scruff cried and yipped pitifully in her sleep, reliving the nightmare again. Brave and tough as she was, she never again would chase after a motorcycle, as surely there was some connection between that noisy bike and the creature from above. And for me, it was an unsettling glimpse at the darker side to my paradise.

* * * * *

For Darren, as a Zimbabwean, our home on Rungudzi wasn't anything out of the ordinary. But I was completely enchanted. Perched on the edge of the African bush and facing wild lands north, it wasn't very far past us that the one-lane highway dwindled to hardly more than a trail. From there the bumpy track could be followed to Zimbabwe's northernmost point, on the shores of the bold Zambezi River.

The vigor of the wide river dominated the Zambezi Valley, an untamed place of few settlements where most of the land was set aside as preserves. Bounding the valley on each side was the perilous Zambezi escarpment, where traversing the few narrow roads through the steep, bush-covered mountains was always a white-knuckle affair.

Yet tragically, the Zambezi's ruggedness hadn't saved her from being ravaged. When I'd first ventured into the valley in 1992, a few secretive rhinos still roamed, of the once large numbers that had made a home in this wilderness. By the time I returned to Zim only four years later, however, the poachers had finished off the last of them. And while elephants and antelope still bravely roamed the valley, as in all of Africa with its swelling number of desperately poor, the wildlife was ceaselessly threatened. For the rhinos, their horns made them the most chased down of all the animals. Often the body was left to rot, with only the horn hacked off to be sold in the Middle and Far East, where the price paid for just one horn could vault a poacher into millionaire status within his impoverished village.

But as I sat on our peaceful veranda, looking out over the bush-covered hills to the north, I pushed the troubling side of Africa to the back of my mind and took in her beauty instead. I imagined the rugged mountains beyond Rungudzi's border, stony and steep, home to furry rock rabbits and sharp-eyed baboons. I pictured the eagles soaring above ridge tops, before catching a downdraft over the escarpment to glide into the tranquility below. Looking out from my sunny veranda and thinking on the untamed places beyond, I felt that most powerful element of Africa. Her awesomeness of nature; so commanding, magnificent, and measureless.

And for me, equally inspiring was Africa's minutiae of life. In the frigid Arctic where few critters crawled about, the frozen winter landscape had sometimes seemed so sterile. For me it was the whirl of insects that brought the world to life, the crickets' rhythmic trills giving vibrancy to each day, the harmonic frogs taking over at night. Our house on Rungudzi was a place where the outdoors and inside had no real boundary, since without screens on the many windows, always open to a soft breeze, an intriguing multitude of creatures casually came and went as if members of the household.

The most abundant visitors at our Rungudzi house were insects of the flying kind, and the easygoing wasps especially considered it a perfect place for homemaking. Their distinctive black and yellow striped legs dangled down, elegantly I thought, long and straight when flying. I actually didn't mind when they breezed through as casual guests, although it was quite another thing to have them littering the house with their tiny mud huts like pencil erasers. The cook Zvitendo and I were constantly destroying these little dwellings, meticulously built, which when the crusty walls were broken revealed a clump of squirming albino offspring.

When looking to set up quarters, the wasps particularly honed in on the wide and round, old-fashioned keyholes. They certainly had a choice of locales, since locks were to be found in every door, closet, drawer and cabinet, a ready-made home that only needed a layer of mud-plastering inside to finish it off. It always seemed that just when I needed to lock something up, I'd find the keyhole firmly cemented with mud. Even more revolting, one morning I grabbed my bathrobe from its hook on the bedroom door, and as I sleepily strolled off my hand brushed something rough, clinging to the pocket. To my disgust the wasps had built a crusty tennis ball-size mud neighborhood, complete with a half dozen entrances, now securely attached to my robe.

While the wasps were completely harmless, the devilish bees were another story. Not many things made the adrenaline shoot through my veins faster, than hearing the seething buzz of a swarm racing in my direction. It was always unexpected when a deafening mass would suddenly swell thorough the open windows, looking for fresh territory to set up fort. I'd bolt from the office or bedroom, slamming the door behind me, and make a dash for the bug spray. Meanwhile, Zvitendo was hurriedly locking up the windows throughout the rest of the house. Edging myself through the cracked door of the infected room, I'd fire off strong blasts of repellent at the intruders. To this the horde would rage even louder, but at least they'd make a break for the open windows at the back. I cautiously followed behind, spray blasting, before shutting the windows tight after them. For many minutes the angry mob then circled the house in a whirlwind. When finally they went away, in their wake came the most soothing hush.

What also appealed to those on the wing, were the two bare bulbs that hung in our long living room, one above our coffee table and the other where we dined. The stark globes blaring in the blackness of evening were magnets to many insects, who pushed past the drawn curtains, the windows open to the summer breeze. Darren and I found it impossible to eat our supper with the light on over the table, because a throng of many-legged visitors would end up struggling in the quagmire of sauce or gravy on our plates. My solution was to put the light on at the other end of the room as a decoy, while we ate by a candle's dim quiver.

The problem was, that later when we sat comfortably in front of the TV, a raucous crowd of flying beetles, moths, winged ants and other guests now whirled madly round the bulb overhead. They continuously slammed into each other or the piping hot bulb, knocking themselves into a loss of flight control or ricocheting off the ceiling. The chaos above meant Darren and I were forever being pelted by mini cannonballs, the snap of a hard-shelled beetle against my cheek or bare thigh particularly stinging. Yet I still liked their company, the room exploding with life and vitality. And anyway, I could always switch lights and send the rowdy gang back to party over on the dining side of the room.

Stopping by less often were, what I considered to be, a friendly pair of bats. They usually slipped in at dusk, while Darren and I sat on the veranda looking out to the bush and talking. Later as I strolled down the hallway, I found myself eye to beady eye with the rascals, as they silently swerved in low arcs towards me. I'd duck at the sight of their awkward flapping, sure they were about to lose control and career into me. Other times, while I relaxed in bed reading they'd softly swirl in, before making a confused exit out the bedroom door like tourists who'd taken the wrong off-ramp. I was actually glad to see these eaters of the sneaky, malaria-carrying mosquitoes. The bats were the good guys ridding the world of evil.

Also waiting until dark to peek out were the shy geckos. They lived inside our house, and being territorial, the same one never strayed from a certain bedroom, bathroom or closet. I was amazed at how their colors varied from slate-gray to pinkish-white, depending on the decor of their chosen room. Two of the geckos must have lived in the house at Rungudzi for years, as even Darren had never seen such strapping fellows, being ten inches from nose to tail tip. They spent most of their time snuggled up behind the pictures on the walls, or a favored hideout of my world map hanging behind the couch. Throughout the evening their round tongues would flick out with lightning speed, to rid us of yet another wicked mosquito.

Other welcomed housemates were the colorful songbirds in the garden, and I spent countless hours peering through binoculars at all the interesting beauties. I felt protective of the bird families who chose to weave their homes of twigs and grass in our garden, like the Paradise Flycatcher pair who made a well-hidden nest in a tree at the corner of our veranda. This delicate bird of a rich russet color, with a crested black head and eyes ringed in bright blue, was mesmerizing to watch as he performed a fast, fluid, gymnastic ritual, to catch insects in midair. During the breeding season the male sported a flowing tail several times longer than his body, mixing his routine with a whirl of elegant "ribbons".

The tree of the refined Flycatcher almost touched that of his boisterous neighbor's. A Southern Masked Weaver had built in plain view an ostentatious home, being a dozen hanging oval nests of bright green. This tireless fellow, feathered in vibrant yellow with a black mask and distinctive red eyes, was always chittering loudly, and having heated debates with other avians who mistakenly ventured into his territory. I was especially fond of this gregarious chap, who was so energetic and took good care of his reserved little brown wives, who mostly stayed tucked inside their well-built homes.

While beyond the fence of my home lay forces I could not control, for these humble beings living under my protection, I would do everything within my power to keep them safe.

Chapter Eleven

|||||||||||||||||||||||||||||||||||||||||||||||||||||||||||||||||||||||||||||||||||||||||

The time had raced up on us, and with only two weeks before our big day, we still had lots to sort out for our wedding. It'd been easy to choose the magnificent setting of Darren's sister's home in the Lowveld, and we'd asked the friendly young Anglican priest there to marry us. On a visit down several months earlier we'd met with him to work out the details, and had been a little surprised when he told us there were religious duties to fulfill as well. Even so, we were happy to do whatever was asked.

The next thing we knew, the weeks had flown by and here we were still delinquents in the church's eyes. Added to the frenzy of trying to get our home in order, had been the hurdle of living a seven hour drive from the priest. I felt embarrassed about our tardiness, but to my relief he didn't seem overly concerned. However, being remiss didn't come without consequences, and he calmly informed us that if he couldn't marry us within the rules of his institution, then he wouldn't be able to marry us under civil law either. To this startling revelation he did offer a solution though, suggesting we be legally married by a magistrate, and then he would still perform a religious ceremony at our wedding as planned. He'd obviously seen this coming, and I guessed we weren't the first to be in such a spot.

This sudden news did put us in a bind, since the waiting lists in Harare meant there wasn't time to organize a court marriage there. But before I let myself panic, I decided to look into the services of our nearest magistrate, who happened to be in little Guruve town. Fortune was on our side and I managed to book a time slot with the court secretary, who before hanging up the phone, added that we should be sure to bring along two witnesses. I hadn't thought about this small detail and commented that we hardly knew anyone here, to which she helpfully replied that even a couple of strangers would do perfectly fine.

There had to be a better option than just snatching someone off the street, so Darren quickly rang up Alan to find out if he might be back from Harare in time.

"You're getting married! Of course I'll be there," Alan said with enthusiasm, volunteering to drive back early. "I wouldn't miss it for anything."

That was one witness at least, so we just needed to track down another. As my mind tumbled through the options, I thought back to a week earlier when Alan had introduced us to another couple recently arrived in Guruve; an attractive and worldly pair, like none other to be found in this little town. He was a Dutch doctor, tall and blond, while his charming wife had a Cleopatra look, with smooth olive skin and ebony hair. Not long before, a new hospital in town had opened its doors, and because of the generosity of the Dutch government who paid his salary, it now had a physician in Dr. Steinberg. He and his French wife of Moroccan descent lived only a block from the courthouse, and when I asked the friendly Yamina if she would be our other witness, she happily agreed.

"What do you think we should wear today?" Darren said casually to me as he poured his morning coffee.

"Oh, well, I hadn't thought about anything other than the usual farm clothes for our little errand into town," I remarked. Then smiling, added, "But I guess getting officially married does call for a bit of dressing up."

We really considered the upcoming September 4th ceremony as the true day of our wedding. Yet today's event was special in its own way, and probably did call for something better than shorts and sun-faded t-shirts.

An hour later as we trundled our car through dusty Guruve town, being quite the spiffy pair we stood out as a conspicuous novelty.

By the time we arrived at Yamina's house Alan was already there. Together the four of us set off on foot, stirring up puffs of russet earth as we walked the few paces to the courthouse. I was surprised to find a small and tired-looking masonry building, and being surrounded by the rustic town, looking like something out of an old Western film set. Even so, it did have a kind of stateliness, or at least it had in decades past when its plaster facade hadn't been crumbling. The portico held a whisper of dignity with its two classical-style pillars, framing a carved mahogany double-door that still stood nobly from its chipped walls. Painted across the top of the high front was the faded black lettering of the town's old colonial name, Sipolilo.

We easily found the secretary's office nearby, and I guessed its original use must have been as a cramped storeroom, since it was only the size of a walk-in closet. Like all government offices I'd been in, the place was revoltingly filthy, its floor layered with years of grime, walls smudged and yellowed. The bare bulb had never been replaced, leaving only dim light to push through a grubby window. Two desks and a filing cabinet completely filled the cubbyhole, and the four of us had to wait outside on the porch while the three hand-drafted marriage certificates were meticulously written out by the clerk, ever so slowly, one at a time. Such is the pace of Africa, and we pleasantly passed the time chatting outside. Eventually the clerk proudly presented her handiwork, and then Darren and I, Alan and Yamina, each signed the certificates by standing in the doorway and leaning over to the desk.

With that important task accomplished the cheerful clerk then beckoned us to follow, leading us into another room, which although more spacious was still dingy and dark. It turned out to be the magistrate's office, and at least it could be said that the dimness provided a solemn mood for the proceeding. The magistrate seemed pleased to be of service, politely commenting that we were only the third white couple he'd married. Then he asked me and Darren to each raise our hands in turn and repeat his lines, and within a few minutes all was said and done. After brief congratulations all around, everyone walked back outside from the unlit office, where the glare of the late morning sun was startling, and for a moment the four of us stood unsure of what to do next. It all seemed an anti-climax. At least Alan had the good thinking to bring his camera, and we decided to commemorate the day with a few pictures. There wasn't much choice of a backdrop, so Darren and I settled for posing under a tree in the shabby front "lawns". The once manicured grounds of this noble institute of justice now only weeds and dirt, encircled by the remnants of a dying hedge.

Darren and I hadn't expected anything more, and were simply glad all had gone smoothly enough. As we strolled back to Yamina's house, I glanced down at the handwritten marriage certificate in my hand. I thought how this simple piece of paper was a special token of the step we'd taken, but even more, an important document I'd better carefully guard. I knew to replace it would be no easy matter, as the other two copies would undoubtedly become faded away, while entombed amongst thousands of others at the back of some forgotten, damp room. I wryly reflected how this humble record of our union was in itself an irreplaceable gem.

A quick minute later we were back at Yamina's, where she cheerfully swung open the door and beckoned us with, "Please, won't you come in."

"Yamina, you've been so kind, but really we don't want to impose," Darren said as we hesitated.

"Oh, but it'd be a pleasure, it's nice to have company for a change," she graciously insisted.

I knew what she meant, because certainly nothing like a bridge club or aerobics class was to be found in this little town.

Upon stepping into the inviting coolness of her home, for a moment we stood speechless. Feeling a rush of delight, I smiled to think that it wasn't an anti-climax after all, as we were greeted with a splendid surprise.

"Yamina, this is wonderful. You're too good to us," I exclaimed.

She had beautifully laid the table for a celebratory brunch, with colorful ceramic mugs steaming in the aroma of fresh coffee, delicious jams brought from Holland for golden toast, a platter of juicy grapes and plums, and a frothy jug of milk to go with the wooden bowl brimming in crunchy grains. In the center stood a vase of bold sunflowers, and along with bright napkins and cheerful plates, the spread was a work of art. Yamina obviously had that French flair for making even the most basic fare into a meal of cultured delight. I was touched by her thoughtfulness, especially because we'd only met briefly once before. Then Darren and I became completely lost for words when she bestowed gifts upon us, while Alan, always the gentleman, stepped forward to present a bottle of champagne.

With true magic, Yamina had created a cocoon of enchantment out here amidst the dust, poverty and decay. Single-handedly, she had made our simple marriage in this obscure little corner of Africa, into an unforgettable memory.

* * * * *

An irrepressible joy ran through me, as Dixie stepped spryly from the horse trailer. Clattering down the ramp, she paused to hold her regal head high. Swishing an arched black tail over muscled flanks, with large eyes she confidently took everything in. Up in the Arctic a horse of my own had simply been too expensive, so for me she was another bounty of Africa. I smiled wide as I stroked the sleekness of her dark-chocolate coat, reaching up to cup satiny and perfectly curved ears in my hands. Then tracing the velvet outline of her nostrils with my fingertips, her cushion of breath was warm against my palms. An elegant thoroughbred is truly one of nature's greatest masterpieces.

The red brick stables where Dixie stayed with the farm horses was a short walk from our house, in a sheltered spot tucked halfway down a bush-covered hill. Walking there, I always paused to look upon the facing hillside, where as the weeks went by its cleared brown slopes blossomed into green fields of tobacco. When the planting first started, I watched each day as the tractors bumped along pulling trailers loaded with seedlings. The field workers were mostly women, although from where I stood they were only a sprinkling of colorful dots on the facing slope. They eased about the specks of green that over the weeks had bloomed into rows of bright splotches, mushrooming until the hillside was laid with a striped fabric of green.

By now we were several months into summer, often with blistering temperatures in the nineties at Rungudzi. So when the end of November came round, the arrival of the four-month rainy season was welcomed like an old friend, its cloud cover and seventy degrees bringing relief to a parched land. As I hiked down through flaxen grasses to the stables, the moist air had a plushness to it, kept soft by a mellow breeze. The clouds seemed so low I might be able to touch them, while swaths of mist clung to the ridge above the distant tobacco fields.

These mornings were irresistible, and I would venture out from the stables on Dixie, her whisking tail brushing at my elbows as we wound our way down through dew covered bush. Hugging the narrow trail were branches garlanded in droplets, so by the time we emerged into the fields at the bottom we were moist with freshness.

Guiding Dixie round the edge of the cropland, I followed a path guinea fowls had left sprinkled with their polka dot feathers of gray-black. On one side of us pressed an airy wall of tangled bush, while on the other, stretching across the furrowed fields, were neat rows of tobacco plants. As we clip-clopped by, workers raised up from their weeding and slowly turned, looking with curiosity at the unusual sight of a lady in their midst, while politely calling out *Mangwanani* (Good Morning).

These outings were one of my favorite ways to enjoy time with Africa. Each day that passed made me feel a little more whole, and like I, too, was part of the greater force of humanity, nature and life.

Drawn by a beckoning path, Dixie and I picked up a brisk trot for awhile. Being naturally surefooted, Dixie loped along the craggy trail as smoothly as if on a sandy beach. Soon the sheer pleasure of our energy mixing with the morning sun, birds sailing above, drew us into a steady canter. Weaving along the curved edge of the fields, rugged bush pressing on one side, Dixie masterfully placed her feet among the roots and loose stones, while striding along in relaxing rhythm.

Meanwhile, Scruff was off somewhere sprinting through bush where Dixie couldn't go, making a great sport of flushing up the partridge-like francolin, and the larger charcoal-colored guinea fowl. Sometimes I could hear her yip-yip-yip sharply in delight as she high-tailed it after a darting rabbit.

One of my favorite tracks to follow steered us to a small lake used for irrigation, formed from an earthen dam. Nearing the place we had to jog through reeds taller than our heads, often disturbing a flock of finch-like Red Bishops. They'd burst from their hiding place of bright green in an explosion of neon-red, an awesome sight against the blueness of the open sky.

A vitality pulsed through Dixie as she vaulted up the side of the dam wall in powerful surges. I soaked up the energy as we cantered along the dam's crest, two stories high and scarcely wider than a horse on top. The grass had been allowed to grow thick and tall to protect the wall from erosion, and it reached up to my waist as I sat on Dixie, who held her head high to see over it, her rhythm animated as she pushed forward and through.

Bounding through the feathery grass above the treetops, with only the broad sky stretched out on each side, we could have been dancing on clouds. Dixie's hooves, cushioned by the grass, beat as soundlessly as if she were cantering on air. The dam wall dropped off sharply below us, with tall grass blocking the view underfoot, so only to be seen was the expanse of calm water far below. The surface of the Earth seemed to start down there, at the water's edge, and I felt beyond the reach of gravity.

Sometimes on a Sunday Darren would join me on a ride. On our way home we'd always steer a course to pass by one of Rungudzi's small dams. By this time it would be late morning and starting to heat up, Scruff plunging in for a cooling swim while the horses waded in after. As they stretched their muzzles down to draw in long gulps, from the saddle Darren and I gazed out across the sparkling water to the strong hills curving round us.

"I feel so privileged to have a home in this grand wilderness," I said as I took it all in. Never guessing how fleeting our time here might be.

* * * * *

When Darren and I had decided to let down anchor at Rungudzi for a while, it was partly to stay close to Brooklands, since there was a chance we might be able to buy the farm on auction. We were still sentimental about the place and felt some obligation to look after her, being as she was, in limbo at the moment without a caretaker. And living on the crest of hills to her north we had an open panoramic over which we could watch. Until a new owner was found, we seemed the natural guardians of this small piece of Earth.

Although we were now well into summer, the peasants still hadn't taken mercy on the land and let up with their bushfires. Looking, as they did, upon all the earth as communal grounds for livestock grazing, and hunting down the last of the wildlife. The scourge of blazes was set alight faster than could be snuffed out, with every farmer around tackling them almost daily. It became a substantial resource drain for all, including Alan, whose tractors and trailers, water bowsers, shovels and tools, were all whisked away from their important farm tasks to instead be used on fire containment. Backpack sprayers, meant for applying agricultural chemicals, were instead kept filled with water on standby for bush-fire duty.

Late evening was most popular with the peasants for setting the fires loose, and for weeks we could expect to hear the night guard clanging at our gate, calling Darren to go fight them. Usually we were already deep in slumber, and when hours later a hollow-eyed Darren dragged himself home, he was as ash-covered and smoky as the battlefield he'd just left.

But one sun-filled day, it happened to be in the afternoon when Darren had to rush off. The alarm had been raised that a blaze was raging on Brooklands, the place an easy target for burning since it was hemmed in by resettlement on two sides. With no owner living there to notice and douse the flames in its early stages, the fire had already swelled to a nearly uncontrollable size. If it swept onto Rungudzi to the north, or Bradley's farm to the south too fiercely, it could become an unstoppable wave, making cinders of farm buildings, expensive machinery, crops and workers' homes.

With Darren and the entire workforce soon gone, I was left as the only soul on a deserted Rungudzi. I tried to keep myself busy, but my mind was too distracted, and after several hours decided to drive over to Brooklands and find out what was happening.

As my car rumbled over the cattle grid at the gate, I immediately sensed a hush. Every blade of grass seemed to be holding its breath. Feeling unnerved by the stillness, I wasted no time in heading to the middle of the farm where a plateau of old cropland would give me the best view. There, as I gazed round in every direction, I found the stark abandonment eerie. Usually someone could be seen walking down the road, stray cattle from the resettlement area grazing about, or youngsters making their way to the dam with homemade fishing rods. Now, chillingly, even the birds had vanished.

I caught sight of Darren's motorbike propped up down a road and warily made my way toward it, all the while feeling bated by something sinister. As I crept the car toward the bike, past it I could see other discarded equipment—an empty water bowser on a trailer, a backpack sprayer hastily laid by the side of the road, a shovel half hidden in the grass. I was near the edge of the open grassy area now and decided I'd better stop, before the track closed into the bush, where I might have to hastily wheel the car around in the face of onrushing flames.

Should I wait here? Surely they couldn't be far from all this equipment. But curiosity was getting the better of me. Soon I was tramping off down the road, through bush that was becoming taller and thicker. Where was everyone? Why didn't I see any smoke? Just then, from around the next corner came queer laughs, and a moment later two scruffy and disheveled women workers suddenly appeared. They were smudged with soot, their hair looking wild, and brandishing tools for fire beating. Their wide-open eyes flashed piercing white against their dark skin, and their taut grins hinted at a presence almost evil, as if they'd been invaded by something fiendish.

Despite the disturbing spectacle they made, I decided to cut in on their cackles to ask if they knew the whereabouts of Darren and the fire. They could barely focus on me or my question, too caught up in the thrill of the most exciting thing to have interrupted their monotonous existence in sometime. I was able to gather though, that the blaze with Darren and others in pursuit, had swept down into the valley.

After I'd left the plateau the road had followed the slope downward, and with the wind blowing down into the valley, I now realized this was why I hadn't seen any smoke. More workers were now trudging their way back up, although these looked weary, with heads drooped and tools slung low. They'd been battling the fires almost every day for weeks now, and for them it'd become an exhausting routine.

As I carried on walking, workers steadily passed by me in more numbers, then eventually faded to a few stragglers. I had hoped to come across Darren but it was obvious that he, along with the tractors and the rest of the crew, must be somewhere else. Pausing for a moment to consider what to do, up ahead I could now see charred terrain. I guessed that the fire must have come this way before the wind turned it around, sweeping it off in the opposite direction. Then startlingly, I noticed thick smoke begin to stream out of the bush on one side of the track, and seep into the brush on the other. A shudder went through me as I then heard a distant roar mingled with crackling. To my astonishment it quickly became deafening, while above the bush, I now saw streaks of flaming orange leaping up to the serene blue sky. In a matter of moments I was looking upon the fire in all its fury, this massive wall of savagery racing through the bush towards me. Yet in spite of the danger I held my ground, overwhelmed with anger at the evil ravaging this beautiful piece of earth.

The wind momentarily inhaled, and for a few seconds the fire fumed where it stood. I was alone and felt as if I were facing Satan himself. Without words I raged back, but knew I was only like one of the spindly trees that could be easily swallowed up. In another moment the wind gusted again and the flames came crashing forward once more, bullying me back to the protection of the barren road, where there was nothing for the blazing creature to devour.

Sullenly, I turned my back and slumped off, feeling beaten. We had tried to protect her but had failed. I hated the thought, but knew Darren and I must forget about Brooklands now, leaving her to her fate. It was a crushing weight, that of having to give up hope and surrender.

When I arrived back at the car, a tired-looking Darren stood talking with the farmer to the south. Bradley was shaking his head in dismay, "I can't keep taking my guys and equipment away from their work," the New Zealander said with frustration. "If the peasants want to set fire to Brooklands, then I guess that's what they'll do. But I can't waste anymore resources on this place. From now on, just let it burn."

Darren, too, had more than his fill of the endless firefights. As it was, keeping up with safeguarding Rungudzi was difficult enough. I felt such despair at the waste of it all. Brooklands was no longer productive and contributing to the vitality of the nation, nor staying as a place of beauty instead, somewhere to invigorate the soul. So while her economic contributions had already been lost, now her wildlife and magnificence were as well.

Those long months during which the bushfires raged was such a depressing time. Even indoors I couldn't get away from them, since everything in our house was perpetually coated with a layer of ash. Running my hand across the desk, my palm and fingertips came away dirtied with soot, and anything left out was soon covered with black grit.

That evening after the fire at Brooklands, Darren and I took refuge on our familiar veranda, where a drink was definitely in order. We faced north towards much of Rungudzi, where a few fires smoldered away, although all we could see were their smoky tufts against a pale sky.

We sat silent for some time, looking out through the smog towards the murky sunset, neither of us feeling like talking. Slowly the
muted sun faded away and the blackness of evening engulfed the
land, now revealing the fires themselves, which stood out threaten-
ingly in boiling crimson.

I wanted to pretend they were innocent campfires, but knew
they'd been purposely lit in an arc near Rungudzi's fence line with
the communal land. The buck that sought sanctuary on Rungudzi
would be caught in a ring of flames, forced to leap over the tall fences into communal territory. There, chances were they would soon
find themselves tangled in snares, or hunted down with spears and
packs of dogs.

Yes, I could picture all too well the brutality of the blazes, leaving behind scorched, leafless trees and burnt soil. I knew that slow-
moving creatures like the chameleon and tortoise would not be able
to escape the flames, although I hoped the many lizards, snakes
and mice, along with crickets, beetles and moths, could flee to safer
ground. And what of the larger animals, such as the squirrels, rabbits, warthogs and many antelope? Would they get safely away? The
angry flames would reach up into the trees, and snuff out baby birds
in their nests of dry grass and twigs. Would their parents abandon
them in time to save themselves?

I thought of the Paradise Flycatcher chicks in their delicate nest
tucked away in dark branches before me, glad they were secure
within the bit of space I could protect for them. Yet the fact that
they, along with the frogs, geckos and others whose home was within my fence, were safe and sound, was only the smallest consolation.

Feeling forlorn, I tried to tell myself that bushfires are a nec-
essary part of nature. But I also knew that when the same land is
burnt year after year, it eventually reaches a point of doubtful re-
covery. My heart ached at my helplessness to stop the misery. How
many more years could nature sustain herself under such duress?
It seemed that all Darren and I could do was sit there in the darkness, silent, watching the fiery monsters and feeling of sadness and
defeat.

Chapter Twelve

|||||||||||||||||||||||||||||||||||||||||||||||||||||||||||||||||||||||||||||||||||||||||

Rungudzi Farm was not on the road to anywhere, so rarely did we have the treat of a visitor popping in. When a friend did hazard the trek out, bringing welcomed laughter and cheer, the occasion was better than if Santa himself had tumbled out the chimney.

A year earlier Darren and I had met Willem, a Dutchman, who had come to Zim as a less expensive and sunnier locale to study for his pilot's license. His résumé already looked impressive, with a master's degree in economics, and plenty of years spent wearing a suit and tie, making his mark on the business world. At the same time, his adventurous stirrings had put him ashore in the Middle East, still working in his profession. Yet for Willem, simply living in a foreign place hadn't calmed his restlessness, and eventually he shipped his suits back to Holland, and headed to Africa in search of his cure.

Willem had that catching *joie de vivre* of someone still taking in his newly found freedom. He hadn't made plans for more than a few months ahead. Wherever he ended up, I couldn't picture him back in a suit coat and stiff white collar. Instead, the mementos he wore from his forays into Argentina were perfectly fitting, a soft leather jacket and tall vaquero boots. He smoked French cigarettes and drank Scottish whiskey, and along with his round wire-rimmed glasses, reminded me of the likes of Teddy Roosevelt.

Venturing out to spend a few days with us, the evening Willem arrived we packed a cooler with orange juice, vodka and bags of chips, to set out for the opposite corner of Rungudzi's twelve thousand acres. As the three of us hopped into the doorless, roofless, hoodless Mazda pickup, hardy little Scruff sprinted out ahead, leading the way in her jackrabbit clip.

None of the bush-covered farm was flat, but we first eased through sloped cropland where, as always, flocks of guinea fowl foraged. Scruff could never resist upsetting the peace, giving chase after these fair-sized game birds, feathered black-gray with specks of white, bright blue gobble upon their heads. The instant she caught sight of them she was off like a bullet, determined this time she would outwit one and take home a prize, even if the birds were as big as her. Without fail, the guineas dashed about in scattered panic, their feathers fluffed high in an arc, their feet jerking quickly over the rough earth. They'd screech in desperate cackles and total mayhem seemed to reign. But as our pickup lazily caught up, the chaos instantly defused, the guineas all casually taking flight as one fluid motion low in the sky. Without any hurry, they lightly settled on a field further off. I always had a laugh at this game the birds played with Scruff, only our more formidable presence spoiling the fun.

As we puttered along, there was no avoiding driving through bush scarred by fires, the most recently charred still void of life. Even Scruff was subdued, jogging along in front of the pickup through a vast blackness, only naked, scorched trees perched lifeless amongst the scattered boulders. That's what really stood out, the rocks. I'd passed this way many times and the large rocks had always been there of course. It was only when every blade of grass, every bit of undergrowth, and each fallen leaf had vanished, these boulders were all revealed. Leaving a land that looked to be from the outer reaches of the solar system.

In some burnt areas, tiny shoots of green had begun to peek up through the sooty ground. With the charred forest now open, any bit of life stood out distinctly against the black backdrop. I thought how the few antelope that might still be around, would have nothing amongst which to camouflage as they nibbled the sweet shoots. It was a poacher's perfect setting.

Eventually we found our way into healthy bushland again, where the msasa beetles were out in force. Although we couldn't see them they lay thick in every tree, their deafening mix of clicking, zinging and buzzing sounding like a thousand electricity transformers. This sheer vigor of life helped push to the back of our minds the injured earth we'd just passed.

The roar of the beetles eventually faded away, and an hour of driving led us to the spot I'd named the Monastery. After parking, we hiked up a few paces through bristly shrubs to the overlook. For several minutes we stood in awed silence, gazing over a breathtaking landscape of bold hills. Directly below us, the gentle currents of the Dande River carved a boundary between Rungudzi and the communal lands, whose pale valleys wrapped around the hills and then disappeared out of view. Crops were planted on any suitable patch found amongst the slopes, and we could just make out a group of cattle ambling home. Their cowbells mixed with the bells of others we couldn't see, the mellow ringing from the different valleys filtering up to us as one whispered hymn. When mingled with the far off voices of people calling to each other, by the time the sounds rippled over the ridge tops and reached our ears, it all turned to song.

We settled onto the warmth of smooth boulders and filled our tumblers, then leaned back to enjoy the magnificence of it all. As the soft light of evening began to fade, the songs of the valleys grew quiet, and indigo darkness slipped in. Soon the shimmering moon gave a feel of satin to the purple night, while now and then the shrill barks of baboons, living amongst the most rugged terrain, rang clear through the still air.

The three of us lay sprawled on the warm boulders, gazing up to the millions of stars and feeling like we were floating amongst them. It was a powerful rush to be a part of the great universe, and intoxicated by the grandeur around us, we all made an unspoken wish that this extraordinary interlude would never have to end.

* * * * *

"Really? You want to go check out the local school?" Darren said to Willem with a bit of astonishment. "I can't imagine why. But hey, if that's what you do for kicks, I'm happy to oblige," he continued good-naturedly. "We can head over to the government school this afternoon."

The students of the school on the resettlement property next door either lived on one of the resettled farms nearby, or were children of workers from Rungudzi and Bradley's place. Plus Brooklands of course, before it closed up.

The dirt road was narrow and bumpy, and I was surprised at how long it took to drive the short distance. At least the lack of development could be said to have one plus, and I was relieved to see this piece of ground still healthy. The trees and shrubs hadn't yet been clear cut, and replaced with overgrazed land. The peasants' homes lay scattered with plenty of stout bush between them, each place a cluster of huts and crudely made livestock pens. I had also expected more cropped areas, but the patches of cornstalks were innocuous amidst the dominant bushland.

I wasn't surprised to see that virtually everyone on this resettled property lived the typical subsistence lifestyle. Grazing their goats and a few cattle, keeping a clutch of chickens, cooking over an open fire, and growing a square of white corn to dry and crush into meal. Theirs was a toilsome existence, their crops being planted and reaped entirely by hand. It meant first clearing an area of shrubs with a *badza*, a sturdy blade between an axe and blunt sword. Then since most didn't own an ox, each spent long hours hoeing, sowing, weeding and harvesting. At the end, cobs were laid in the sun to dry, after which the women carried them in buckets atop their heads to a grinding mill. A shed-size affair where they were charged per pail for the service.

"One of the more enterprising fellows living here is employed by Alan as the driver for his ten-ton truck," Darren explained to Willem. "He grows a few acres of tobacco which his family tends, plus owns a grinding mill and kiosk. You know, one of those shacks used as a store, with a window counter that opens to customers standing outside."

Being a driver was a real benefit, because when he went to town to pick up Alan's supplies, he also brought back purchases for his store.

"Here we are, we've found it," Darren announced as he steered around a corner and we came upon the school. "Although it looks like classes might have finished for the day."

As we drove up I felt a tinge of sadness, it was such a desolate looking place. The grounds were cleared of trees, with the only grass being yellowed patches on a sports field, recognizable by the warped poles at each end meant as soccer goals. The rest of the school ground was clean-swept dirt. The classrooms consisted of a half dozen simple concrete structures, starkly whitewashed and open to a bare courtyard, in the middle of which stood a lonely pole holding up its faded Zimbabwe flag.

Darren parked the truck and the three of us made our way towards an office where we heard voices. The two men who greeted us looked understandably puzzled, as we explained that we'd come to have a look round their school. But they were friendly enough, especially the one who was a teacher, a jovial fellow with a winsome smile. The other, square-shouldered and composed, turned out to be the headmaster and was more subdued. I put it down to what looked to be a never-ending struggle of trying to educate with meager resources. All the same, the teacher, a tall man with a lean frame and easy gait, proudly led us off to show us the instructors' work, more than half of whom it was unfortunate to hear were without training beyond high school.

In spite of the austerity, I'd found a welcoming simplicity to the school grounds. Yet a peek inside the classrooms left me instantly dismayed. Although clean and tidy, it was heartbreaking to see them in such an abysmal state. The weak light of small windows was consumed into the grayness of concrete floors. And while each classroom did have some child-size chairs, none were in one piece. A line of several without seats was spanned by a warped plank, and ones with back legs missing were wedged against the wall for support. The rooms were small, so when the headmaster told me up to sixty students were in a class, I tried to picture how they'd all fit. Surely the spare little classrooms would be so packed, that moving around would be impossible.

"There doesn't look to be enough chairs, and certainly not enough tables, for that many students," I commented with concern to the headmaster.

"No, some of the students have to sit on the floor and do their work there," was his matter-of-fact reply.

In one corner I noticed a carefully stacked pile of yellowing and tattered books. With curiosity I wandered over and picked one up to have a glance through. It was completely unexpected to find stories written to the backdrop of 1950s Britain, tales odd enough to me, and surely even more bizarre to these African schoolchildren. But I knew to even have these books was a luxury.

Despite the obvious poverty, I did find the classrooms had a cheerfulness. Bright posters of African scenes decorated the walls, while colorful drawings and Cut and Paste projects hung proudly displayed. On chalkboards, teachers had carefully written out grammar and math problems in neat handwriting.

The last of the buildings was still under construction, going slow, the teacher explained, because of lack of money. The concrete walls and floor were finished, and Alan had paid for the roof which was now up, but no windows or doors were coming anytime soon. I supposed that buying a chalkboard first would be more important.

"And when the building is finished, what about chairs and tables? Plus books and supplies?" I asked, my voice echoing as I peered into the empty shell.

"We're not too worried about that, we can stretch what we have," the teacher responded brightly. "We're just excited to have another classroom, as space is so tight."

The irony of it, was I knew this to be a place of privileged children, those with parents could afford to send them to school. Although the fees might only be US$2 per term, by the time uniforms and supplies are bought for several sons and daughters, sometimes food on the table was a more urgent priority. I was disturbed at seeing how ill equipped these caretakers of Zimbabwe's future were for their important charge ahead, as the fate of paradise lay fully in their hands.

I thought our tour had ended at the classrooms, but the next thing we were being led out back. We passed by the sports field and left the buildings behind, and I wondered where we were headed. A minute later we found ourselves at the faculty houses, where the teacher and headmaster introduced us to their polite and demurely smiling wives. The ladies were proud to show us their humble quarters, which by Africa standards were above average. This only meant, however, a roof that didn't leak, windows with glass, and several rooms the size of walk-in closets in the States. The "bathrooms" were simply outhouses. Even so, I guessed that the teachers and their families considered their situation in life better than most.

Our little visit was starting to wind down, when we noticed under a shady tree nearby sat a young man carving soapstone, surrounded by his collection of figurines. At once we wandered over with interest. He told us he sold most of his work at an art center in the district, although he'd also just returned from a trip to Holland, taking part in an exhibition of African sculptors. He and Willem were soon chatting away, while Darren and the teacher fell into a discussion about the many issues of land resettlement. This left the reserved headmaster and me standing patiently by, and I thought I might as well strike up a chat.

"So what do the people in these remote places think about the problems of Zimbabwe?" I asked him casually, although realizing I might be bringing up a touchy subject. "How much do they understand about the economic situation, or do they even realize the country is being mismanaged?" Then I pressed further with, "What do they think of Mugabe becoming rich while the rest of them suffer?"

I had indeed hit a sensitive chord, as the headmaster tensed and glanced towards the others. He then answered in almost a whisper, "President Mugabe is only getting what is due to someone of his status, as leader of a nation."

"But his personal wealth is said to be vast," I argued, annoyed at such an outlook. "His wife's spending sprees in Europe are well known. There are yachts and other expensive things he has bought for himself, all through his presidency."

"It is the same as what your president of America gets for his position."

"It certainly is not," I said indignantly. "Our president does not become a man of immense wealth from his office."

"Doesn't your president have a big home? Doesn't he own expensive suits and cars? Go on holidays and have many possessions?" the headmaster insisted.

"Yes," I responded with a little more patience. "But he's a lawyer, he made money in a profession. And besides, his wealth doesn't begin to compare with what Mugabe has amassed."

"There you see. Your president started off with more," he quietly carried on. "With good schooling as a child he was prepared for university, and his family had the means to send him. So he could earn money before he was president. President Mugabe didn't have those opportunities, so now he has to make up for the years of having nothing and get more now."

I knew it wouldn't matter if I told him that President Clinton hadn't come from a well-to-do family. The headmaster would simply say he still had an advantage in life, because he came from a country with opportunities to climb the ladder. It was clear he didn't want to accept, or couldn't understand, the difference between being paid enough to live comfortably and amassing a fortune in public office, and at the expense of his own countrymen. Yet in many African cultures, it seemed accepted that a leader is unquestionably endowed with a right to untold riches.

For a moment we both paused in thought, before the headmaster added in a guarded tone, "What the people in the rural areas fear more than anything is war, and they think that if President Mugabe's power is challenged he will bring war upon them." Finishing gloomily, he added, "And then it will only be the poorest who suffer."

"That's ridiculous," I blurted, still puzzled at the turn in the conversation. "How can they think that voting for a new president would start a war? Besides, Mugabe has been in power for twenty years. No matter how well he's done, it's always good to have new leaders with new ideas. Don't you agree?"

"It doesn't matter what the reasoning may be," he firmly stated. "The rural people simply want to avoid war more than anything else."

At the time, my knowledge of African history and culture was still limited, and I was thoroughly confused by what he said. It was only as I continued to live in Zimbabwe and read about her history, that his comments later made sense. I then realized that when the headmaster had talked of war, I'd envisioned tanks, rockets, and uniformed troops marching about the bush. Whereas what he really meant, was something closer to guerilla warfare. Actually, that term was even incorrect, because what he'd been referring to was merciless intimidation through systematic criminal acts of violence; beatings, torture, rape, and even murder. Later I also learned that in various degrees, political "campaigning" by intimidation had been a regular feature of all the nation's elections.

This grim plight of Zimbabweans had come about because the majority are rural folk, poor people who receive little information about most anything, including personal health care, productive agricultural methods, new skills and basic education. Politics, economics, and the world at large can be vague concepts at best. Particularly when people are struggling to simply make sure they have food on their plates and a decent roof on the hut.

Thus it happens that when you are poor, weak from ill health and an empty belly, live far from police stations or other kinds of support, have only your two bare feet to get you anywhere, and have little knowledge about what goes on beyond your village and nearby fields, your options are limited. When men come to tell you who to vote for, that if you don't vote or cast your ballot for the other guy, they'll know and come punish you—African-style—plus your family and neighbors have already been beaten, you simply comply.

After all, does who you vote for really affect your life in the end? When you can't see how it will ever be anything other than the daily struggle of finding a meal and a dry place to sleep anyway.

Before parliament elections in mid 2000, when one day my housemaid Batsirai and I were both busy in the kitchen, I offhandedly asked if she had registered to vote.

"No, no," she gulped in a whisper, her eyes fixed on the floor while shifting uneasily.

"Well, aren't you going to vote?" I thought this important enough to press the point.

"Oh, no. Oh, no," she stammered back. "I don't want to get involved in that."

I didn't push her and at the time was exasperated, wondering how Zimbabweans would ever better their situation if they didn't try to change it. Yet it made sense later. I could picture the scene at the polling station, where eagle-eyed thugs loitered about and stared menacingly at the voters standing in line. My diminutive housemaid would be wondering if it were really true that the balloting was secret. She'd envision the horrors if anyone discovered she had voted for the opposition. Better to err on the side of caution, she'd think to herself, and vote for Mugabe and his party. Or even better yet, to just stay out of the whole terrible business of politics altogether.

How exactly, I wondered to myself, can a way forward come about, to ensure a better future for everyone here in paradise.

Chapter Thirteen

||||||||||||||||||||||||||||||||||||||||||||||||||||||||||||||||||||||||||||||||

A discreet murmur had been busily making the rounds, putting out the exciting word that a new political party had sprung up. It was late 1999, when anything to do with political happenings, and most definitely about an opposition party, was not something anyone wanted to be blatant about. A citizen never knew when it might lead to, in the very least, a complete thrashing. So news on touchy subjects like politics was mostly by word of mouth—and very quietly at that.

Yet it hadn't always been that way for my adopted home. When Zimbabwe first embarked upon majority rule in 1980 there were several active parties, not surprisingly formed along tribal lines. ZAPU (Zimbabwe African People's Union) was supported mostly by Ndebele people, while ZANU-PF (Zimbabwe African National Union—Patriotic Front) was largely Mashona, the tribe that made up most of the population. A few smaller political parties had also hung out their shingles in those hopeful years of the early '80s.

It didn't take long though, before all except the ruling ZANU-PF were stamped out. Merciless intimidation became the order of the day, and it could save a man's life if he was able to flash a ZANU-PF membership card. Most folk were happy to renounce allegiance to any other party in exchange for this valuable document, which with a bit of luck, would keep them and their family safe from unthinkable harms.

By the time I first visited Zim in 1992, in practical terms there was only the one active party, ZANU-PF. Rocking the boat of the men in power was a dangerous affair, so no one complained too loudly as long as people were fed and not suffering too much, businessmen allowed to create profitable enterprises, roads passable and power lines flowing with current. By the late 1990s, however, the country had fallen into a downward spiral.

The '90s also saw many rural Zimbabweans heading off with satchel in hand, to try their luck at a better life in the city. While living in the far-flung countryside they had mainly subsisted, growing much of what they required and bartering for other necessities. By not needing a lot of cash, they hadn't seen an obvious connection between their cost of living, and thereby quality of life, to politics. But as the new urbanites became more informed and increasingly savvy about personal finances, and therefore economics and prosperity, politics took on new meaning.

On the strength of the growing urban populous came the Movement for Democratic Change, forged in 1999 and headed by the stoic Morgan Tsvangirai, a former leader of the country's largest labor union. Despite its roots, the MDC quickly became a broad coalition of groups besides labor, also appealing to businessmen, farmers, those with a religious affiliation, and an array of others.

The small tribe of white-skinned people in the country also became enthusiastically involved. It had happened that, during the early '80s, two-thirds of whites in the country had said their goodbyes, not wanting their futures caught up in the uncertainty of a new government. Those left behind were less than one percent of Zimbabweans, so the prospect of having any real influence seemed slim at best. Time and resources usually spent on political efforts were thought put to better use on other community needs. By the late 1990s, however, whites began to wonder how much of the country's decline could be attributed to their sitting on the political sidelines. Optimistically, many jumped feet first into active support of the MDC.

At this time, our friend Alan of Rungudzi was in the midst of serving his second term as his district's political rep, a post almost never held by a white man. Several years earlier when he had first run, he'd initially declared himself an independent candidate. To this ZANU-PF officials immediately paid him a visit, offering, or rather strongly "encouraging", him to accept membership in their party. Alan's polite response was, "No thanks, I'd rather be an independent." To which they said, "Ah, but no, we insist!" Alan then calmly replied, "How can I be a member of ZANU-PF, if I don't agree with their policies and what they do?" To this they answered, "Well, if you think there are things needing changed within ZANU-PF, what better way than by becoming a member." Then they added ominously, "Besides, if you don't join and persist with running as an independent, the government will take your farm."

At first Alan was, as anyone would be, angry about the intimidation tactics. But as he thought about it, he decided it might be worthwhile to be in on the inner workings of the party. While his minor elected office would mean very little politicking outside his local community, he would still be able to attend national party conferences and receive bulletins. He figured he'd probably be more useful to his constituents as an informed official, rather than an excluded outsider.

So in late 1999, with all dedication Alan was serving his second term as his district's rep, still as a member of ZANU-PF. Yet the government's actions, being one and the same as the ZANU-PF party, had become increasingly hurtful to the nation. There were the suffocating monetary policies and other moves damaging to the economy, but especially the grim decline in human rights. Soon after the Movement for Democratic Change was formed, Alan resigned his post and decided to run for the same office, this time as an MDC candidate, in the elections to be held in early 2000.

Alan's gracious wife supported him in his political endeavors, often traveling with him throughout his rugged district of mainly communal and resettlement lands, his constituents almost entirely poor peasants. Like the many others now inspired to give the country a new spark, Alan began to help with MDC rallies, mainly by lending his farm truck as transport for the crowds who wanted to attend.

So it was that we had a few months of blissful optimism in late '99, as the emergence of this new party gained momentum. In fact, it wasn't so much a political group, but an organized means for people to join together in fruitful endeavor for their country. Soon everyone was going to MDC rallies—rich and poor, black and white, young and old. The crowds gathered in simple dirt parking lots, where speakers infused everyone with a new hope, stirring all to take an active role in saving the nation.

This contrasted sharply with the ZANU-PF platform, based on the notion that the problems of the country were, to begin with, a result of its brief colonial history. In particular the white element which embodied that past, as well as the evil and manipulative forces of foreign governments and agencies such as the IMF. Also individual land owners, who ZANU claimed ruthlessly kept the peasants suppressed. Plus businesses who horded foreign currency, rather than convert it into unexchangable Zimbabwe dollars. How to react to these menaces? In the view of ZANU-PF, with an iron fist, unyielding pressure, and policies that force them to abandon their defiant ways. And to show how tough we are, to also cut off dialogue with many foreign governments and agencies. We will beat them all back! We will be their pawns no longer! Fight, fight, fight! But this irrational and negative approach, with intimidation as its main tool, wasn't the way to endear the people.

Zimbabwe's president Mugabe and his party, not surprisingly, became incensed with the MDC. They considered it a rebellious element that was gaining too much support. Especially traitorous was the fact that the MDC consorted with white Zimbabweans, foreign countries of white citizens, and white businessmen. It fanned Mugabe's fury against those within the country, and whites were one of the first he cracked down on. Thugs, mostly under the guise of the Zimbabwe National Liberation War Veterans' Association, were sent out to do the dirty work. Alan was told that, in no uncertain terms, if he continued to use his truck to transport people to MDC meetings, it would be torched to cinders. Most alarming, many who openly supported the MDC became the targets for menacing death threats.

Throughout it all, the MDC's unwavering leader Morgan Tsvangirai continued to inspire Zimbabweans. He told of a nation in
which everyone had a better chance in life, by once again helping
businesses to bring about jobs and prosperity, by improving schools
and hospitals, and most importantly, by respecting human rights.
Mugabe was enraged by this blatant defiance, and we all uneasily
waited for the day when the headlines read, "Morgan Tsvangirai
Dies under Mysterious Circumstances."

As the threats and thuggery boiled up, businesses quickly took
down MDC posters and people locked pamphlets away in secret
places. The organization became something spoken of in whispers,
and only in trustworthy company. In the early days of the MDC,
supporters walking along the road would proudly give the MDC
salute as we whisked by in our car. An arm outstretched and held
high, palm up and open, all five fingers widely splayed. Now, only
partly in jest, the new MDC "salute" was a hand pressed tightly over
one's mouth.

I was still new to the country and busy with getting my own
plans on track, so the nation's political scene hovered at the periph-
ery of my life. As citizens, Darren joined some family and friends
to occasionally help with election efforts, but involvement by them
and our white peers soon dwindled. While everyone had thought
they were doing their part as Zimbabweans, this had only brought
death threats and risk to family. Better to leave the ballpark once
again, many thought, and let the majority rule.

Yet while it was relatively easy for whites to retreat politically,
for blacks who had come out in support of the MDC there was no
drifting back unnoticed to the sidelines. The fringe element who
supported ZANU-PF, or more accurately, the thugs paid by ZA-
NU-PF for their "efforts", targeted MDC supporters with calculated
brutality. It started as a shiver of hostility deliberately percolated
through the neighborhoods. By the middle of the following year,
however, when parliamentary elections were close at hand, it became an all-out attack of beatings, rape and torture, aimed at those
who were, or even thought to be, linked to the MDC. The whites
were in some measure "forgiven". After all, ZANU-PF expected

them to back opposition to the government. But blacks not supporting the government were deemed outright traitors. An offense
for which there'd be no mercy.

* * * * *

I could only call it a jinxed Christmas. The first disaster came in
mid-December, when a ripple of disturbing rumors foretold of the
country's fuel soon running out. All the nation's supply was precariously reliant on the government, the only one allowed to import
it. And while everyone anxiously speculated about how much still
skimmed the storage tanks, the government's *modus operandi* as
usual was not to communicate anything about what they were doing, thinking, or planning. So no one knew the real story, although
distributors were private companies and they hadn't been resup-
plied in a month. This had never happened before and it was believed stocks would hold out for only another few weeks. Although
certainly troubling, I figured that a country couldn't exist for too
long without this indispensable resource. So my concerns were a
little eased by assuming some kind of solution would have to come
about.

The rush on hardware stores meant shelves were soon emptied
of canisters, as everyone scurried to make sure they had a stash of
gas or diesel. Darren and I had to borrow containers from Alan for
our holiday travels, since our plan to visit both his mother and sister
would mean fifteen hours on the highway. And our chances of buying fuel along the way were virtually nil.

On top of this, I felt the weight of our personal worries. For
the last five months our energies had been poured into looking for
a farm, yet nothing had worked out. The needle on our compass
pointing us in that direction had seemed so clear, but could it be we
misread the signposts?

As it was, Darren and I now wondered if farming was really for
us. While admittedly Alan's place was more isolated than most, we
talked about whether we wanted to live so far out. It meant long
drives just to do basic shopping, see a friend on occasion, and now,

even to buy fuel. We'd also begun to feel we were missing out on the pulse of things. Yes, it was wonderful to have the breadth of open spaces, to keep our own hours and make a living from nurturing the earth. But we were now seeing the downsides, too. We both felt the constant stress of having to look after hundreds of workers, each needing a home for his family, a way to get to the hospital in an emergency, a supply of maize meal and some ground for a veggie patch, boots and overalls, plus an opportunity for their children's education. There was policing weekend brawls in the workers' village, and dealing with hysterical wives whose husbands beat them. The list was endless and fell to the farmer as provider for all.

Yet an even bigger problem for us was the difficulty of financing. By now banks weren't giving loans for any longer than three years, and interest had climbed to a strangling sixty percent. Costs were soaring, while agricultural commodity prices had tanked. Spare parts had become ever more difficult to find because of the foreign currency shortages, and the unresolved land dramas added more insecurity to the whole situation.

But to write-off farming put us back to our old quandary of how to earn a living. With the country falling apart all businesses were struggling, and we knew starting a venture of any kind could be dubious.

While we tossed ideas about, Darren remembered an enterprise he'd come across several years earlier, before we'd met. It'd been during his lonely drilling days in Zambia, when living out of a tent and working in the solitude of forgotten bush. He and his crew had tramped into the town of Kitwe, looking for a place to leave the rig while they went on leave. In the neglected industrial lot Darren rented stood a small building, and when he wandered over and had a look inside, he was surprised to find an abandoned workshop, complete with a plethora of equipment and tools. As he poked around in the shadows, he discovered it was an automotive engineering shop, a business that machines engine blocks, crankshafts, cylinder heads and other parts when an engine is overhauled. With his curiosity sparked he decided to track down the owner, who didn't hesitate to say he'd sell. His asking price was more than Darren had at the time, but it wasn't unreasonable and could certainly be a possibility for the future.

During those long months Darren spent in isolated corners of Zambia, passing infinite black evenings next to a crackling fire under the stars, he kept his mind busy by plotting out different ventures he might one day put in motion. That rundown machine shop was an interesting prospect. Where would be the best place to set it up? In a city with lots of competitors, or in a small town with less work but no competition? How many employees would he need, and who would be the best clientele to attract?

"I wonder if that workshop is still for sale," Darren said absently one afternoon. He had never mentioned it before, and as I looked to him with an eyebrow raised, he immediately went on to tell me about it. This kind of business would be a man's scene, rather dirty and rough, of which Darren would be running it more on his own. While we had wanted something to do together, we now had to admit that such prospects looked slim.

As it turned out, our decision about what to do soon became more urgent, when at the end of January Alan said he couldn't afford to pay Darren anymore. This didn't come as a surprise, since from the beginning it'd been obvious that Alan's farming operations were too small to support both an owner and manager.

Our options were few, so Darren quickly set about searching for the owner of the workshop in Kitwe. Finding him ended up being easy enough, and yes, it all still sat there, unsold. His price had gone up, but Darren still thought it a good investment. Everything was easily falling into place, and during those long evenings by the campfire, he had already thought through how to get it all started.

We had found our enthusiasm again, and as we cruised along the highway to his sister's for Christmas, our minds tumbled with plans. Streaming along through open fields of wide-leafed tobacco, then past squat soy bean plants waiting for rain, we felt vitally connected to this land, the place where our future would unfold. We drove through a shadowy wood while clouds above grew dense and gray, the power of nature mixing with our own stirred emotions.

As the sky darkened and churned, our drive led us through grasslands dotted with sluggish cattle, the wind growing stronger as we left the shelter of trees. Sweeping across the open fields, the wind shook the yellow grasses and roused the steers, who began to trudge their way home. Cracks of lightning shattered the heavy air, while black clouds boiled and the wind raced with fury, spinning the cattle trough windmills at a maddening pace. Africa was rallying us. Our motivation grew as a torrent of rain burst out, the wind hurling raindrops through my open window, past Darren and out again. We had plans to make, people to see, places to go. As soon as Darren finished up with Alan in a couple of weeks, we'd undertake the fourteen hour drive to Kitwe. From there we'd then head to southern Zimbabwe and make arrangements to set ourselves up.

Chapter Fourteen

|||||||||||||||||||||||||||||||||||||||||||||||||||||||||||||||||||||||||||||||||||||||||

The assault was sudden and fierce. With a torrent hurled down from the sky Cyclone Eline unleashed her wrath, pummeling southern Africa with a vengeance. On the continent's southeast coast, the palmed beaches and forested hills of Mozambique took the worst of the thrashing. Half the country was nearly wiped off the map, and it buffered the deluge that went on to sweep across eastern and southern Zimbabwe. Within hours, rivers swelled to flood plains, bridges washed away, and whole villages vanished in an instant.

In Mozambique the flash floods sent terrified villagers sprinting for the trees, the high branches their only place of refuge from the swiftly moving brown depth swallowing up the earth. There, families clung together for long days, waiting for too few helicopters to come to their rescue. As they balanced precariously, fighting off sleep and with muscles strained as though on a tightrope, amid the branches one woman gave birth to her daughter. For many hours she valiantly battled the fatigue wanting to push her into the churning swill below, when at last from above appeared a South African Army chopper team, to scoop her up and away.

Meanwhile, the rains pattered steadily down in the Lowveld of southern Zimbabwe. Although a heavier than normal downpour, it was the middle of the rainy season and didn't seem out of the ordinary. At Jane and Vic's, the offshoot of the Mtilikwe River in front of their house had spilled its shallow banks, their lowest expanse of lawn awash, with the brown water reaching the first of the stone steps leading to the higher terrace. The placid little tributary had never come up like this before, but it was still a safe distance from the house, and before Vic went sleepily off to bed he simply moved Jane's potted flowers onto the top stair.

Later, in the deep stillness of night, Jane was stirred by the muted sound of soft lapping. Drowsily she slipped out of bed, and in the dim shadows wandered over to the veranda door. When she creaked it open, at once she was shocked into wakefulness. In the silvery moonlight she watched with horror as the dark river washed on and off her veranda in easy waves, her flower pots now bobbing around like buoys on the ocean.

Scrambling throughout the rest of the night and into dawn, Vic and Jane hurried to empty the house of their furniture, clothes and keepsakes. When the first light of morning peeked over the horizon, it revealed an astonishing sight. Sweeping out from the edge of their veranda was a vast, brown sea. Their lawns and garden, and the reedy islet that had rested within the small watercourse, had completely disappeared, consumed by the swollen river which had meandered a mile away. Further downstream, the Mtilikwe had grown to such power and ferocity, that in one big bite it had devoured half the concrete highway bridge.

Over at Hammond on the other side of the district, Spike was away, leaving only Nicky and the workers on the ranch. There the Njerezi, a parched sandy riverbed for most of the year, was running fast and full in front of Hammond's lodge. Without the slightest warning, the river suddenly swelled and overran its banks, sending a murky flood to rush through the painstaking-built prize of the ranch. Vigilant workers raced to call Nicky, who wasted no time wresting a boat down to the lodge, in a desperate attempt to save what she could. But while Nicky swam around inside the kitchen, grabbing pots and cups and throwing them in the boat, she had to watch helpless as the stove and fridge floated off downstream.

Nearby on the sprawl of Humani, a teeming herd of goats found themselves trapped in a low-level paddock with the water quickly rising. Desperately they clambered up against the fence, treading water and barely keeping their heads above the muddy depth. To add to their panic, snakes of all varieties streamed towards them to scramble up amongst their horns, also trying to find higher ground from the rapidly rising tide. When rescuers eventually rowed up in boats, the snakes, many fatally venomous, had to first be cautiously untangled from the goats' horns and left to their watery fate.

Unlike the fortunate goats, thousands of other animals through-out the flooded areas couldn't be saved. Such as the three hundred ostriches that drowned when their thousand acre paddock was swamped. Elsewhere, Vic watched helpless as a troop of terrified monkeys scampered up into the branches of a tall msasa to es-cape the spreading waters. The tree became alive with the shriek-ing hoard, as they watched the strong current rushing by below. It wasn't long before its roots gave way and the heavily laden tree was swept downstream, carrying with it the desperate monkeys scream-ing to the end.

In fact, all trees became writhing, buzzing masses, as every reptile, bird, insect and small creature climbed skyward to flee the engulfing sea. The shrill pandemonium that pulsed out from the branches sent an unsettling ripple to the core of one's bones. Any-one who happened to brush up against a tree trunk, as he waded through water or slipped past in a boat, would instantly have a swarm of ants, beetles, and spiders rushing over his hand and up his arm in a panic for safety. Each creature desperate to escape from the millions of others teeming in the treetops.

Meanwhile on Zimbabwe's southern border, the deep gorge of the Limpopo River was full to the brim and perilously rising. Its high bridge linking Zimbabwe and South Africa was now closed. Usually feeble creeks swelled up hills and onto roads, forcing cars, buses and interlink trucks to crowd atop highway ridges. Many drivers abandoned their rigs, while others climbed on top, only to be stranded on their trailer roofs for days.

In the Eastern Highlands and bordering Mozambique, our friends Trevor and Karen were even closer to the eye of the storm. There was nothing Trevor could do as he watched his young coffee trees and newly planted timber be thrashed by the cyclone, much of it destroyed. The bridge at Tanganda junction on the only paved track into Chipinge, isolated and tucked in the mountains, was carried away by the floods. The community became entirely cut off and within a few days stores ran out of supplies, banks closing because they had no more cash. Trevor and Karen were without electricity for eight weary days, and had to wait two weeks until their telephone worked again.

Having weathered the storm in the Lowveld, Jane and Vic moved back into their house a couple days after the flood. With unease, they noticed there'd been a lot of activity around the place while they'd been away. Revealed, with a shiver, by the many crocodile tracks about. Along with the even more dangerous hippos, whose footprints went right up to the front door. Luckily the water hadn't forced its way inside, but the river was still high and at night they could hear the hippos foraging just outside the bedroom window. They could only guess what the sneaky crocs might be up to.

When the swollen river in front of Jane's house finally seeped back, the view from the veranda was a startling one. There was just one vast scene of gray devastation. Sadly, many large trees in their garden had been carried away, while others, when the soil about their roots had been stewed into soft mud, were now yanked to a sharp angle by the muscle of the current. Most of the leaves and smaller branches were gone, leaving eerie skeletons bent at sickly angles. Where the expanse of emerald lawn had been, now lay mudflats of brown silt. Past it, the small island where the hippos played was strangely void of bush and tall grass, so we could now gaze beyond it for a distance. The whole scene presented an alien landscape, as if the house had been plunked down on a different planet, Jane's award-winning garden now only a memory.

For thousands of ill-fated villagers, mostly Mozambicans, their homes and livelihoods had been completely erased. Their huts and meager belongings all washed away. Their fields caked in silt with crops buried under it, and every last one of their oxen, goats and chickens carried out to an infinite ocean.

I shuddered at this chilling reminder of how fragile fate and existence can be. And in the shifting tide of Zimbabwe, it seemed even nature had her moment of rage, leaving scars upon the land not to be quickly forgotten.

Chapter Fifteen

||||||||||||||||||||||||||||||||||||||||||||||||||||||||||||||||||||||||||||||||||||||||

The fuel fiasco still reigned, leaving our tank dangerously low. But for me to venture from Rungudzi to the nearest station and back, took a gas guzzling hour of driving. So as always I phoned ahead, and was promised there'd be some set aside for me. Yet maddeningly, not for the first time I arrived at the station to discover I'd been terribly mislead. The pumps held not even a dribble. The rest of the country, especially the capital of Harare, was limping along on fumes as well. All that Darren and I needed to scrounge together though, was enough to reach the Zambian border seven hours away, where we could buy as much as we wanted on the other side. Always generous, Alan doled out to us some of his cache of the precious liquid. And we made sure to take along extra containers to fill up in Zambia, so we could at least make it back home.

Several years had passed since Darren had seen the workshop, and before buying wanted to have another good look. This meant undertaking a grueling thousand mile journey to Kitwe in central Zambia, in the middle of the continent and up on the border with the Congo's badlands.

* * * * *

I was impatient to be on the road, having never been to Zambia and looking forward to the thrill of checking out new territory. Darren on the other hand, had spent more than his fill of time there, during the few years before we'd met. Trying to describe the place to me, he wondered if I might find it similar to Malawi. Although he'd never been to this small nation east of Zambia, for a few days in 1992 I had tramped about its peaceful countryside. What both of us did know, was that neither of these lands had seen the modern world filter in as much as in Zim.

Struggling to keep up with the modern age, the little country of Malawi rested to the northeast of Zimbabwe. Long and thin geographically, stretching along her east side and vying in size with Lake Erie, lay the tranquil waters of Lake Malawi. The country was mostly hilly, her ridge tops helping to catch the moisture drifting off the expansive lake. With more reliable rains than in Zim, cropping and raising livestock had been better prospects there. This steady water supply provided Malawi with that essential feature needed for people to simply subsist.

In decades past, the peasant folk of this small nation had thrived in their environment. Her population, like most countries in the world, boomed during the twentieth century. So now, every inch of Malawi had the burden of trying to support ever-expanding, impoverished families. During my visit through this land of kind-natured folk, as I motored about the rutted clay roads I anxiously scanned every hill and curving dell, searching for a patch that wasn't weighted with scraggly rows of crops or foraging livestock.

What especially made this landscape so disheartening, was the fact that these struggling cornstalks were only a pitiful likeness to the flexing fields in America's bread basket. Subsistence farming exacts a heavy toll on the earth. Cleared lands farmed with modern practices and high-yielding seeds, can produce twenty times the food than subsistence cropping. So it follows that under subsistence, twenty times the land must be razed to produce the same rations.

Further dispiriting was to see that most folk lacked a respect for the ills of erosion. Or it may have been that, desperate for land to crop, they planted on erosion sensitive land anyway. Malawi's hilly terrain, combined with her steady rainfall, makes erosion an eternal danger. The sight of cleared hills whose slopes had fallen away in jagged chucks was truly depressing. Soft soil lay exposed, bleeding downstream to the ocean and sapping more productivity from an already strained land.

One of my favorite features about Malawi was her magnificent trees, her climate especially perfect for growing the beautiful ebonies. Like many hardwoods, over decades they could rise to massive proportions. In Alaska trees are of necessity a spindly breed, as otherwise the snowload on their branches would shear them to stalks. For me, gazing upon a woodland of strong timbers was just as inspiring as a raging waterfall or majestic mountain range.

Understandably then, I felt real sadness when looking upon the annihilation of Malawi's forests. The large ebonies had all vanished, even medium-sized ones now rare, with the mahoganies and others also rapidly disappearing. Craftsmen whittling carvings to sell to tourists certainly didn't help the deforestation. More than anything though, it was the clear-cutting for subsistence farming and cooking over a simple wood fire, that spelled the death of Malawi's woodlands.

In place of the resplendent forests, was a land now groaning under the crush of humanity. So when Darren wondered if Zambia was like Malawi, I thought, oh how I pray not.

* * * * *

Darren was relaxed and upbeat, now that he had a clear course to the future and felt his fate was back in his hands. I was also eager as the wheels of our pickup ticked off the highway miles. As we trekked north towards Zambia, I saw a boldness to the land to match our energy. Now late February and near the end of the rainy season, the bush looked healthy and strong, with every leaf and tender shoot strutting itself in vigorous green. For the last hour before the border, the highway cut along the steep Zambezi escarpment, where cascading below lay breathtaking territory. I looked out to a stunning mosaic of dark-green bush, granite boulders, a scatter

of thorn trees laying some shade, swathes of beige earth ribboned
through. A picture of Africa at her most vibrant.

Marking out the border, the Zambezi River quietly churned as
we trundled across the Chirundu bridge and into Zambia. On this
side the drive down was easier, through low mountains of peaceful
wilderness. With an image of Malawi in mind, I assumed I'd see
people far and wide. There, everywhere had been a woman hoeing a
patch of corn or cooking over an open fire, a thin boy herding goats,
or a shirtless man fishing with a net in the river.

As we curved our way down the escarpment and I searched the
hills for signs of settlement, I immediately felt relief. Although I
knew a lot of this land along the river was set aside as park, it was
still heartening to find so much bushland still outwardly intact.
Even if most of the wildlife, especially rhino and elephant, had long
been finished off by poachers. So although the bush was still there,
I knew amongst its shadows much was missing.

A quick two hours from the border took us to the outskirts of
the capital, Lusaka. As Zambia's largest city I envisioned a place
similar to Harare, with skyscrapers, miles of four-lane byways, and
an hour drive from end to end. Yet before me was more of a sleepy
town than a bustling city. Although I'd known Zambia's industry
was only a fraction of Zim's, not until seeing the scant size of her
economic center did I understand how little commerce there really
was in the country.

The tragedy of it was that Zambia did have the potential for success. In the past their mining industry had thrived, and there was
no reason that tourism couldn't increase fivefold. I'd been told that,
even more so than Zim, the country had a better climate, soils, and
terrain for agriculture. If Zambia's agricultural industry burgeoned
to its potential, I guessed Lusaka would soon become a lively metropolis.

Instead, I found Lusaka in a dreadful state. One of the larger
buildings in the center of the city, twenty stories high, seemed typical of the decay. A fire had swept through its midsection some years
back, gutting several middle floors, leaving glassless windows and
the interior's black hollow clearly visible. Yet unbelievably on the

floors below, florescent lights revealed busy offices of people going about their work, as though completely unaware of the charred remains lingering above their heads. But that was how life and business went on in much of Africa. Everything around falling apart, no hope of it being repaired, leaving me to wonder how a country had continued for this long without collapse.

As I watched these scenes of a struggling city pass by, with a buzz of commerce but in a grubby and lethargic way, I supposed it was inevitable that Zambia's transition into an independent nation would have its growing pains. There'd been such a chasm to bridge, when in 1964 this predominantly tribal society decided to adopt many of the western ways of its several thousand European settlers. Most of these immigrants had first stepped down from their ox wagons onto Zambian soil in the 1920s, after the discovery of copper. At that time, the Africans in the country still lived the same ancient tribal lifestyle they had for hundreds of years. In the early twentieth century, with a stream of Europeans turning the footpath north into a well-beaten track, highways and railroads soon reached across the land, followed by unending miles of telephone and electricity cable. Western-style government and legal systems were established. Then in the 1950s a crowning glory to modernity towered up on the Zambezi River, when the Kariba hydroelectric dam harnessed and tamed the mighty waters.

Soon after this 1964 arrived, when the British handed the country its independence and the Zambians found themselves rulers of a changing land. I tried to imagine what it must have been like for them to have inherited the many Western cultural, political, legal and civil systems. Before the arrival of Europeans only a few decades earlier, the wheel had not been in use and Zambians had no written language. By the 1960s, it had been one generation since European settlements of any significance appeared in Zambia. Most Zambian government officials, utility executives and schoolteachers, would have grown up in a thatched hut without plumbing or electricity. The people of Zambia had faced many hurdles in the country's early years, and I could see they were still working hard to get past them.

* * * * *

"These roads can be utterly painful," Darren grumbled as he negotiated our pickup through Lusaka. "I see they haven't made improvements since I was here last."

"Yeah, I know you warned me they could be frightening, but
this is downright dangerous," I declared, wide-eyed and checking
my seatbelt.

Ahead of us lay a maze of potholes so deep, large and numerous, that traffic traveling in both directions zigzagged down the
road, careening between the holes and swinging across both lanes.
All I could see was what seemed to be complete chaos, as vehicles
darted in every direction. In fact I did notice an informal protocol,
which was simply to drive on the shreds of pavement still remaining
between craters. The problem was that cars sprinting in both directions wanted to use the same shred of asphalt. And while residents
of Lusaka were old hands at navigating, rather too quickly, down
their familiar streets, out-of-towners like us had to desperately maneuver amongst it all, hearts racing and a prayer on our lips.

"Well, at least there are roads," I observed, looking on the bright
side. When I'd visited Malawi in '92 a single battered, although admittedly paved, byway had been the only drivable link through the
countryside. Tracks going off were so badly rutted or washed away
that even a donkey cart often couldn't negotiate them. Certainly not
a feature to help commerce thrive.

Once out of Lusaka and sailing along the two-lane highway
again, I let out a sigh of relief. The road was now peacefully quiet,
its sparse traffic another symptom of Zambia's lack of prosperity.
I wasn't allowed to relax for long though, as even out of town lay
treacherous potholes, Darren slamming on breaks when a dark
patch suddenly appeared. After thanking our lucky stars we hadn't
snapped an axel hundreds of miles from anywhere, we cautiously
continued on, keeping eyes peeled for the next labyrinth of craters.

As we pressed on through a lonely countryside, I did notice one
informal industry that seemed popular. At intervals along the road
peasants were selling bundles of charred black sticks, something

like charcoal. To make these, a supply of trees was axed down and then burnt underground. I felt a knot in my gut at the sight of so many beautiful hardwoods turned into charred shreds, knowing there'd be no replanting of this precious resource.

Further along the deserted highway, other barefoot Zambians wearing threads were trying to earn a few bucks by selling meat, in its crudest form. Upon hearing the rush of our truck's approach, some fellow would leap out from the bushes to lean into our lane, and with an outstretched arm frantically shake a still feathered dead chicken by its bloodless feet. Then a few miles down the road, on offer might be a beef quarter, a fawn-sized antelope, or a limp furry rabbit. While I wondered who might actually be buying such delicacies, Darren cautiously veered around each flailing peddler, worried he might slip in his desperation for a sale.

Occasionally we traveled upon stretches of highway where a few potholes had recently been filled with dirt. Rather than the efforts of a government works department, it looked like more poor folk creatively trying to earn a dollar. As we sped along, scrappy teenagers sitting by the road sprang up when they heard the approaching hum of our tires. Grabbing a shovel, each stood expectantly next to a pile of dirt and a pothole, stretching an open palm towards our truck. I doubted this "occupation" earned much of a living, although enough of them stood by potholes over the hundreds of miles we traveled to make it seem there must have been some money in it.

By the time we arrived in Zambia's second largest town of Kitwe it was late Friday afternoon. The little community had obviously wrapped up business for the week, since the streets were virtually deserted.

"Well, I can say one thing," Darren commented with a wry smile, as he scanned the empty lanes. "They've made improvements to the roads since I was here last."

"Really, how so?" I replied, noting his bit of sarcasm.

"The town council has simply torn up the last shreds of asphalt and put the lanes back to dirt," he explained. "This way at least, a grader can smooth out the roads now and then. And when potholes do appear they'll be rounded, rather than sharp-edged pits in pavement that bend tire rims."

Guiding our pickup through the shabby town, Darren steered a beeline to where he had stayed many times on his passings through remote Kitwe. This inn of sorts sat in a common neighborhood lot and from the outside was only a plain concrete wall, just like all the other houses on the street. But as the high metal gate slowly rolled to one side, a beautiful oasis was revealed beyond. I felt the weight of the surrounding decay lift from my shoulders and soothing relief come over me. As we pulled inside our tires crackled enticingly on the white gravel. Before us lay an alluring expanse of lawn, fringed with a plushness of ferns and multicolored blooms. Next to the walking path, miniature waterfalls showered over rock sculptures, giving a restful melody to the fading day.

We left our bags in our room and made our way across a cushion of lawn. The crystal pool lay undisturbed in the growing shadows, as we strolled past to where tables sat invitingly on an open-air veranda. Burgundy bricks formed a short outside wall, holding back large strelitzia, philodendron and cycad plants that cast swaying shadows over the dining tables. Amidst the warm evening air, we settled into comfortable chairs and relieved our parched taste buds with tingling sips of wine.

Kitwe sat only a stone's throw south of the Congo, an untamed land stretching for a thousand miles from north to south and almost as wide. With impenetrable tropical forests, daunting rivers, and downpours that disintegrate roads, any attempt to explore, or even traverse, this vast domain was a near impossible feat.

The Congo's seat of government lay in the very west of the country, and during dry spells a person might be lucky to reach the southern districts in a journey of weeks. During the rains, however, it was hopeless to even try to trek overland from one end of the country to the other, leaving the south as a place unto itself. Here, the reach of the central government was even further weakened, in territory where roads and telephones were already scarce. Most of the businessmen in southern Congo were hard-edged entrepreneurs, in a place not unlike the early American West. Each community had to devise its own way of keeping law and order, and bandits thrived dodging between far-flung settlements.

Zambia was a world of modern amenities then, compared to southern Congo. Many businessmen from across the border made frequent trips to Kitwe, the closest Zambian town. With few places to lodge, most stayed at the Sherbourne Inn. Having these steely nerved buccaneers, who of necessity must be shrewd and cunning, milling closely nearby, gave the mood an edge of daring intrigue.

Fingering the cool moistness of my wineglass, I let my eyes follow a toughened patron sauntering up to the bar. In the dimming light of evening his body looked stiff from a long hot ride, a whisper of dust coming from what appeared to be worn leather chaps. But no, it was just the shadows playing tricks. And was that a holster at his hip? No again, only my imagination filling in details veiled by a fading sun.

Darren and I dined on a supper of Nile perch, made all the more delicious because surrounding us lay hundreds of miles of untamed land. Not only had the ingredients made a long and complicated journey to our plates, we knew that for a vast distance such cuisine could not be bought at any price.

"Let's go have a drink at the bar," Darren said after we finished dinner. We strolled over and settled onto stools next to a burly man, who I was sure could be intimidating if he wanted. Instead, I found myself mesmerized by his translucent blue eyes, glinting brightly from light-chocolate skin. He must have been a frequent guest here, because the proprietor of the inn soon came by and greeted him like an old friend.

When Darren turned to the big man, at first he was reluctant to be drawn into conversation. But after awhile Darren's friendly approach had him feeling comfortable enough to talk. His smooth accent was of no particular place, an exotic mix from speaking English in Zambia, French in the Congo, and probably several African languages. Darren and I felt an instant camaraderie with him when he told us he'd been born and raised in Zimbabwe. He was a true son of Africa, with both a Shona and Matabele grandparent, an Afrikaner grandparent (that is, a white African with centuries-old

Dutch, French and German ancestry) and an English grandparent whose father and mother had been early pioneers to Zim.

His was an interesting story, as we learned he was a copper merchant, buying the ore in its roughest form in the Congo from peasants who mined it by hand. When he had filled a semi truck with copper he would bring it to Zambia to sell. He told us his greatest risk was during transport, as often these trucks ferrying tons of copper were hijacked. A fortune could be lost, and there was no way to insure against such perils. After a few drinks he then fell into a wistful mood, telling us about his wife and children living in Lusaka, and how he missed them.

At a table nearby lounged another traveler from the Congo, whose wife had come along. As Darren and the copper merchant fell into a discussion on the finer details of mining, my attention wandered to the couple. I overheard the wife telling the inn owner she was excited to be in Kitwe, as it'd been some time since she'd made a trip out of southern Congo where they lived. I stole a glance over and could see they were well-to-do. She looked chic and cultured, and talked with anticipation about all the shopping she had planned for the next day. "How wonderful it is to be in civilization again," she gushed with elation.

Kitwe as civilization! I considered we had traveled somewhere beyond such. And I certainly couldn't imagine being excited about shopping here, even if it was the second largest town in Zambia. There was less in this place than in the tiniest American town. Only the industrial sites were larger than might be expected for a little community, since mechanics, welders, carpenters, and sheet metal constructors were all in demand in a place where the repair business was the largest industry going. Certainly not a locale to find *haute couture.*

Instead I found other things that lured me. An aura of high intrigue and fortunes to be won. Lands promising copper and gold, diamonds and gems, and forests of hardwood timber, albeit laced with the taint of dubious business deals. A frontier where vast riches could be made, but where all could slip from your grasp in the blink of an instant.

* * * * *

Before us stretched the last daunting stage of our Zambia expedition—the five hundred mile obstacle course of disintegrating highway back to Zim. Darren had wrapped up the deal to purchase
the workshop equipment and we headed back on a route through
southernmost Zambia. From the border town of Livingstone, resting high on the banks of the Zambezi River, it would be a quick hop
over to Victoria Falls town on the Zimbabwe side.

After a long day's drive, Darren crept our pickup over the cen-
tury-old bridge. While the treacherous Zambezi boiled underneath
us, the colossal falls towered above, pounding down in a deafening
rush. I was humbled by its awesome power, feeling like an insignificant creature as we inched across the thread of a bridge, hanging over the wide gorge chiseled out by the river's steady pulse. The
explorer David Livingstone had named Victoria Falls, although the
Africans living here had more aptly called this misty, roaring behe-
moth The Smoke That Thunders.

As we eased our way back into Zimbabwe, I immediately
thought back to the cultured Congolese woman who'd been so enthusiastic at having crossed into Zambia. I too felt I was passing
through the gates of civilization, as we left Zambia's border town
of Livingstone and drove into Victoria Falls, where the contrast
couldn't be more glaring.

Livingstone looked like so many other towns found in Africa—
a relic of times past. Most of the buildings were dilapidated 1950s-
style houses, their yards fronted by stout hardwoods that neatly
lined the streets, as though this had once been a quiet little town
in the States. In another setting the trees would look majestic. But
surrounded by a crumbling town and sitting amidst garbage and
weeds, they seemed limp and dreary. Alongside them lay roads dotted with potholes, while none of the buildings, fences, or signs had
been repainted in years. Even the traffic lines on the streets had long
since been worn away. Weary pedestrians trudged along lanes of
few vehicles, and only a couple of dim shops appeared to be doing
any business.

Then—POW! Crossing over the river and stepping into Victoria Falls, was like pulling into Vegas from out of the desert. The place was flashy and vibrant, with smiling tourists strolling along landscaped grounds among new buildings and busy shops. The bustling streets were repaired, and when the yellow stripes in the middle of the road caught my eye, I realized I hadn't seen such a phenomenon for days. This was the modern world!

The pace in the little town was enlivening. Business thrived. There was even a Subway sandwich shop with its familiar yellow sign, along with funky gift stores and Internet cafés. In the many chic hotels were flashing slot machines and the whir of roulette wheels. While hints of Africa did show here and there—a littered parking lot, a peeling old building, a verge of uncut grass, and a scattering of poor folk dressed in rags—the town was strikingly better off than its dreary neighbor just over the bridge.

So why the difference? Simply, the bustle of commerce and economic opportunity. For Darren and me, like all Zimbabweans, Zambia was an unsettling reminder next door. And as Zimbabwe's economy kept dwindling away, we all whispered the prayer, "just as long as we don't become like Zambia." Plunging into that same black hole of decay.

Chapter Sixteen

||||||||||||||||||||||||||||||||||||||||||||||||||||||||||||||||||||||||||||||||||||||||||

S tepping out of the car, I stretched my arms wide with renewed vigor. It was a relief to finally be off the road. A late afternoon shower had cooled the day and I drew in a breath of clean air, sweet smelling and fresh. We had reached Darren's sister's home in Triangle, close to Chiredzi where Darren had decided to move the equipment and set up shop.

Our drive through Zim from Victoria Falls had been on quiet highway, and by late afternoon we had made our way through the Lowveld, where the aftermath of Cyclone Eline was still to be startlingly seen. Snapped tree limbs and clumps of debris were tangled high in the trees, astonishing evidence of the height to which the rivers had swelled. Bridges were only beginning to be repaired, and over the Mtilikwe we nervously crept across a precarious patchup, the gap between what remained of the bridge and the cliff-like bank being only piled high dirt. Many roads were unpaved and still deeply rutted, the fuel shortage making the situation worse. Graders and backhoes that could have been busy helping to get life back to normal were often left standing because of their empty tanks.

Yet amidst the wreckage, the sun-baked little town of Chiredzi still thrived. In fact, compared to the rest of Zim which was suffering from the depressed economy, and certainly in conspicuous contrast to Zambia, Chiredzi seemed to be booming. Darren and I felt further encouraged by all the business owners who told us they were humming with work. The largest industry in the district, that of growing and processing sugar, was also doing well. Our decision to set up here had undoubtedly been a good one, as everyone we talked with was confident our business would be a success.

"Let's take a picnic basket down to the river this afternoon," Darren's sister Jane said to me, while Darren was out with his brother-in-law on the last day of our visit. Jane's daughter Shawna joined us, as we pushed our way through yellow grass higher than our heads, down to where the cyclone had carved out a fresh sandbar. Spreading a blanket, we nestled onto soft sand, the tall grass pressing close and creating a cocoon around us.

"Now, let's see what your future holds," Jane said bewitchingly, as she pulled tarot cards from the basket. A mirror of water sparkled next to us through an opening in the grass, while I carefully selected the cards that would show my fate.

"Ah yes, this is good. Very good," Jane pronounced thoughtfully, confirming that, indeed, the course Darren and I had chosen was the right one, and everything would work out just fine.

* * * * *

"I'm sorry to have to do this to you," Darren said, "but you'll have to pack up the house and manage all the moving by yourself."

"Don't worry, I understand," I replied. "You've got a big job ahead of you, readying all that equipment for its long journey to Chiredzi."

"Yeah, I'll probably be gone for a couple of weeks."

Our few days in the Lowveld had been successful, having found a premise for our business and a house to rent. So now we were back on the road again, first to Harare where Darren would return directly to Kitwe without me. Driving the long miles north I felt wistful, excited that our plans were moving forward, yet also knowing I would miss our little Eden on the edge of the bush.

A gentle rain had pattered down most of the day, but by early evening when I arrived home the sky had cleared to powder-blue. I wandered out to the veranda where I could settle into the molded comfort of my woven-grass chair, and feeling peaceful, watched a brawny sun dip towards the horizon, making the droplets on every leaf sparkle. While I breathed in the misted evening's intoxicating scent, I smiled to see my favorite birds—the dainty Blue Waxbills—delicately pick seeds from the bird feeder, until the rowdy Masked Weaver pushed his way in. Nearby, iridescent starlings shimmered blue-green and purple, as they hopped about on the lawn. Flocks of ribbon-tailed swallows swept high across the sky, while perky lizards darted about on the low brick wall in front of me. Even the trees seemed content, swaying to the subtle rhythm of the wind.

The beauty and splendor of the farm was more poignant than usual, because an ominous presence had recently arrived there. While Darren and I had been away a group of squatters had settled themselves on Rungudzi. Although this was unheard of in the past, in recent days a handful of other farms in the district also had strangers showing up to camp out, a part of a growing trend throughout the country. At first everyone assumed the squatter problem was related to the ever present issue of land distribution, which had seen many dramas over the years. This simply seemed another development in the never-ending saga, to which farmers took the position they would just leave the squatters alone, until a solution could be found.

As usual, there was nothing clear coming from the government. Mugabe's stance was that the peasants had simply moved onto commercial farmland of their own accord. He said he sympathized with the squatters, and with a low smile asked how he could go against the "spontaneous" will of the people. As always, he made no mention of a plan to resolve the situation. We all knew his unspoken wish was that the four thousand farmers, other than the few who supported ZANU-PF, would "spontaneously" pack their bags, go live in another country, and leave their farming businesses behind for Mugabe to do with as he pleased.

Not long after the arrival of squatters on farms, the Zimbabwe National Liberation War Veterans' Association announced they were the ones organizing what became known as the "land invasions". Most of the squatters, however, were women with children in tow, and men too young to have played a role in Zimbabwe's civil war, which ended twenty years earlier.

While the national farmers' union was hastily coming up with a plan to deal with the situation, squatters became increasingly aggressive in occasional confrontations with farmers. Tensions between them and farm workers also heated up.

Yet on Rungudzi, the situation remained calm. The squatters had picked a particular knoll on which to camp, and hadn't ventured over to the farmhouses or other buildings. Nor had they wandered near my horse riding trails, so I never came across their unsettling presence. Alan firmly instructed his workers, who were very unsympathetic to the squatters and even felt some animosity towards them, to also keep their distance.

One moonless evening soon after I returned to the farm, I strolled over to Alan's for one of those pleasant interludes at his inviting bar. He was always a reassuring sight, as he sat looking proper in a crisp white shirt, yet all the while relaxed and welcoming. We had only just poured our drinks and begun to catch up on news, when a faint beat of drums and distant singing floated subtly into the room. It seemed to come from the squatters' camp, although this wasn't particularly alarming, since often in the evenings the Africans sang and stirred up some music. A similar rhythm was often heard coming from Rungudzi's workers' village, especially on weekend nights. And when I visited friends on their farms it wasn't unusual to hear the pulsing beats drifting through the darkness.

But this time, the sound coming from the squatters' camp was distracting. A reminder of trespassers nearby and surely a whisper of things to come. To which I felt a gloomy uneasiness slip into the back of my mind.

In a corner at the other end of the room, Alan's TV was tuned to the government station. Our conversation had taken a distracted turn, as both of us tried to brush off the low chanting which had crept into the room. When the evening news announced that a spokesman for the War Veterans' Association was to make a statement, we put down our drinks to wander over and listen. He got straight to the point, and with steely words threatened that if ZA-

NU-PF lost seats in the upcoming parliament elections, the Veterans would take to arms and war would break out.

Straight away, my puzzling conversation with the headmaster came to mind. I remembered him saying that the peasants' greatest fear was of war. Clearly the spokesman's pointed declaration was a calculated move by the ruling party—that is, the government— to announce on national TV that voting for the opposition would mean just that: War. It was an outright threat to Zimbabweans, that if they didn't keep the ruling party in power their worst fear would become reality. I had thought the headmaster was being ridiculous when he'd said people would continue to vote for Mugabe because they were afraid of war. In fact, he'd been exactly right.

After this menacing announcement on TV, scarcely ten minutes passed when the throb from the squatters' camp pumped up to a bolder pitch.

"A couple of the squatters must have snuck down to the workers' village and watched the news on their community TV," Alan commented calmly. "They've probably gone back to their camp and told the rest of the group all about it."

As he spoke, the drums and chanting grew louder still. We both silently wondered if they were making their way towards the house, to which Alan casually stood up and sauntered over to the window. Taking a drag on his cigarette, he pushed the curtain aside and peered into the darkness. All the while keeping his cool and looking unworried, possibly as much for his own benefit as for mine.

"They've stayed at their camp on the hill," Alan said to me as he contemplated the blackness outside. "Sound travels clearly at night. They aren't coming this way."

He then poured us each another drink and we tried to continue with our light conversation. But really it was impossible, as how could we speak of simple matters like what our families were up to, the funny thing the dog did, or an irritation that seemed so minor now, when the fabric of the nation was unraveling around us?

"Well, I guess I'd better wander home," I said quietly, since we both seemed to have run out of much to say. "Goodnight Alan, you were great company as always."

"You'd better take a hand radio with you, just in case," he cautioned. "Let me give you the frequencies and show you how it works."

"Thanks, you're the best," I said as he then walked me to his gate, both of us subdued. "See you tomorrow."

"Yes, see you in the morning. Sleep well," he bid me, briefly laying a comforting hand on my shoulder.

"You sleep well too, Alan," I called back as I walked away in the darkness, feeling a sad foreboding that, somehow, nothing in our lives would ever be the same again.

* * * * *

A couple days later I strolled over to Alan's to join him for morning coffee, where I found him busy on the phone and CB radio. This was often the case when I happened to pop in and I didn't pay much attention. After making myself a cup without him, I settled into one of the carved dining chairs, high-backed and comfortable, at his burnished Arthurian table. The room's curved outer wall was windows from end to end, framing a peaceful panoramic of his hilly farm resting in the morning sun. Out the open windows, silky green-blue peacocks with brilliant tails wandered by on the lawn, and the whistling of songbirds lilted through the garden. But while I gazed out across the landscape of strong bush, pieces of a disturbing conversation caught my attention. With unease, I gathered that something dreadful must have happened to the headmaster.

"How absolutely terrible," Alan, composed as always, began as he walked into the room. Then shaking his head in disbelief, explained, "Last night at eleven, the headmaster of the resettlement school was so severely beaten by so-called ZANU youths, he's now in the hospital."

"Oh no, that's horrible!" I gasped, unable to imagine the soft-mannered headmaster, with whom I'd talked a bit of politics, arguing with someone, let alone launching into a fight. "Why was he attacked?"

"It has been blamed on his support of the political opposition," Alan answered in a flat tone.

"That doesn't make sense," I argued. "Only a few months ago he defended Mugabe to me. He seemed supportive of ZANU-PF."

"Well, he isn't actually a political guy," Alan commented in response. "He stays out of politics."

"I don't understand, there must be some kind of explanation for it," I then remarked more to myself than to Alan, upset by such seemingly random brutality.

After a minute in thought, Alan went on to coolly explain. He said that during Zimbabwe's 1970s civil war, the guerilla groups that later formed ZANU were backed by China and other communist countries. Part of the support given by the communists was military training, with Mugabe himself even taking part. Tactics taught by the Chinese included how to control the people by intimidation, and towards this end, one method was to break the local leader or another influential figure in the community. This was supposed to create fear amongst the folk, and once intimidated, their suppressors believed they were controlling the populous.

Alan paused, gazing out the window over the peaceful landscape. "In rural Zimbabwe, the local headmaster is looked upon as a community leader of sorts. Regardless of his views or actions, or even a lack of such, he is often a target for violence. Then when the locals see that even an influential person in their group cannot defend himself, they simply do as they are told. Hoping that they and their families will avoid a similar fate."

Alan paused once more, then added with an edge of bitterness, "It's really just terrorism."

I thought back to my conversation with the headmaster, remembering how he had furtively eyed the others standing nearby, when I had started to discuss Mugabe and voting. I was miffed with his evasiveness then, but now it was all clear.

Without a doubt, the premeditated steering of this placid country towards a dark path had begun.

Chapter Seventeen

W hile I'd miss much about the farm, I'd be leaving one nerve-wracking trauma behind: the harrowing drive from Rungudzi to Harare. The two-hour journey always started safe enough, since there was little traffic along Gota Hill Road from the farm to the "highway". But once on this single-lane of asphalt, a terrifying blur of buses and trucks careened through the hills, a scatter of turtle's-crawl ox carts thrown into the confusion. Most frazzling was that as I speeded along, motorists coming in the opposite direction drove towards me head-on. With only one car's width of pavement, we both jerked our wheels sharply to the outside, the tires on the driver's side clawing for a grip in the dirt, as the inside ones claimed half the paved track. The stream of large vehicles had battered away the earthen shoulder, so that a cliff of tarmac now threw my sedan into a stunt car angle.

Each time I traveled from the farm I had this daunting hour of wide-eyed navigating, running the gauntlet through hills with too many blind turns, at any moment a crazed bus driver suddenly flying towards me at Indy-car speed. My car then under fire in a bulleting spray of rocks, left in a cyclone of dust and blinding me at the wheel. No relief was so sweet as to eventually glide onto the calmer waters of a two-lane highway for the final hour of driving.

Upon pulling into Harare my most pressing errand was to settle our bill with the shipping company, who was trucking the workshop from Kitwe to Chiredzi. It meant exchanging greenbacks for Zim dollars, and I still couldn't believe the exchange rate had now started to slide. Although the official rate was still thirty-eight Zimbabwe dollars to one US, there was now a black market rate of forty-two to one. I found it all too ironic. The currency exchange had been key to our farming plans, but immediately after giving up such ambitions, the rate had promptly dropped.

There was, of course, a reason for the devaluation. Chiefly because the fuel crisis exacted a huge demand on the country's foreign currency needs. The government had not kept up payments to suppliers and they cut Zimbabwe off, so now any fuel purchases had to be paid for upfront. As further pressure on the exchange rate, countries providing Zim with half its electricity also felt the sting of default, and were threatening to flick off the switch.

With the government now snatching all foreign currency that came in through official means, such as banks, no hard currency was available through normal channels for anyone else. Soon it became impossible to buy imports such as industrial chemicals, fertilizers, spare parts for vehicles, and retail items like toothpaste, batteries and light bulbs.

Yet what if a Zimbabwean needed some international currency to take a trip outside the country, such as for critical medical treatment or another emergency? What could they do? Their only option was to go outside official channels and make their own currency deals on the black market. But of course, a higher price had to be paid. Actually, this informal currency trade that sprang up wasn't really called the black market. It was known as the parallel market, and from the start became the usual way of business for companies as well as individuals.

With errands accomplished, on my last evening in Harare I insisted Darren's mom Georgie let me treat her to dinner. Following the tranquility of the farm, the busy restaurant felt like a carnival atmosphere, everyone lively amidst decor of bright red and blue, the place awash in luminous light. A peppy mix of music played, as I savored some of the best pasta to be had on any continent. I felt revitalized, being amidst society and indulging in a little luxury. For the moment it was easy to forget the troubles and enjoy living in this extraordinary land, at once fascinating, beautiful, and puzzling, which still had me under its spell.

* * * * *

The next day I made tracks back to Rungudzi, and although sad to be leaving, knew it was a good time for Darren and me to make our exit. The squatter crisis throughout the country had quickly gone from bad to worse. Because the War Veterans' Association had announced they were the ones invading farms, the squatters became known as "War Vets". However, most were not veterans of Zimbabwe's 1970s civil war.

In the Guruve district, many farmers now had these so-called War Vets camped out on their places. With each passing day, the situation became more electrified. Plus, an unbelievable piece of information had come to light. It turned out the squatters were actually being paid a daily wage by the government to hunker down on farms. This certainly put a whole new meaning on things, and while everyone was still reeling from the idea of premeditated robbery, the Commercial Farmers' Union's advice to landowners was to try and keep things calm. The CFU had just won a High Court order declaring the occupations illegal and ordering the invaders to leave all properties. Regrettably, however, this was not to be the end of it, as the government had no intention of complying with the court's order. Instead, they gave the police firm instructions not to remove any War Vets.

As each contentious day went by, it brought more property damage to farms. Help to farmers by the police was virtually nil, even when it came to harassment of workers. Although some officers at rural stations did try to respond and maintain a rule of law, it was usually only one or two and they had little effectiveness. The police had already become woefully inept even before the squatter situation, because the fuel shortage meant most police vehicles had empty tanks. To enforce the law on foot or bicycle was obviously impossible, and soon farmers were driving to the station and ferrying a cop to the scene.

For the moment, the best farmers could do was try to keep some sort of status quo. Hopefully limiting the harm to their workers, minimizing the damage to their farms, and most importantly, keeping their families safe.

In our district of Guruve, the local CFU chairman had a band of War Vets parked on his place, who had begun to shake their fists about and demand he meet with them. Keeping his cool, he agreed to a few coming to his house as representatives for the group. The next day, while several let themselves in through the front gate, the rest of the gang lingered outside the fence and glared in, edgily ready for any excuse to surge forward and pounce.

The farmer and his wife calmly greeted the three War Vets, who seemed to have come looking for a shouting match. But when they tried to stir things up, the farmer gently raised his hand and said, "Before we begin, can we start with a prayer? Let us all join hands and take a moment to pray for God's help."

Before the War Vets could think of a comeback, the man and his wife had bowed their heads and taken the thugs' hands in their own. The three tough guys were momentarily stunned, and by the time the farmer ended with amen, the hyped-up ruffians were subdued. A calm discussion then followed, and after that, even though a small group stayed on the farm, clashes fizzled out.

On Bradley's place south of Brooklands, the War Vets there had begun to mark out boundaries for plots to be divvyed up between them. An ill-omened rite that had become common on many "invaded" farms.

One sunny afternoon, when Bradley was making his usual rounds through the fields on his motorbike, a couple of placid War Vets flagged him down. He recognized them as regulars in the group of hangers-on, although these two hadn't been on the farm as of late. He was certainly not pleased to see them back. When he pulled up, they politely informed him they had only just returned, to discover that a different clan of War Vets had settled there. These two wanted Bradley's help in protecting their claim, since they had been the first squatters to have arrived on his place.

"You remember us, don't you?" the mild-mannered pair explained with childlike innocence. "We were the first ones to have come here. If others show up you must tell them we have the right to this place."

By now, the last shred of Bradley's patience had run out. The previous month had been unbearably stressful, with hundreds of farms inundated by often hostile War Vets, the workers harassed, property damaged, a wholesale cutting of trees, plus the political violence like the pummeling of the innocent headmaster next door. The government was not listening to court orders and the police were useless.

It became impossible for Bradley to contain himself any longer. Still sitting astride his motorbike he burst forth into an animated tirade, furiously bouncing up and down while venting his frustrations, telling the War Vets exactly what he thought of them. Before he'd finished ranting the two made a hasty departure and, in this case anyway, were not seen again.

So situations were contained for the moment, but such frictions were surely an ominous prelude of things to come.

* * * * *

Although I still wanted to argue with the gods, in the end I had to concede they'd actually been looking out for Darren and me. They had decided for us farming was not to be, or at least not now. For the last year and a half I'd been ever more frustrated, wanting to make my dream come true of a home on a farm in Africa. But now I was immensely thankful not to have become embroiled in what was called the "land invasions". Everything would have been at stake for us, since Darren and I would have put our life savings into the undertaking. Money that had been dearly paid for with countless hours of back-breaking work and sacrifices made. I knew many people in just such a circumstance who had risked everything to make a start, and now whose livelihoods, down to their last penny, might be snatched away.

My last evening on Rungudzi had arrived. The War Vets were still camped out on the knoll, but I never saw a hint of them, not even a waft of smoke from their campfire. The house was packed and empty, with no TV to watch and the stereo in its box. There would be no guests tonight, but the beautiful garden was company enough. Everything was serene and peaceful, and I felt content.

I settled onto our familiar veranda to watch the sunset's changing hues of red and orange melt across a wide horizon. All the Earth was solemn. The birds were subdued as they went about their end-of-day tasks, and even the insects, frogs and other creatures of the bush uncommonly hushed.

I sipped wine from a coffee mug since all the glasses were packed, feeling the poignancy of the empty house lingering behind me. The chapter of our stay at Rungudzi was finished now. What a peculiar sensation it was, to be about to turn a page of my life and start a new chapter, not knowing what would be written there.

As mystic darkness eased in, I could hear a distant rhythmic thumping of drums carrying through the hills. A breeze drifted through the silky air, steeped with the sensual, rustic scent of Africa. I thought back to when I'd first arrived here. I was a different person then. Yes, somehow I had changed.

Sitting there in the gentle warmth of evening, the subtle music lilting through the darkness, the air fragrant with earth and life, Africa felt tangible. I now realized what Africa had done for me. She had given me my soul. Or at least she had completed it. For the first time in my life I felt like a whole person. I whispered out to her, "thank you, my friend." And then said a silent prayer that the future boded well for both of us.

Part Two

Chapter Eighteen

||||||||||||||||||||||||||||||||||||||||||||||||||||||||||||||||||||||||||||||||||||||||

G ritty little Chiredzi town had all of three banks, three gas stations, and three small grocery stores. The largest settlement for hundreds of miles, my new home was the usual mix of old and new Africa. As a backdrop were its colonial leftovers of civility, those neatly laid streets lined with sturdy flamboyant trees, and dignified white masonry buildings. Yet all of that was overwhelmed by the new—litter, potholes, ceaseless dust, peeling paint and battered cars, along with careworn peasant folk. Luckily the three-bedroom house Darren and I had rented not far from our business was welcomingly neat and in good repair. Only the yard was neglected, and in shadier spots hardy plants had survived as a tangle of overgrowth, while in the places where the Lowveld sun beat down throughout the day, lay only hard-baked clay.

I knew I could rejuvenate the lawn, and most fortunate, out the back of the house banana, grapefruit, lime and paw-paw trees had managed to survive. Even better, a towering mulberry bush stood by the fence, its gangly limbs hung with clusters of red-purple berries. As a kid growing up in the Arctic, it was inconceivable that fruit trees could actually grow right in a person's yard, like something out of Eden. Yet here I was now, staring at my very own and feeling as if a slice of heaven had landed on my doorstep.

The inside of the house was cozy and inviting, and it was a prize to now have parquet mahogany floors instead of gray concrete. Another luxury was the light coverings, after the blaring bare bulbs at Rungudzi. I was also happy to find a fireplace to chase away the chill in winter, since homes in Zim didn't have central heating. And I especially liked how the many windows made the house cheerful and bright, plus they even had screens to keep out the multitude of insects which thrived in the Lowveld heat.

Our first couple of weeks in Chiredzi was chaotic, with the house in a tangle of boxes, stacked furniture, crumpled newspaper and messy suitcases. The workshop had also been coming together in a tumultuous effort, the first feat being to offload the massive machines from the flatbed by crane, then muscled inside and into place. Next, the electricity system had to be revamped. Then a small office built, plus tools, worktables and supplies bought, and employees interviewed. Amongst it all, our bookkeeping was to scratch a note upon the manila envelope from which we grabbed cash.

But as the frenzy about us calmed and order prevailed, our home eventually took shape. With boxes unpacked, curtains up, and mementos on the shelves, my new surrounds took on a comforting familiarity. I'd never lived in a small town before and found I enjoyed the convenience. The grocery store was a quick two minutes from our house, the horse stables a few minutes in the opposite direction on the edge of town, and our workshop only blocks away. Situated in the midst of it, our neighborhood was typical small town. Well, probably not in the US, but in Africa anyway. Each day I watched our mailman bicycle slowly along the quiet neighborhood streets, sitting purposefully upright with his cap squarely atop his head, and an important air to his methodical pedaling. Stopping at our gate, he'd dutifully retrieve a letter from the wire basket between the handlebars and give tinny rings on his thumb bell. Even the private overnight mail service, the local version of FedEx, made deliveries in town by bicycle, their company name of Swift proudly painted on the wooden box perched over the back wheel. Then twice a week the garbage collectors came by, simply managing with an oversized drum on a trailer, pulled by a chugging tractor.

Yet with a big sigh, I wished it all was as idyllic as its first impressions. Because soon I was introduced to the more vexing quirks of the neighborhood, my sanity first tested by the fondness which many residents had for keeping roosters. This came promptly to my attention at the obscene hour of four a.m. during our first night in the house. Initially I thought it only our next door neighbor who had an affinity for this obnoxious creature, since the piercing crows from our fence seemed all that was penetrating our bedroom like a fire alarm. But then one morning not long after we'd moved in, I happened to venture outside just before dawn. Instantly I was stopped in my tracks, astonished to hear the shrill staccato of a hundred roosters, in varying decibels, reverberating through what would have been the quiet morning air. My neighbor's fowl, just a few yards from where I stood at my kitchen door, was in the midst of a pre-dawn dueling contest with the next nearest scoundrel. I listened as one crowed heartily, to which the other answered with a mightier and longer refrain. Then the first would reply with even more sinful vigor.

While I had enough of a challenge trying to sleep from four a.m. to seven as the well-rested cockerels let loose at full volume, then most nights the neighborhood dogs performed during the ten-until-three time slot. Our fence was only a few feet from our bedroom window, and our other neighbor's dogs thought this an excellent place to hold stage. The Lowveld heat meant we had to sleep with the windows open, and the operatic dogs took full advantage of their captured audience.

After a couple of weeks, feeling frazzled from sleep deprivation and desperate for relief, I decided to drop in at the town council. I wanted to ask for a copy of the regulation stating roosters weren't allowed within town limits, which I was considering showing my neighbor. The red-brick council headquarters was the most impressive building in our little community, as a town hall should be, with its two stories of offices surrounded by well-kept grounds of spacious lawn and tall trees.

I parked my car in a neatly marked spot and made my way to the front doors on a clean stone walkway skirted by flowers. Inside the building I stepped into a grand center. The expansive lobby had a sweeping staircase that led to a circular balcony, off of which were the second floor offices. It all looked impressive and I thought to myself, "I'll find some action here!"

The building was quiet with an appropriate air of respectability. In my quest for the regulations, I was not too surprised to first be passed from one office to the next, before eventually being given the name of the person supposedly in the know. I had to return several times because he was always in a meeting, but finally managed to track him down. He then said he couldn't help me but someone else, who was out sick that day, could. The following day this fellow then passed me on to another, and round and round it went. Eventually I had to admit that this response, or lack of it, was only to be expected. By now I'd discovered that the offices found off of the airy center lobby were really just dark and dusty cubbyholes. And that which at first had seemed to be a quiet, professional aura, was more like the leaden gloom of a morgue. I was about to admit defeat, when the last person I saw gave me an answer, of sorts.

He matter-of-factly explained that the town regulations had expired some years back, and the council had never voted in new ones or extended the old. He seemed to be implying that, in a legal sense, there were no town laws and therefore no rules to be enforced. Indifferently, he said the old rule had allowed fifteen fowl per household and all could be roosters. I was suspicious about this, and when I asked to see this regulation he couldn't produce it. I wondered if he was just making this up to get rid of me, but by now I was tired of trying to rouse some response, or even a sign of life, from the blank stares of the council workers.

The whole episode left me frustrated, to say the least, at how the citizens-at-large apathetically disposed of civility and the law. And while this simple indifference to having town regulations may have not seemed to them to have any real consequences, it was exactly this kind of attitude that set the tone for events to take a more calamitous turn.

Chapter Nineteen

||||||||||||||||||||||||||||||||||||||||||||||||||||||||||||||||||||||||||||||

Amid the whirlwind of setting up our home and business, Darren and I were too distracted to notice happenings beyond our little sphere. When we did finally stop and turn on the news, we were startled to learn that farm invasions had become more numerous—and more violent. The troubles spread like a cancer, with unrest now creeping into towns and all tentacles of society.

In an attempt to cool the boiling waters, a peace march was approved by the court and scheduled to pass through downtown Harare on April 1st of 2000. Zimbabweans from churches and professional groups, activist organizations and workers' unions, came to stand side by side. Upon taking their first steps forward, however, the police faced off with the citizens. When marchers refused to disperse some were arrested on the spot. Thousands of others determinedly continued on, and with the police outnumbered, the government unleashed thugs from the downtown headquarters of ZANU-PF. Surging forth, brutal bullying was used to break things up, with marchers and anyone else who had the misfortune of being around attacked. So much for the "peace" march, I thought with disappointment.

In its new wave of crackdowns, the government required permission to hold a rally, with most requests denied as a supposed threat to law and order. The Mugabe regime had become paranoid, taking no chances when it came to perceived threats to his omnipotence. Their success at ignoring Zimbabwe's laws soon gave them the arrogance to disregard international agreements as well, going so far as to open the British Embassy's diplomatic mail on its arrival at the airport. The paltry excuse of the Mugabeites was they suspected it carried pamphlets printed for the opposition.

This latest stab of rifling through the diplomatic bag was part of the ongoing antagonism the Zimbabwe government had kept up with the British for years. Mugabe felt the Brits owed an open-ended debt because of the past colonial connection. Along this line, the Zimbabwe parliament passed a ludicrous bill, declaring the British must give the Zimbabwe government money for farms. In the back of my mind, I heard a tinny echo of Jimmy Buffett's *Banana Republics* as theme song to Mugabe's latest performance. It was a moot point anyway, since over the previous twenty years the British already spent US$70 million on land redistribution and had reaffirmed their pledge for more funds. Mugabe's frustration now was that money was no longer being handed out as unconditionally as in the past.

Alas, life in the Third World always has its supply of dramas, particularly when it comes to politics. So although the escalation of farm invasions and War Vet aggression were cause for concern, most of us still believed problems could be resolved. Dialogue continued between all involved—the Zimbabwe government, foreign governments, farmers and the War Vets' Association—such that it seemed only a matter of working out details.

Then suddenly, with a nerve-shattering crack like a lightning bolt, our small world imploded. On April 15th 2000 a farmer—David Stevens—was brutally murdered. A shockwave splintered through the country, destroying any last illusions of paradise. Over the previous months we had all wondered just how far Mugabe would let the violence go, and now we had our answer.

What made the slaying of David Stevens so profoundly alarming were its particular circumstances. To begin with, although it'd been years since a farmer was killed, it wasn't unknown to Zimbabwe's history. Plus in recent months we'd heard barbaric stories of peasants and other black Zimbabweans being tortured and murdered. Admittedly these deaths were farther from my reality, mainly because journalists were not allowed to cover happenings in the communal areas and townships. Much of the news in the country was spread word of mouth, and since most of the violence didn't happen on the doorsteps of people I knew, I had little knowledge of the blacks' struggles.

When we first heard about Stevens' murder it was, as usual, through the grapevine. He farmed in the northeast of Zimbabwe, quite far from us in Chiredzi, so initially all a stunned Darren and I knew was that a brutal killing of a farmer had taken place. But as we talked to friends and more facts trickled into the verbal pipeline, further details came to light.

David Stevens was a conciliatory man and highly thought of by all who knew him. He had done much to help his community, such as loaning his tractor and driver to plow peasants' lands bordering his farm, and other neighborly acts of goodwill. And this is what Mugabe didn't like. Farmers doing more for the people than the government itself, as surely this was a threat to his power. Stevens was also considered fair and well-liked by his workers. In fact, it was his efforts to look after their welfare that set the stage for his murder.

Like so many others, David Stevens had War Vets camped out on his farm. They had unleashed a barrage of harassment in the workers' village, with the worst beatings for those accused of being MDC. Stevens had supported the MDC, and workers of farmers who backed the opposition were targeted by War Vets—that is, government thugs. Meting out violence upon the laborers was often thought a more effective way of menacing the farmer than threatening him directly. For one, the farmer was mobile. He could simply get in his car and drive to safety. Or phone for help. In the very least, lock the gate of his home's fortified fence. Whereas the workers had no way to escape from their tormentors. Trying to protect their staff from the government's campaign of violence put the farmers in a tricky situation.

The enraged workers on David Stevens' place had taken enough from the War Vets and had actually succeeded in chasing them off the farm. But peace was short lived. The thugs soon returned in force and a mini battle was in danger of breaking out. Stevens stepped in to try and keep the sides calm, with the confrontation explosive and tense. Suddenly amidst the tussle, Stevens and his foreman found themselves seized upon and dragged off.

Meanwhile, during the standoff five neighbors had been alerted. They arrived at the scene just as the War Vets were racing away in Stevens' Land Rover, kidnapping him and his foreman. The other farmers swung in behind, only to be under a volley of fire from Stevens' stolen shotgun. In desperation they veered off and sped to the nearest police station. But the cops were uninterested in their plight. Even more to their shocked surprise, the captors promptly marched in and seized upon them too. The police simply watched as the farmers were wrested off from the station.

The five men were hauled to the War Vets' base, where one was thrown into a room with Stevens and his foreman, both of whom were a hideous, battered sight. After the three were tortured for several more hours, one small miracle happened. The groaning neighbor was yanked up from the floor, and gruffly told he could leave. He later discovered a sympathetic woman in the War Vets' camp said she knew him and had made a plea for his clemency. Yet horrifically, his release only came after he was made to watch as a bullet shattered through his friend Stevens' face, swiftly followed by the foreman also being coldly shot dead. The foreman's lips were sliced off and then taken to Stevens' farm village, where War Vets flaunted them before the foreman's family, friends and neighbors, as an example of what happened to anyone supporting, or even mentioning, the MDC.

Throughout the long night, the other four farmers were mercilessly beaten with iron bars, rocks and fan belts. By the next morning they were nearly dead. After this, the War Vets chucked them all into the back of a pickup to get rid of the bodies. Two were tossed out close to a river, where they managed to stumble to safety despite their crippling injuries. The other two were dumped elsewhere, too badly mutilated to stand. Half conscious, they dragged themselves to a hiding place, worried their attackers might return. Luckily they were found by a kind boy who led the right people to them. A favored method of torture by thugs in Zimbabwe was to make their victims lay face down on the ground and then pummel their backsides. One of the brutalized farmer's buttocks were so badly pulverized there was nothing left, and he'll have trouble walking for the rest of his life.

Yet the bewildered nation's trauma didn't stop there. On the same day as the slaying of Stevens and his foreman, another double murder shocked the country, and all too clearly showed the lengths to which Mugabe was willing to go. The driver for Morgan Tsvangirai, the opposition leader, along with an MDC organizer, were traveling in the rural district for which Tsvangirai was running for parliament, when their car was ambushed by a ZANU gang. Word quickly spread that the sedan had been set on fire, the men trapped inside and dying an agonizing death.

Such unspeakable horrors left the nation in stunned disbelief. The surge of beatings and intimidation had been hard enough to keep at bay, but now there was calculated murder at the encouragement of the government and with the complicity of the police. I wanted to shout, "No, no, no! This is all going the wrong way!" Things were supposed to get better for my friend Africa, not worse. I was overwhelmed by a feeling of powerlessness, watching her swept up in this vortex of destruction.

* * * * *

The shock of these murders still quaked the country when, chillingly, three days later tragedy struck again. The date was April 18th, Zimbabwe Independence Day and a national holiday.

As a precaution, Martin Olds had already sent his wife and family away from their farm, to stay in the town of Bulawayo. Recently, sinister threats had been hurled at him, as was happening to many farmers. But up to this point the thugs had yet to act upon their words, leaving a farmer to decide whether it best to stand his ground, or give in to the intimidation and hightail it to safety. Like

most in his situation, Martin Olds was trying to strike a balance
between the two.

On April 18th he was readying himself to head to town and
spend the holiday with his family. When about to climb into his
pickup, from out of nowhere a convoy of armed men swelled up
outside his fence. Dashing back to the house, Olds immediately
rang a neighbor, along with the police, telling of his urgent need
for help. In the meantime he needed to keep the situation calm, and
with few options, went out to speak with them. But the mob hadn't
come to talk and instead fired upon him, their bullets shattering his
right leg, crumpling him to the ground.

Desperately, Olds managed to drag himself back inside, where
he quickly splinted his leg with a plank. On his shortwave radio, in
an anxious plea he called out to nearby farmers, who swiftly joined
together and sped off to the police. But at the station their efforts
were futile. The disinterested officers said they were aware of the
War Vets being at Olds' farm, and casually told the farmers that the
mercenaries were unarmed. Then further to the farmers' amazement, they added that everyone should just stay out of it. Guessing
his neighbors would react to Olds' call, the cops had already put
up a roadblock on the way to his farm. At the same time, another
friend was circling his plane over Olds' house, clearly seeing it was
under siege and radioing that the situation was dire. Yet still the police were determined to keep the farmers, and themselves, far away.

All the while, Olds was trapped in his farmhouse with bullets
ricocheting around him. Soon fire bombs were hurled in through
the windows. Bravely he returned gunshots as best he could, trying
to hold them off. But with the house about to be engulfed in flames
there wasn't much time left. Still, he knew his neighbors were aware
of his plight and was certain help must be on its way. Throughout
the ordeal, War Vets stood guard at his workers' village to keep any
of them from running to his aid. As a last effort Olds took cover
from the fire in his bathtub. Eventually though he had to escape the
blaze, and when he stumbled outside on his splinted leg, the War
Vets rushed upon him, smashing his head with a tire iron before

blasting rounds into him as he lay unconscious. His valiant struggle had lasted three horrifying hours.

With Olds now dead, the convoy of War Vets casually drove back down the farm road and past the others at the roadblock. Only then did the police allow the farmers to go to Olds, the cops themselves waiting several hours before making their way to the crime scene. Ironically, years earlier Martin Olds had received the Zimbabwe Medal for Valor, and he showed his courage again the day he died.

With the verbal pipeline already well greased, the story of Martin Olds' death quickly spread around the country. Shock on top of shock creates a state of temporary numbness. The nation was paralyzed. Most incomprehensible was how the police had been on the side of the murderers.

While Martin Olds had been fighting for his life, Mugabe was giving his Independence Day address in Harare. In the past, this speech had always been made with much pomp in a stadium. But this time Mugabe opted for the distance of a televised broadcast, saying he wanted to save money. Many suspected he was worried a live ceremony would be met with demonstrations.

Darren and I watched a few minutes of his speech on TV, disturbed at his menacing ravings. We couldn't bring ourselves to watch it all, as it was just too appalling to see the president intent on fracturing an already distressed nation. With a face twisted in hatred, he called white Zimbabweans, and in particular white farmers, enemies of the state. He then went on to rant about one of his favorite topics, colonialism. According to Mugabe this was the root of all Zimbabwe's problems, and those handful of decades under British rule had somehow doomed Zimbabweans to eternal suffering.

"We won't bow down to imperialist attitudes of a superior race, a superior color, a superior culture," was his bitter propaganda, his words making a jittery populous even more on edge.

This inciting talk, together with the murders condoned by the police, only served to encourage the War Vets—along with criminals in general—to rape, pillage, threaten, kill and intimidate without restraint. In the anxious days following Martin Olds' murder,

Darren and I joined friends to watch CNN and the BBC on satellite TV. We all became obsessed with the top of the hour as Zimbabwe made headlines on each channel, everyone rushing to stand in front of the TV and watch silent and transfixed. Journalists trying to report around Zim were being harassed by War Vets, but some footage still made it through. Camera views were furtive and on the run, showing such horrors as a fleeing farmer's dogs being bludgeoned with iron rods.

In the troubled weeks after Stevens' and Olds' deaths, we continued to hear rumors of more murders of blacks linked to the MDC. Farm workers were also indiscriminately harassed and beaten, sometimes their homes burnt along with all their worldly possessions.

Some farmers were taken hostage, including Roger of Humani, while driving about his ranch one morning on his daily rounds. He was flagged down by War Vets, fellows he knew well because of their many previous encounters, since most had been resident poachers on his property for years. This time, however, they were more hostile than ever before. With a sudden lunge, they grabbed him and ushered him back to his house. For many tense hours they held him outside, while trying to figure out exactly what to demand, probably hoping a ransom would be offered. All the while, Roger's large family steadily gathered at his home in a show of support. By the time sundown came the War Vets simply released him, seeming to have lost interest in the meaningless affair. In other cases though, they did manage to blackmail a bounty out of kidnapped farm managers.

Our good friend Terry, an affable fellow, grew roses for a living and suffered a barrage of anonymous telephone threats. After being told his ears would be cut off, like many farmers now, he slept in town and only in daylight ventured out to his place. Another friend had his crops slashed by a mob, his equipment destroyed, sheds broken into with tools stolen, and guards so severely beaten they landed up in the hospital. While in some cases policemen did try to stand up for law and order, often they too became the thugs' victims.

Many government schools closed for weeks as violence against teachers and headmasters became out of hand. One rural private school also closed for awhile when War Vets squatted there, declaring they intended to take the school's land, too.

Predictably, embassies were flooded with people wanting to renew their passports or apply for visas. We heard rumors that embassies had drawn up plans for evacuation of their citizens. And sadly for Zimbabwe, foreign governments were now telling travelers to avoid our once idyllic country.

Oddly for me though, I still felt at peace about my own life. It was actually strange, watching such terrible news on TV about the country I lived in, because our doorstep in quiet little Chiredzi was as lazy and placid as ever. Certainly the atmosphere was subdued, but day-to-day life still ticked along as if this week were no different than the last.

Plus, we had the usual scraps of hopeful news to cling to, which for the moment kept suitcases in the closet. While Mugabe was in Cuba, Zimbabwe's vice-president declared that squatters should leave farms. And in mid April 2000, the government, the Commercial Farmers' Union, and the War Vets' Association announced they would meet to resolve the situation. By the end of April, a delegation of Zim government officials was in London to talk with British ministers, since Britain's longstanding desire for Zimbabwe to be a prospering nation had kept close ties over the years.

Yet regrettably, upon his return from Cuba Mugabe took an opposite stance from his vice-president, saying he supported the War Vets' actions. Nor was progress made on any other front. But it was the fact that each week we had some new shred of hope that kept us going.

And while we all desperately hoped for the nation's salvation, every conversation was dominated by talk of what shore to land on if forced to leave. In fact, the recent years of a dying economy meant a stream of Zimbabweans had already left their homeland. Most were professionals and tradesmen who didn't own land or a business to be left behind. Many had family in South Africa and moved there. But even more put the problems of Africa behind them for good, striking out across the oceans to the stability of Britain, Australia, New Zealand, Canada and the US.

For those who did own a business, including farmers, the decision to leave was troublesome. Many citizens had sunk everything they had into hard assets, since the devaluing Zimbabwe dollar meant savings accounts were strictly not an option. Better to keep money in land, equipment, houses—*anything* but Zim dollars. For many, their life savings was now in assets impossible to sell, since no one wanted ventures in a place of such turmoil. For numerous businessmen and landowners, if they left Zim they would arrive on a distant shore virtually penniless. Not to mention the millions of Zimbabweans with no capital of any kind, and without the choice of buying a ticket to flee their strife-torn land.

Beyond the practicalities of leaving, for many people, Darren among them, the reality was Zimbabwe was their home, the country of their birth, the land of their ancestors, and the place where friends and family lived. And for others like me, it was still a paradise. Yes, Zimbabwe was falling apart. But the fact that her foundations were crumbling only made it all the more important to not leave just yet. I desperately wanted to believe this marvelous corner of Earth could be saved. Surely my prayers would not be in vain.

Chapter Twenty

||||||||||||||||||||||||||||||||||||||||||||||||||||||||||||||||||||||||||||||||||||||||||||||||||||

A midst the chaos, life went on. As always, each day dawned in a flood of sunshine and warmth, Mother Nature doing her part to keep up the optimism. Nothing stops the clock from ticking forward and the weeks had taken us to the last Saturday of April. Nicky's birthday in fact, and her best friend Jenny was throwing a bash on Humani.

The ranch rested in the heart of the Save Valley Wildlife Conservancy and our last hour of driving took us through this million acre oasis. Darren steered along a wide dirt road flanked by hardy bush, where I was glad to see the wildlife still looking as untroubled as if in Eden. As we drove past, long-legged gray kudu studied us from the bush, watching with large Bambi eyes and perking oversized ears. Penciled down their sides were half a dozen white stripes, while upon delicate heads they balanced tall spiraled horns, looking unwieldy. At the last moment they scooted silently off, and in unhurried bounds glided through a web of branches and scrub. I noticed how they leaned their heads back, cleverly tucking their massive horns along their sides, free of the tangle of bush. With fluffy short tails, white underneath, they waved good-bye and slipped into the shadows.

As we drove leisurely on, we came across charcoal-gray wildebeest cantering in small groups, sporting stubby black manes and tufted long tails. With black faces of Romanesque profile, I thought

they looked peculiar in their rocking-horse gait and head too big
for the body. Their funny black horns grew sideways, before curling up at the tip. Hearing the crackle of our pickup on gravel they
would stop and abruptly turn, every head in the herd snapping up
in curiosity, while swishing the black tufts of their tails. A moment
later they whisked themselves away, playfully shaking their bristles
of mane and kicking up their heels as though they hadn't a care.

Ever present were the numerous impala, fine-boned and red-
dish-fawn with white undersides. Daintier than the kudu and wildebeest, their spiraled horns were refined, curving gently back and
up. As our pickup nipped past they darted off in their characteristic
leaps, the long grass tickling their bellies as they flew easily over it
and away.

The sandy road finally led us to Jenny's parents' place, an unassuming masonry farmhouse. Roger and Ann's home had been built
five decades earlier by Roger's parents and added on to over the
years, sitting protected by mahoganies and a shrubby green garden.
Many friends had already arrived, plus Darren's sister Jane and her
family. Nicky was there with her mom and sisters, along with a half
dozen bachelor safari guides who worked for Roger. I always looked
forward to these socials, getting together with dozens of others who,
like me, were bound to this stoic land.

Drifting among the group was a smiling Jenny, at ease in her role
as hostess and a perfect embodiment of sunshine. Her warmth and
sunny spirits brightened any room; her radiance complimented by
eyes of sky blue and locks the color of a soft orange sunset. Joining
the party was Jenny's boyfriend Butch, a skilled pilot and respected
safari guide. When I'd first met him, I saw a sternness with a cynical
edge. But Jenny's glow had melted the coolness, and I now found
Butch to be relaxed and engaging, flashing his wide grin often.

Our festivities got off to a fortifying start with a barbeque of
marinated impala kebabs, followed by a lively game of cricket on
Ann's expansive lawn. Before long, however, someone suggested we
all head down to the banks of the Turgwe River and continue the
party next to its soothing waters. Coolers were soon packed and the
boisterous crowd tumbled out to the front of the house, piling into

four-wheel drives collected there. Our Isuzu pickup was the lone two-wheel drive, and Darren brought up the rear down to the river.

The epic flooding unleashed by Cyclone Eline had left in its wake a clean sandy beach, carved out along the water where before had been thick bush. Arriving in an exuberant swell, everyone leapt out of trucks and grabbed drinks from coolers. Darren's friend Marius turned up the stereo in his Land Cruiser, as easy laughter mingled with the rippling river. This swathe of pristine beach, protected by strong bush, was a marvelous patch of still unspoiled paradise. Relaxing there, I had that wonderful feeling of knowing there was no place on Earth I'd rather be.

Amid the ruckus, Roger's sister sat down neatly on a crate, to carefully unpack her china tea set from its wooden box. While her floral dress fluttered in the breeze, with ritual slowness she lifted out each cup and saucer wrapped in tissue, then carefully assembled her tea service on another crate in front of her. I sat comfortably on the soft sand nearby, leaning back on my hands and looking on. I thought with a smile how her dainty tea setting seemed as natural there on the African riverbank, as a roaring campfire would be.

The small beach overflowed with an irresistible energy as the noisy bunch ran and fell about in the deep sand, casually attempting to play another ball game. The temperature was perfect this time of year, in the low eighties during midday and cooling nicely in the evening. As the sun sank towards the horizon its golden rays made the river sparkle. Several of us collected graying branches washed up on the bank, fatalities of the cyclone, to build a cozy bonfire. Eventually everyone drew round its warmth where we softly talked the hours away, in tranquil darkness next to flickering flames. Nature's simple magic better than any action-packed amusement park could be.

Gradually, the collection of trucks on the dunes became fewer. Only after most were gone did we realize our light-weight Isuzu wouldn't make it up the sand. Luckily Marius was still there and could tie our Isuzu to the back of his 4x4. There could be no hesitation going up the deep sand, as the Land Cruiser strained forward with engine groaning and wheels throwing up grit, our Isuzu heav-

ing over the swells behind. We lunged forward between clumps of
tall grass and logs, lurching side to side over the rough terrain in the
pitch-black night. Darren and I laughed and reveled in our dose of
recklessness, the day exactly what we needed to chase our worries
away.

Invited to stay the night at Humani's safari camp further up the
rushing Turgwe, a dozen of us met for nightcaps under the thatched
roof of the camp's little bar. Our lofty perch sat on a hill rising up
from the river, and from out of the infinite night the hoarse barks
of leopards, answered by hyenas' whoops, floated up to us through
the silky air.

"You've certainly enjoyed yourself this evening," I commented
to Darren as we later headed off to our chalet. He'd had far more to
drink than usual and was unsteady on his feet.

"Here, let me help you," I said with a little laugh as he leaned on
my shoulder. Stumbling along in the blackness, he pulled us down
to the ground in a jumble. I got us on our feet again, but after a few
times of this gave up. We lay on soft grass gazing up to the brilliance
of the cosmos, the stars and planets astonishingly numerous in the
African bush on a moonless night, and I felt dreamily content.

The next morning we all met for breakfast, the long table set
out in the fresh air and laid with a feast of creamy porridge, fresh
mango, eggs and salty bacon. The mood was light and untroubled
as everyone cheerfully chatted. But then it all abruptly ended, when
Jenny's sister Sarah came to us with unsettling news.

"A warning has come over the shortwave radio that a group of
War Vets could possibly be headed to Humani," Sarah flatly stated,
keeping emotions out of it. Details were hazy, but her announcement was enough to bring our weekend of fun to a shuddering halt.

Everyone soon collected outside Roger and Ann's house to soberly discuss the situation. It was really just speculation whether
any War Vets would show up. And if they did, would they become
aggressive? Everyone was calm, yet subdued, as we weighed the options.

In a moment of reflective hush, Ann suddenly sprang into
action, running back to the house and declaring, "I've got to get

my eggs!" A whisper of motion in the high branches above made me glance skyward, where I saw several vervet monkeys swinging through the treetops towards the hen house. The commotion stirred everyone to exhale. In a way it all seemed so absurd, like running from a ghost. But we knew even a vague warning had to be taken seriously. Butch, for one, wanted to keep his Cessna 206 safe by flying it off the ranch and out of harm's way. All were unanimous that Darren's sister Jane and her young children should not stay on Humani. The only road out might have War Vets coming down it, and they were known to erect crude roadblocks. It was chilling to think of the possibilities, should Jane and the kids find themselves surrounded by thugs in the middle of the wilderness.

The best thing would be for them to fly out with Butch. Her husband Vic could then drive by himself and meet them in Chiredzi. Darren was worried though, about Vic being alone in what might be hostile territory, and insisted on following him in our pickup. Since there were enough seats in the plane, it was then decided I would also fly out.

Butch wanted to waste no time in getting off, and a few minutes later everyone had gathered out on the grass airstrip. No one said much as Butch silently went about his pre-flight checks, not even the warm mid-morning sun able to chase away the chill of anxiousness that hung in the air.

A pensive Jane climbed into the front of the plane with baby Jeanette on her lap, while Nathan, Shawna and I settled into the seats behind. Butch then pulled himself up into the pilot's seat, glancing round to make sure we were all fastened in. As he buckled his own belt, Jenny stepped up to the open door. Gently laying a hand on his leg, she raised her eyes to look steadily at him, her sunny glow clouded.

She said nothing, but as Butch held her gaze and placed his hand on hers, he quietly comforted her with, "Don't worry, I'll see you soon."

A moment later he turned the key and the propeller spun feverishly into life. With a noisy whirr we taxied toward the end of the airstrip, while those standing in the pale grass slowly waved good-bye, every face solemn and strained. I watched out the window as they grew smaller, also feeling anxious. I wondered whether Darren and Vic would meet with trouble on the road going home, and about the chances of harm coming to the friends staying on the ranch. How crushing it was to have to leave loved ones behind to face uncertain dangers, while I soared up to the safety of a clear blue sky.

Butch pushed the throttle in and the plane made a bumpy rush along the grass, at first seeming to strain against its load of heavy hearts. But then as the wheels left the troubled earth we lifted easily up and away. The airstrip ran parallel to Humani's citrus plantation, and as we climbed skyward its rows and squares gave the Earth a look of tidiness and civility. Did chaos really rule down there? But then as we gained altitude, the orderliness of the plantation was engulfed by miles of wild bushland for as far as the eye could see.

Upon leveling out a minute later, Butch made a sweeping turn toward the conservancy's main road. Within another few minutes we all felt a little better, as there was not the slightest sign of War Vets upon it. For the moment anyway, we could lean back in our seats, knowing danger wasn't imminent.

As I peered out the window, below was a land languid with autumn, although only the mighty baobabs had lost their leaves. The bush was still a deep green, while scattered amongst it soared the massive gray trunks and twisted branches of the baobabs. From the air they stood out boldly against the sameness of vast bush, the hefty trunk of even a small baobab three yards wide. Large ones had girths several times more, and from high above they looked like upended driftwood, their tangle of gray limbs seeming to be roots instead. I could see how the African legend came about that baobabs are uprooted trees, savagely replanted topside down by an angry god.

Eventually we left the skies over the conservancy's untamed bushland, and in striking contrast, flew above the Mkwasine sugar estates with its thousands of acres of cane fields. A plush green carpet lay over the earth in patterns of squares, fringed by the glittering waters of the irrigation canals. At this simple change of scenery I immediately felt relief, as though the aura of our lives had regained some civility again.

What would have been a two-hour drive from Humani to Chiredzi was a quick hop in the Cessna, and in less than a half hour we were landed and parked. From the small airport we walked to my house where we then phoned Vic and Darren, to say we hadn't seen any War Vets on the road. We all rested better when, a couple hours later, they arrived safely home.

In the end, no War Vets showed up at Humani that day. But I knew the tide had irrevocably turned. I now had to accept that my imperiled home, this beautiful country, was condemned to suffer.

* * * * *

It soon became glaringly obvious, that the country's troubles weren't really about land, but about possessing absolute power. This was made clear when offices of the only non-government daily paper were maliciously bombed. The explosion at *The Daily News* happened at night, so fortunately no one was hurt. But it was a menacing sign. The regime had turned a new page to suppress freedoms, with its thirst for a stranglehold on the people not yet quenched.

The troubles were clearly politically motivated and many felt if we could just bear through it until after parliamentary elections, peace might be ours again. The government announced voting would be the last weekend in June, giving a sliver of hope that, if we could just hold on till then, the violence and harassment might be only a bad memory.

With elections in a matter of weeks, there was still a mountain of obstacles to overcome. The voters' role was twenty years outdated, including names of many dead folk while excluding numerous eligible voters. Also, the government had yet to define constituency boundaries, making it impossible for parties to announce candidates. This was an obvious ploy to add disarray to the voting process, the government wanting to frustrate the oppositions' efforts.

Along with everyone else, Darren and I looked toward parliamentary elections with uneasy optimism. Parliament had always been filled with ZANU-PF members and nothing more than a rub-

ber stamp for what Mugabe wanted to do. It would take an overwhelming win by the opposition to change it into an effective body.
Even so, with Mugabe continuing at the helm, the country would
still be at the mercy of his whims.

It was against this backdrop of countrywide violence and a nation with an uncertain future, that on the 1st of May 2000, Darren
and I quietly opened the doors of Chiredzi Engine Reconditioners
for business.

Chapter Twenty-one

||||||||||||||||||||||||||||||||||||||||||||||||||||||||||||||||||||||||||||||||

While I stood chatting with Darren and his sister on the edge of the group, in curiosity I glanced round the shaded lawn at the others. I felt at home with my new neighbors, who were mostly sugar cane farmers or safari operators. I was naturally at ease with people who, like me, found their happiness in the outdoors, sunshine and a sense of freedom.

Nearby, a fit middle-aged man, with thick black hair and purpose to his step, walked past. Seeing him, Darren called out, "Hey there, Tore! It's been ages." As Tore then strode towards us to say hello, Jane added, "How nice to see you. You're looking well."

"I don't think you've met Cindi yet," Darren said and introduced me.

Tore politely asked me the usual "how do you like Zim" questions, which somehow led to the favorite subject of horses. At this, Tore's eyes instantly brightened.

"I have some beautiful Arabians on my ranch," he told me, suddenly enthusiastic. "They're great horses, lots of fun to ride. I bought them from Sam down in Beitbridge. Would you like to come riding sometime?"

"That would be nice," I gave as a courteous answer, not expecting it would come to anything. "Thanks, Tore."

"Call me anytime and I'll arrange it," he insisted, treating me like an old friend. "You'll enjoy the ranch. It truly is spectacular."

A couple weeks later was Africa Day, a public holiday, and having only recently arrived in town Darren and I hadn't made plans. Early in the morning the phone rang, and when Darren hung up he casually announced, "We're going out to Tore's ranch today. He asked if you wanted to come ride his Arabs, and I told him you'd like that."

"Aren't you going to ride with us?" I asked with suspicion, wondering what Darren was getting me into.

"I don't know," he replied too offhand for my liking. "I guess."

"I suppose I should wear my riding pants," I then remarked more to myself. I was feeling apprehensive, although surely if someone had Arabians they were as proud of as Tore was, they'd be all of well-kept, well-mannered and well-trained. Yet I did wonder why, when I'd visited him and Janet, Sam hadn't mentioned his Arabs. But if his sleek and finely-bred Brahman cattle were any proof, the horses would be magnificent indeed.

An hour later Darren and I pulled into the safari camp on Tore's ranch. He stood talking to one of his workers nearby, but upon seeing our pickup immediately strode over to greet us. Right away, I uneasily noticed a change. At our first meeting he'd been dressed in a neatly ironed white shirt, new jeans and polished loafers. What I should have taken as a warning though, was that unruly black hair of his, peppered with gray. Now as he walked to our truck his thick hair was even wilder. The look matched his faded shirt with sleeves rolled up, dusty jeans and boots that had trekked many miles. I suddenly felt out of place in my shiny black riding boots and fashionable jodhpurs. As I climbed out of the pickup, he welcomed me with a mischievous grin and a glint in his smiling eyes.

"The horses should be here any minute," he said with cheerful spunk. "Why don't I show you the camp first."

The three of us walked the few paces to the chalets, where I found myself awed by the splendor of the place. "This is absolutely beautiful, Tore," I exclaimed. "What a wonderful spot."

The safari camp rested on the bend of a strong river, churning calmly past. Twinkling sunlight showered down through the lofty trees all around us. Tore had built several thatched chalets, one of which was constructed on top of, or really as a part of, a rocky outcrop. Large boulders had been left as nature placed them, to serve as steps, walls and floors. In fact, this cozy chalet built into a hill seemed more of a fox's den or eagle's aerie, than the usual rigid structures made for humans.

"Okay, here are the horses now," Tore announced. "Are you ready to go for a ride?"

"Are there only two?" I asked skeptically. "Isn't Darren coming along?"

I knew Darren would be happy to stay behind, but I wasn't sure about riding off into the wilderness with this wild-looking character as my guide.

"No, you two go ahead," Darren said, smiling to me as he settled onto a spot in the shade. "I don't mind waiting here. You and Tore go enjoy yourselves."

I warily eyed the rugged little steeds, who were absolutely nothing like what I expected. I supposed a hint of Arab blood could be detected from some distant lineage, but these were through and through bush horses. They were small in size like most hardy equines who lived an un-pampered existence, with narrow chests and knees only a few inches apart, looking too spare to carry the weight of an adult. But they were certainly well-fed, with coats clean and brushed, although they had the longish hair of bush ponies which gave them a scruffy look. Upon their backs were McClellan "saddles", meaning unadorned smooth wooden frames under which lay colorful rugs. Now I definitely felt out of place in my jodhpurs, and wished I'd worn jeans and chaps instead.

In one easy motion Tore slipped onto the sprightly bay, a deep brown color with flowing black mane and ebony tail. I was told to ride the gray, since he was calmer, although he was blind in one eye. This might be very interesting, I thought to myself nervously.

"You'd better leave your dogs behind," Tore warned. "There's plenty of crocodiles around here."

Darren called bite-size Scruff to him, but I thought our lab-ridgeback cross should come with us. Tagging along with the horses was his favorite sport, and being a lanky young dog he could easily run for miles.

My flyweight charger stood quietly as I put my foot in the stirrup and swung up. I then checked the girth to make sure it was good and tight. The middle of what there was of a saddle was open, and against my thighs from underneath the soft rug, I could feel the horse's strong spine and flexing lean muscles.

"Are you ready?" Tore asked without waiting for a reply. "We'll see you soon," he called to Darren as he wheeled his gelding around, then burst into a gallop and disappeared into bush.

At this, my mount didn't hesitate to launch himself off his toes and bolt after Tore's horse. I was surprised at the zip of this scraggly equine, and as we shot off, for a moment wondered how safe I'd be. But I quickly noticed that my horse responded well to me. After several minutes of racing through the bush, I could also see he was clever with his feet, as he galloped confidently along.

The track into the woodland soon petered out and we were now sprinting through unmarked bush. Speeding along, we dodged jagged stumps and leapt over old logs, veered around thorny shrubs and ducked under low branches. I mostly left my horse to steer our way as plainly he'd traveled these parts before, seeming to know every tree and log while negotiating it all effortlessly. I simply leaned forward into his gallop, kept my seat near the saddle for sudden turns, and tried to stay in sight of the dodging tail of Tore's horse ahead.

My big black dog had sprinted out in front, careening through the bush in all directions, mad with enthusiasm at being in open spaces again. As we raced headlong I heard him barking hoarsely far ahead, although I couldn't tell if his bawls were of the frantic kind, or if he was simply suffering from overexcitement. Then in the next second, also from a distance, the clear barks of many baboons ricocheted through the trees. The guttural echoes were almost a predatory sound, sending a chill to my bones. I instantly imagined the baboons' sharp teeth ripping apart the soft flesh of my hound.

"Is my dog all right?" I called apprehensively to Tore, as our horses slowed to a trot. "Do you think he's in trouble?"

"I don't know, but we'd better find out," was his answer as he spurred his mount into a gallop again. My own little steed seemed to enjoy the urgency and leapt forward with vigor. As we raced along I uneasily spied a ravine looming ahead, and expected Tore and the horses to slow for the vertical drop. But in front of me neither he nor his mount slackened their pace, and the next thing they disappeared over the edge. I was tempted to rein in my horse, but guessed he had probably crossed this place many times and knew exactly where to put his feet. Before I could finish my thought, in an instant we flew over the ravine's edge. Automatically I tilted back in the saddle, forced my eyes open and braced for a jolt at the bottom. But to my surprise, this clever little animal landed with the gentleness of a hare. He then sprung up the steep opposite side in rocketing bounds, while I gripped fistfuls of white mane and held tight at each powerful lunge, amazed at the pluck of this scrappy creature.

Suddenly we bounded out of the bush and into sun-flooded openness. We looked upon a magnificent river scene, where we found my dog rushing about and barking idiotically. A troop of baboons of every size was scampering over a collection of boulders, to reach the other side of the river. Our horses came to a prancing halt amidst a cacophony, as every baboon on the opposite bank and in the facing trees, was letting forth a bark, scream or grunt. All giving encouragement to the last tiny youngster struggling to cross the wet boulders. I watched as the little fellow hesitantly hopped from rock to rock, his extended family tensely looking on, their yells surely meaning, "Hurry up! Come quickly!" Suddenly, he slipped and fell in the water. At this a piercing collective shriek burst forth from the troop. One adult then promptly darted back, helping the small chap the rest of the way.

The baboon family seemed so good-hearted, I felt guilty at having had visions of them ripping apart my hound. But then, the truth still was that they could be ferocious when pressed.

"Keep a lookout for crocs," Tore instructed as we walked our mounts along the bank, and he scanned the river for a place to cross. He wasn't worried so much about the horses, but for my dog. Finally he found a good spot, and we wound our way down to water clear and shallow, the horses gingerly making their way through slippery rocks to the other side.

Once on the opposite bank, Tore didn't hesitate to move into a quick clip, weaving us through thick bush before once again meeting up with the curve of the river. I noticed the bank was even higher now, as we cantered along far above the water. I made sure to keep my horse a few paces behind Tore, so I might catch a hint of what he'd do next. As I expected, he wasn't looking for the easy way home. Without warning he plunged off the embankment and down into the sandy riverbed, then quickly galloped off through shallow water. I presumed my reliable steed would follow, but instead he just gave Tore and his horse a sidelong look as we galloped on above, the downside becoming higher and steeper. I decided I'd better make a move, since the terrain up top was becoming more precarious, and at least going down was all sand if we landed in a crumple somewhere between here and the riverbed.

With only the slightest of encouragement my brave mount pitched over the edge, leaping out as far as he could for a flatter landing. His hooves sunk into sand above his ankles and for a moment he struggled to keep his feet under him, our forward momentum threatening to send us tumbling head over heel. But in another second we were flying down through the river, as I watched for dark patches that could be deep holes. All the while trying to catch up with Tore, who never once glanced back.

When we arrived back at the safari camp, my exuberant dog close on our heels, Darren casually walked up. Patting my horse while I dismounted, he said to me, "So did you have a nice ride? How's the ranch, is it quite stunning?"

Tore went off to take care of some business, so I strolled back to the shady lawn with Darren. "Actually, I didn't have much of a chance to take in the view," I told him honestly. "But what I did notice was spectacular."

"What do you mean you didn't see much?" Darren asked, giving me a quizzical look. "Weren't you looking around you?"

"Frankly, I was too busy hanging on and ducking low branches. Didn't you see us take off out of here at a mad gallop?"

"Well, yeah. But I thought you were just trying to sprint away before the dogs could follow. I figured you brought the horses to a walk a short distance from here."

When I filled Darren in about our exciting ride, he chuckled and declared, "That sounds like Tore. I'd guess he was testing you. I hope you enjoyed yourself anyway."

"Yes . . . I did. Very much," I said reflectively. "And I certainly hope I passed the test!"

Then too, I was glad for every chance to spend a day exactly as this with Africa. And as a bonus, with Tore I'd just made another extraordinary friend.

* * * * *

As the days brought us to the end of May, our first month open for business, I took stock of the situation. It hadn't been a good month for the country. War Vets continued to cause havoc, while police had their hands tied, either by decree from those above or for a lack of vehicles and fuel. This encouraged criminals to have a heyday.

Yet while the police did little to respond to crime, they and the government's Criminal Investigation Organization spent their time carrying out searches on farmers. Nicky's sister had her farmhouse intrusively searched for firearms, the notorious CIO even pulling up the floorboards in their zeal. I was stunned, accustomed as I was to regard illegal searches as a cardinal sin. But I noticed that most simply tolerated it as part of life in Africa. Or more likely, this grin-and-bear-it attitude was because they had few options, unless they wanted to abandon their homes, livelihoods and country.

On Humani, things weren't going well either. The War Vet contingent had eventually arrived and made themselves comfortable in the safari camp where we'd stayed. I could certainly agree that these nicely built chalets made an inviting hangout. Most of these hooligans were already well known to Roger, being the resident poachers he'd clashed with over the years.

At the police station, Roger was told nothing could be done to evict the "War Vets" since it was their land anyway. It didn't matter that when Roger's parents settled in Humani's rugged wilderness in the 1920s, no African villages existed there. Early maps labeled the area "Unfit for Habitation" because, in fact, nobody managed to live there.

Regardless, the War Vets on Humani—that is, the troublemaking poachers of only weeks earlier—would be allowed by the police to stay on the ranch. In Humani's workers' village, home to five hundred souls, the hoodlums simply marched in to bully and beat the folks there. Like outlaws will do, they demanded food and whatever they wanted, and went on a campaign of terrorizing. A favorite tactic was to force villagers to lie face down on the ground, and then beat their buttocks and bare soles with rods or leather straps until they couldn't walk. Many workers laid charges at the station, but the cops did nothing.

Throughout the country, War Vets stormed into villages and rounded up everyone other than toddlers and the very old. Workers and their families were then marched to a camp set up for reeducation, all night forced to sing and parade to ZANU songs, and be lectured on ZANU ideology to which they had to give the "appropriate" responses at the "appropriate" intervals, or risk a bloody beating. Occasionally someone was pulled from the crowd and given a thrashing, as an example to anyone whose zeal might waver.

I also heard that some farmers had been escorted off to attend these "reeducation" sessions. With disbelief, I wondered what I would do if faced with such insanity. In astonishment, I listened as Nicky told me that her cousin's husband, a burly ex-rugby player with a forceful personality, had been made to "dance" and chant ZANU songs in his workers' village. When I talked to him later, I was amazed at how he took it in good humor. As he saw it, his cooperation meant there shouldn't be any violence meted out on his family or workers. Yet I knew the unsaid was that everyone living in Africa understood certain aspects to life here, especially political dramas, just had to be endured.

I considered it'd all gone too far, however, when I heard the next alarming story about our friend Jean. One afternoon while working in her tobacco barns, she suddenly found herself surrounded by thirty hyped-up War Vets, who grabbed her by the elbows and immediately marched her off. She was forced to run barefoot along a secluded country road, chanting ZANU songs while they struck the back of her legs with sticks. But she wasn't alone. During the ordeal sixty of her workers, although mute with fear, chose to run alongside her.

Amid the initial commotion, a worker had slipped off to alert nearby farmers. Jumping into pickups, several rushed to her aid. By the time they caught up with Jean her barefoot run had spanned ten miles. A negotiation for her release then ensued, the thugs trying to intimidate the farmers by roughing them up a bit, too. The men kept their cool, and after they, Jean and her workers compliantly recited ZANU slogans, then chanted and "danced" to ZANU themes with the appropriate amount of enthusiasm, they were allowed to go.

I also worried about Nicky, living out there in the back of beyond, as she too had a run-in with War Vets. Driving to Chiredzi one morning she was held up by a small band, who had thrown together a crude roadblock by dragging logs and large rocks onto the conservancy road. Although unarmed, they were agitated and tense. Nicky was nervous, but managed to bribe her way past with cigarettes and a promise to bring bread on her return.

Our beacon of strength, the leader of the opposition Morgan Tsvangirai, was thrown in jail on a trumped up charge of inciting civil unrest. Commercial farming lay in ruins. Tourism had come to a screeching halt. The mining industry was withering, mainly because of the government's currency policies. Then insurance companies in Zim scrambled to change their policies to clearly state they would not cover losses due to political turmoil. Amongst it all, unsurprisingly the Zimbabwe dollar slid to sixty-to-one with the greenback. This was a crushing 300% devaluation since my arrival in the country two and a half years earlier.

Meanwhile, everyday life in our little town was as mellow as always. Even with the country disintegrating around Darren and me, our little business, which we hadn't expected to carry itself for its first month anyway, managed to pay the bills. Somehow we had at least come out even and it seemed a good omen for us personally. Like everyone in the country, we looked toward next month's parliamentary elections as a last hope for salvation.

* * * * *

With a few weeks to go before elections, everyone I talked with held either of two opinions about how the cards would play out. Many reckoned, if carried out fairly, the political opposition, mainly the MDC, would win the most seats. But plenty of others guessed Mugabe would rig the elections, ensuring a ZANU-PF "victory" so he could hold on to a majority in parliament to rubber stamp his decrees.

From what I could see, the deck certainly didn't look stacked in the MDC's favor. Many of their nominees had been forced into hiding because of risk to their lives. In the very least, those running on the MDC ticket had to keep a low profile, or risk retribution from ZANU thugs. Added to the impossibility of openly campaigning, the party was allowed virtually no coverage in the state-run media.

While scraps of news about attacks did reach my ears, at the time I didn't fully understand the extent of the violence since media coverage was almost zero. Only later did I learn of the harassment that went on, and against the voting populous, too. Often when a ZANU-PF political rally was to be held, thugs went around to nearby homes and "insisted" everyone attend. On farms, War Vets threatened workers that if the ruling party didn't win the upcoming vote, retribution would be merciless.

Although Mugabe announced he would allow election observers, when the time came he granted permission to only a chosen few, then severely restricted where they could go. Once again, he successfully orchestrated the process to exactly how he wanted it, saying to the world, for example, that he had allowed observers, while at the same time keeping them completely ineffectual.

There were some factors we hoped might work to the MDC's advantage. Just about everything in the country was falling apart, and in a logical world this would be a mark against Mugabe and his party. Fuel was scarce, the rare deliveries sold out within hours.

Power cuts were now a frequent affair and the phones were down
more than usual.

Many companies put their employees on a four-day workweek,
with a painful twenty percent pay cut. Business owners sat at their
desks reading magazines since they had nothing to do. There were
no customers because no one was spending a penny, or making the
slightest decision, until after the elections. Everything in the country was completely on hold.

One morning during our second month in business, and with
the power out again, I drove the short distance to our workshop to
see how things were going. My heart sank when I saw Darren. He
sat alone at the wooden plank which served as a desk, in the gloomy
darkness of the windowless workshop. The telephones were down
and the water off, the shop disturbingly quiet without the usual roar
of the machines, which couldn't operate without electricity. But
it didn't matter anyway, since there wasn't much work to do. As I
leaned down in the empty silence and put my arms around him,
I was filled with a crushing sadness, hating to see him so beaten
down by this shroud of disintegration.

Darren's hopes and plans—everything he had worked toward—
was fading away before him. He had come so close to making it all
happen, of establishing a business in his country, finding someone
who shared his dreams, and settling into a home. But now the hard
won goals were slipping from his grasp just as he reached them.

I thought how even Mother Nature seemed to have lost the desire to try, the weather unusually dismal. Clouds and showers were
rare this time of year, but here it was overcast and drizzly, some
mornings with fog down to the ground. It reminded me of coastal
Anchorage weather, and in a strange way, made me feel a little comforted.

For me at least, gazing out the window past our garden pond
to the shifting fog, I still felt privileged to live in this unique corner
of the world. After each rain shower eased, I watched as a crowd
of burping frogs lazily ventured out from the pond's depths. Frogs
were a rare creature in Alaska, leaving me forever captivated. But

even more fascinating, the exodus of the frogs brought to our yard the prehistoric looking hammerkop bird. The long feathers on the back of his head, or *kop* as it's called in Afrikaans, gives him a hammerhead look. This mystical avian, with stick legs and long narrow beak, frequently visited us for a meal of porky amphibians. I thought to myself, surely such an extraordinary guest must bring us good luck.

When evening settled in, the fog mysteriously vanished and the night revealed a slowly rising moon. This was another gift of Africa to me, the brilliance of moonshine. I had read stories of how the brightness of a full moon could expose a danger lurking in the dark, or save a life by illuminating a path through the woods at night. But really, I couldn't understand how the placid moon, floating in an infinite black sky, could make a difference to anything.

But in Africa I found out. Sitting on my veranda after nightfall under a full moon, amazingly, I could see everything. I could have read a book. Why now, after more than thirty years, was this a discovery? Partly was the fact that when camping in Alaska—the Land of the Midnight Sun—summer nights were never dark enough to show the potency of the moon. But even more, it was because in Africa where so much is stripped away, that so much is revealed. As I now sat taking in the deep night, around me no homes pierced with outdoor lights, and no street lamps flooded out glare. In the unblemished night, the shimmering glow of moonshine was another bounty of Africa. And that's why I didn't want to leave most of all. I wanted to see what other gifts I knew she still had to give.

Chapter Twenty-two

||||||||||||||||||||||||||||||||||||||||||||||||||||||||||||||||||||||||

"What do you think we should do this weekend, during elections?" Darren said to me, although we both knew the answer before he asked. No one could guess whether a storm of violence would erupt, and being only a three hour drive from the South African border, like many we had considered slipping south just beforehand. But as that weekend—the 24th and 25th of June 2000—drew closer and the quiet rhythm of our small world remained unchanged, like most of our friends and neighbors we decided to stay put.

With only a few days to go, an uncomfortable muteness took over the country. These elections were the same as important senatorial ones in the States, but amazingly, I saw not a single political advertisement. When I did errands in town, I noticed people went about their business in a careful and furtive manner. Any farmer or rancher who had a staff beerhall kept it closed. During the week before and throughout the weekend of elections, no one uttered a peep about politics. Other than the radio announcers, that is, soberly encouraging everyone to go out and vote.

The first morning of balloting began with a well-needed prayer, broadcast over the radio by the Coalition of Churches. On that Saturday, Vic and some of his workers dutifully drove to the polling station in Triangle. After patiently standing in line for an hour, upon making it to the front, to their disbelief the attendant said they weren't on the register. Each duly presented his voter registration card listing this station, yet still they weren't allowed to cast their vote. When all was said and done, we learned that this problem of legitimate voters being turned away at the booths had happened throughout the country.

By the end of the first day, turnout had been dismal. Everyone was subdued, the roads quiet and shops empty. A countrywide hush held the land, as though we were a nation in mourning. On the second day even fewer citizens showed up at the polls. The voting process in Zimbabwe had become so overshadowed by thuggery that folks just didn't want to have anything to do with it.

Still, we were anxious to hear the outcome. Everyone kept close to their radios and TVs, with the first results coming from the second largest city of Bulawayo and surrounding Matabeleland. Mugabe was a Mashona, so it wasn't a complete surprise when these early announcements from Matabeleland showed MDC candidates as winners. We hadn't dared to think that the opposition could actually win seats, and for a breathless moment hope revived. Eagerly watching the tally on TV with friends, we couldn't help but assume the nation might be rescued.

But gloomily, the next batch of results showed ZANU-PF as winners, a party tainted by oppression. Dark clouds once again rumbled over our spirits. In the end, the outcome was nothing like anyone expected.

The tally showed ZANU-PF with 62 seats, the MDC with 57, and a lone seat to a third party. No one had guessed the vote would end up so closely split. But because 30 of the 150 seats in parliament were appointed by the president, it still left the opposition without the two-thirds majority needed to pass laws. Without the opposition having a majority, we despondently realized big changes wouldn't be coming soon.

No surprise, observers concluded the vote had not been "free and fair". Besides the far-reaching intimidation and violence, there were the voters turned away because they weren't on the register, while some ballot boxes had been briefly "misplaced". This could easily happen, with no security at night or during transport. Even if no dirty dealing was involved, the process was a shambles. The MDC immediately filed complaints with the court, contending some seats had not been won fairly by ZANU-PF.

Along with the entire nation, Darren and I gave a sigh of relief, as at least now parliamentary elections were over. Could everyone just get on with business as usual? Would we be allowed to go about our simple lives in peace? Did this mean a slackening of strife in our once placid country? The future was uncertain. Zimbabwe had never crossed this threshold before with two political parties, both strong for different reasons. Each day, each week, and each month for the foreseeable future would be unpredictable. To the detriment of an already struggling nation, long term planning was now erased from the Zimbabwean frame of mind.

* * * * *

An uncomfortable quiet steeped in Zimbabwe for the first week after elections. I supposed no one knew what was to happen next. Like everyone, I assumed that simply making it past elections wouldn't solve our problems, and more than anything, the economy was key. Yet the economic collapse, given a mortal blow by all the political strife, was the product of Mugabe's misrule.

Mugabe, however, had covered his tracks well, cleverly creating what began as an effective smokescreen. For a time he succeeded in turning the world's attention away from his brutal crackdown and draining of public coffers, with a tragic portrayal of poor peasant versus rich farmer. His diversion worked because an obvious dilemma existed, with millions of Zimbabweans scratching out an existence on communal lands that were now overgrazed and over tilled, trees axed down and soil swept away.

Something needed to be done and foreign governments thought making generous cash handouts to Mugabe for buying land would solve the problem. Yet settling peasants on farms at the cost of commercial enterprise hadn't raised living standards and improved people's lives. With modern techniques and equipment, certain agricultural ventures can be viable. But a peasant battles a climate, terrain, rain patterns and soils that are not sympathetic to subsistence.

This was true to the extreme in southern Zimbabwe where our friends Sam and Janet lived. For hundreds of lonesome miles the terrain lay as flat as a pancake sizzling in a frying pan. In this parched land the scant rainfall is measured in millimeters and a scorching sun beats down on a shadeless, breezeless landscape. It's a place where you feel forever thirsty, and thankful to only be passing through.

On our visits to Sam and Janet, we reached their house upon a track of coarse sand, our pickup swishing against its grainy looseness. Looking out the window at the sparse bush, I wondered what their Brahman cattle actually ate, since the brittle shrubs looked too inedible for even a starving beetle.

Yet unbelievably, Janet told me the government wanted their austere ranch. Their place bordered a communal area, and as I now stood with Janet looking out across their barbed wire fence towards it, I couldn't believe the landscape could be even more desolate. The startling contrast made me notice that behind us, the rocky ground of Sam and Janet's place was actually scattered with tuffs of brown grass. The thorny shrubs looked thick compared to the communal side of the fence, where woodstuff for a nightly fire had long since been plundered.

As Janet and I scanned the bleak expanse of the communal acres, she explained with frustration that the peasants look over the fence and think a privileged farmer got the good land. When in fact, both pieces of ground looked exactly the same fifty years ago. The saddest part was that most of them probably didn't understand why their ground had become a desert, nor could they remember the time when their land, too, had looked like Janet's side of the fence.

The difference in landscapes was because Sam and Janet's place hadn't been overstressed. In this arid territory avoiding overgrazing was vital. But Janet told me how townsfolk would buy cattle, a favored "investment" in Zim, and leave them on communal lands to be looked after by a relative. For the cattle owners in town, the communal land was a bonanza of free grazing. But when combined with the communal folks' own livestock, means devastation for the veld.

Then too, trying to grow crops in this harsh locale was a waste of resources. Still, the peasants here did sow their patches, despite the expense not justifying the meager yields. Ever optimistic, they continued to plant year after year, hoping Mother Nature would bestow unheard of good rains. Yet I knew that even if the rain were generous, the sandy earth could not provide the nutrients for a bountiful harvest.

Throughout the country the story was the same. In the southeast where Darren and I lived was still a severe climate, restricting crops to mainly sugar and citrus, and only with irrigation. Driving west for hundreds of miles, no crop land was to be seen. Other than of course, the peasants' bleak patches in the communal areas. Western Zimbabwe's heat and unreliable rain meant cattle, ostrich and wildlife ranching were the best ventures. Even in the north, where Darren and I had lived on Rungudzi, there were scorching temperatures and scant rain.

The rugged Eastern Highlands was the only region with semi-regular rain, but it was hilly country at best. Timber and coffee were the most feasible, although these yield returns only after years of hefty investment. Simply not an option for the peasant living hand to mouth.

It is the gentle countryside around Harare in north central, at most a quarter of the nation, which gifts the best agricultural land. East of Harare was known for its tobacco, which likes sandy soils that drain well. To the west lay expansive wheat fields in heavy red clay.

In my curiosity, I discovered that peasants traditionally settled where land is sandier and more easily worked by hand, or ox and simple plow. But sandy soils provide fewer nutrients, making fertilizers a must. Food crops on the other hand, such as wheat and corn, thrive in the red clay. The same stuff the brick-makers use, the dense red earth also baking concrete-hard in the sun. Loathsome to a poor peasant trying to scratch a furrow in cemented ground.

Yes, I knew Zimbabwe's story. Before modern wells, dams, canals and manmade lakes were built, her lack of year round water kept the population sparse. The advent of modernity in the twentieth century attracted many people to her. Some from Europe, the Americas, India and elsewhere, although most from other African nations where jobs and living standards were less. Many Zimbabwean have parents or grandparents from Zambia, Mozambique or Malawi, making her a land of immigrants of all shades of color.

For years I was stunned at how journalists eagerly fell into Mugabe's trap, telling of a struggle between poor peasants cramped on communal lands and those who had all the "good" land. Did they mean ranchers like Sam and Janet, who managed to make a profitable enterprise out of barren, God-forsaken ground? Or was it just those growing crops, like Alan up in the rocky hills of Rungudzi? He struggled even with the hardy tobacco plant, and then only because he contrived a few small irrigation dams. Or was it our friend Trevor on his rugged coffee farm bordering Mozambique, whose land should belong to the peasants? Like Roger's parents on Humani, when Trevor's family settled on their place decades ago, no one else, native or newcomer, lived there. Or perhaps it was the wheat farmer on his land of baked, stone-hard clay, who should concede his farm to the peasants. Admittedly as I drove past, even I jealously yearned to possess those golden fields.

As I watched all the struggles around me, I knew that having the masses scrape out a living was not what anyone desired for the nation. All landowners and businessmen wanted the peasants' lot to improve, because if each Zimbabwean had extra dollars in their pockets, that money would create a thriving economy in which everyone had a better life. I was only one of many searching for a way to save paradise.

Chapter Twenty-three

|||||||||||||||||||||||||||||||||||||||||||||||||||||||||||||||||||||||||||

"This has gotta be the best bargain going," I thought to myself, feeling buyer's satisfaction at getting a deal. A farmer near Chiredzi provided a weekly veggie service of twenty-five pounds of vegetables for the equal of US$1. Most weeks my packet included lettuce, cucumber, tomatoes and carrots, green or red peppers, broccoli, cauliflower, a variety of squashes, turnips, beets, corn on the cob, radishes, sweet potatoes, spinach, cabbage, beans and so on. In Alaska, where fresh food stuff had to be flown in, this was a cornucopia of provisions. The parcel was abundantly more than Darren and I could eat in a week, and the bag supplied our housemaid and gardener, too. The farmer had arranged with Tore to use his workshop as the collection point, so each Wednesday I stopped by there.

Tore's workshop rested at the edge of our small town, on a fair-sized lot with plenty of hardy trees and long grass, the surrounding tracts thick with bush. He operated his transport business from here and a couple of broken-down semi trucks always blocked the drive. The place had a junkyard look, with its bounty of old tires and rusting drums, discarded parts piled everywhere. However, Tore seemed to know where each much-valued item was "stored", and was sure every scrap would have an important use later.

Parking my pickup along the dirt drive, I carefully stepped amongst the scatter of a dismantled engine to make my way inside. An old house served as the workshop, its porch heaped with a wealth of clutter but with a path kept clear to the door. Inside, a central room with an oil-stained concrete floor was used as an exceedingly crammed storage area. The space wasn't well lit, blurring the crowded interior into a uniform grayness. Against the walls, ceiling-high shelves were packed to overflowing and thick with undisturbed dust. To reach Tore's office at the back, I followed a trail carved out between the stacked-to-the-roof "collectibles".

Stepping inside his office, to my right soared even more tall shelves stuffed with an assortment of goodies. The front of each shelf was lined with tacks and nails, holding such treasures as a salesman's forgotten business card, a yellowed receipt, or a loose key. On the opposite wall above his desk hung an enormous corkboard thickly covered in clippings and papers. A third wall was decorated with a collage of snapshots, showing Tore's wife and three daughters, his ranch, friends and special places. The farthest side was taken up by a large window, a tangle of bush pressing close outside.

Of course Tore's desk and bookshelf, and the large table next to it, were heavily scattered with papers, books, notepads, ledgers, telephone and adding machine, spare parts, tools and so on. The boxes and other whatnot on the floor left little standing room. The place had a gritty feel, made especially so by the dull light, yet all the same I found it inviting.

Each week when picking up my veggies, I looked forward to dropping in at Tore's office for a quick chat. He was always a cheerful sight, his face lit by his winning smile. I'd happily sit down as he offered me his guest chair, a shabby relic from the Sixties, and our quick chat predictably turned into a two hour discussion. Tore always had some helpful, although often unusual, advice to solve my problem of the day. Once I told him we'd had a lot of mosquitoes at our house and I was having it professionally sprayed. He then politely informed me that the repellant didn't work. His advice instead, was I should simply let all the spider webs build up in the corners and nooks of the rooms, allowing the spiders to keep the mosquitoes under control.

"See, like I've done," Tore said, pointing up to the high ceiling. As I cast my gaze upward, I saw that where the walls joined the ceiling was an uninterrupted mass of spider webs, encircling the entire room. The webbing was several layers deep, an intricate spider metropolis with hundreds of residents. Smiling, I told Tore that while I liked the idea of natural insect control, I didn't think a tangle of spider webs on the ceiling of my living room would fit with my decor. And it'd certainly be a creepy addition to the bedroom.

Each week the conversations Tore roped me into were usually along a philosophical line. Mostly on the subject of religion; his favorite topic. He'd passionately launch into detailed, almost scientific, explanations of redemption, sin, heaven, and man's relationship with God, which I sometimes struggled to follow as he fervently rushed on. In his enthusiasm and desire for me to understand, he'd dump out the contents of his "briefcase" and rummage for a pen. Then eagerly draw flowcharts of circles, squares and arrows to illustrate the process of salvation, and the spiritual path man makes in his journey to heaven. All the while exclaiming, "This is truly amazing! Isn't this exciting?"

Tore's "briefcase" was a beat up metal ammo box, its green paint peeling, and filled with an array of essential items. Scratched reading glasses with one "arm" missing, a flashlight pumped by hand to keep the bulb glowing, Tore's battered cell phone, a watch that didn't work, crumpled dollar bills, loose keys for long-forgotten locks, a screwdriver, a calculator, sunscreen, twice as many caps as pens, a multi-use Buck knife, coins, a tube of ointment, and enough scraps of paper for a ticker tape parade.

One afternoon as I was leaving the bank, I happened to see Tore. He stood filling out a deposit slip with his open ammo box on the counter next to him. Somehow, at least in Africa, this seemed perfectly normal. I stopped to say hello and a smiling Tore asked how things were going.

I wasn't in the best of moods and usually didn't like to grumble, but it'd been a frustrating day. I first launched into my banking woes, as even though Barclays was an international bank, in Zimbabwe it

still ran in a pre-modern mode. I had just been told the check I was
depositing from an out-of-town account would take two weeks to
clear. As with anything in Africa, time is not of the essence, even
with banking transactions. Added to this, the bank's check-making
machine was broken so I couldn't order another checkbook.

The thing about it was, my trip to the bank wouldn't have irri-
tated me so much had I not just spent four hours in line at the fuel
station. And during the hottest time of day without a hint of shade.

Upon arriving at the station, I found the line already stretching
down the street, as word quickly spread that some fuel had been de-
livered. I felt lucky though, because the string of cars spanned only
two blocks when I slipped in behind. But as I waited on the sun-
baked asphalt with the day ticking by, the line didn't seem to move
at all. My patience was nearing its breaking point, sweat was trickling down, and I wondered what the heck was going on. Had the
power gone out, stopping the pumps from working, as sometimes
happened? Finally my pickup crept onto the station's lot, where with
exasperation I saw the reason for the holdup. Mild chaos reigned at
the one diesel pump, with vehicles pushing in from all directions,
leaving cars lined up in orderly fashion like mine as the most un-
successful at edging near the pump. Now no one could barely move.
A dozen big trucks and buses had also crammed in, creating a ferocious knot of vehicles that blocked all ways in or out.

By this time, however, I was in sight of the pump and stubbornly determined to keep my place. As I stood there baking next to my
pickup, hoping for a wisp of breeze, I noticed that the pavement under my feet and everywhere around was solidly flattened with litter.
The spectacle was the ultimate in filth, topped with a layer of grime.
Standing now at this fuel-station-cum-oversized-gutter, I realized
I'd become so used to the town's grunge that it scarcely registered
with me anymore.

When I finally made it to the pump, everyone was being limited
to twenty-five liters, or less than seven gallons. Meager rations indeed for the four hours spent to get my hands on it. But once again,
tasks in Africa weren't measured by the time they take. What was

important, I had to remind myself, was I'd been able to complete what I set out to do.

Tore listened to my ranting with a patient smile. He was in a particularly good mood this afternoon, telling me that living in a place like small town Africa kept a person in touch with reality. Well, one thing I could agree with, was that in Africa I did regularly find myself thankful for my good fortunes.

The trouble was, the good things in life were steadily lessening for all Zimbabweans. With inflation and unemployment at frightening levels, everyone's quality of life was eroding away. And when such minor accomplishments as keeping the trash picked up seemed impossible, I had to wonder how Zimbabweans would ever manage to get their nation back on track.

* * * * *

With the nuisance of elections behind him, Mugabe could get back to his real priority of the land grab. He started to publish a weekly list of farms he wanted to acquire, as yet another plan to snatch commercial farmland, since his initial schemes had been thwarted by the courts. It was now obvious that his tactics were meant as a harassment of those who didn't support ZANU-PF rather than as a legitimate resettlement plan.

One sunny Saturday, while I sat on bleachers watching Darren's nephew in a school rugby match, I found myself talking to a farmer's wife. She and her husband grew tobacco on their farm east of Harare, having bought the place eleven years earlier when it had no infrastructure and was lying idle. Her story made me reflect back on mine and Darren's plan to get into farming, by starting simple and building things up. The couple had put in tobacco facilities, a home, fences, boreholes for water, cattle dips and so on. In late 1998, when foreign governments were still giving Mugabe money to buy farms, they decided not to contest the government's notice to buy theirs, reasoning it better to start life again sooner rather than later.

After months of dragging things out, the Zim government abruptly pulled out of the deal. From the point of view of Mugabe's

camp they saw no benefit in taking property from someone willing to give it up. Plus by now, acquired farms were being gifted to
Mugabe's inner-circle, and since theirs sat on a communal boundary, none of his cronies wanted it. Selling on the open market was
now unlikely, so their choice was to either keep trudging along and
hope for the best, or abandon it all and bankrupt themselves.

Besides the land uncertainty and War Vet harassment, farmers
like our friend Jean had plenty of other problems, too. Although
international buyers paid with US dollars, Zimbabwe law required
farmers to be reimbursed in Zim dollars at the official exchange
rate. So for every US$1 of tobacco Jean sold, she received Zim$38.
Yet her imported fertilizers, chemicals, and spare parts had to be
purchased at the parallel rate of Zim$60 to US$1. This equated to
an astonishing 50% increase in expenses and meant a farmer's business had to have a whopping 50% profit margin to break even. Also,
like many farmers, the bank told Jean they would no longer give her
financing because farms, as collateral for loans, risked being taken
by the government. But with interest rates at 60%, who wanted financing anyway.

Thus, Mugabe had successfully created so many obstacles for
farmers, that eventually they may have no choice but to pack their
bags and turn their backs on the land. To which he would be unquestionably delighted.

Chapter Twenty-four

|||||||||||||||||||||||||||||||||||||||||||||||||||||||||||||||||||||||||||||||||||

Sprawled within hundreds of miles of thorny bush and thirst-stunted trees, lay the Chiredzi River Wildlife Conservancy. Buffalo Range was the largest of the dozen ranches making up this unspoiled refuge, while Darren's sister and brother-in-law also owned property there, bordering a communal area. Vic and Jane kept a lusty herd of Cape buffalo, which unfortunately had to be incarcerated in a large pen and fed hay and pellets, waiting for the time when a sturdy game fence was up on the communal boundary. Only then could the buffalo be allowed to range free over the conservancy's rambling acres.

The problem was, as soon as a span of fencing was up on the boundary, it was immediately dismantled by peasants living on the communal side. Then, while this section was being repaired, another was being taken apart. The peasants found it a simple matter to chop down poles and cut wires, in order to expand the grazing for their goats and cattle. It became impossible for Vic to guard the many miles of boundary, so this struggle to keep a secure fence line went on for years. All the while, the unfortunate buffalo were forced to live in their cramped paddock.

The main reason the buffalo couldn't be released without a secure barrier was veterinary laws. They had to be kept separate from cattle on communal lands to prevent spreading bovine diseases such as the dreaded "hoof and mouth". Also was the fact that buffalo are known to be aggressive, and to have a herd cavorting

amongst the villages would lead to serious, if not fatal, clashes sooner or later. Not least of all were the financial considerations for the
private enterprises which had carried the cost of breeding up these
magnificent beasts, each valued at US$10,000. Allowed to roam the
communal lands, these expensive animals would eventually end up
in someone's supper pot.

In the end, Vic realized he was fighting a losing battle to keep
the game fence up, so having found someone who wanted the herd
he despondently sold the proud buffalo. After several years in con-
finement they were finally free, and we could only hope they'd be
safe and thrive in their new home.

On the ranch next door to Vic and Jane's, our friend Terry's
parents were employed as caretakers. War Vets had pretty much
taken the place over as their private poaching grounds, this group
being especially belligerent. Terry's parents couldn't drive around
the ranch without being menaced. It was impossible to ride horses
about the place or fish in the dam. Even on walks close to the house
they could hear the rabid barking of the War Vets' hunting dogs,
followed by shrieks of a terrified antelope caught in a snare. The
poachers soon realized it was even easier to approach the horses
while they grazed, ramming a wire through soft nostrils to lead
them away, then peddling the meat to villagers as "zebra meat".

My buddy Tore's hardy ranch, where I had joined him for a
horse ride, also rested in the Chiredzi River Conservancy. He now
had ninety War Vet families living there, taking advantage of the
easy pickings by indiscriminately killing his cattle and game. Not
even his regal sable antelope were spared, worth US$5,000 each.
There had been a time when owning a breeding herd of valuable
game had been a good investment in Zimbabwe, where investing
earnings outside the country was illegal and a person had few options for his "pension plan". Another popular option for financial
planning had been to buy real estate, such as his ranch. But now,
like so many in Zim, at the age of fifty Tore risked losing his entire
life's savings. And there were certainly no government programs to
help break the fall.

On one of my Wednesday trips to Tore's workshop, I was disturbed to find him in the dim light of his office, sitting at his desk looking haggard and distant. This was so unlike him and I had a difficult time even finding out what troubled him. I suspected that like everyone, it wasn't a matter of a single problem, but rather the many impossible difficulties that became more overwhelming each day.

As he stared out the window, Tore mumbled a few words about problems on his ranch. Then turning to look intently at me, said, "I don't know what to do, Cinz. The War Vets, along with their families, want to meet with me today. They've told me they'll burn the ranch if I don't give it to them. So what can I say to these folks? I understand they have so little and are also desperate to improve their lot."

We both sat for a minute, lost in this infinite, unanswerable question. Then Tore simply stated, "All I can do is ask them to join me in prayer. I will ask God to help each of us with our troubles. I'll pray that the dark shadow hanging over all of our lives will be taken away."

* * * * *

Six harrowing months had passed since War Vets started camping on farms. It'd been six miserable months of scarce fuel, enduring long lines at stations. We had now suffered through three years of economic ruin with the plunge most rapid in the last six months. To put it simply, I felt battle weary.

Living in this dusty, litter-strewn town also wore on my spirits. I found doing errands depressing. Everywhere was garbage. That is, other than in the middle of the grubby sidewalks, where pedestrians kept the trash pushed into the gutter on one side, and up against the buildings on the other. Scruffy peasants wandered about languidly. A blind woman always sat on the curb holding her empty bowl, and skinny children begged for coins outside the grocery store.

Even the ordinary task of going to the post office wore on me. I could see the place had been built with pride those few decades ago, alluded to by its small landscaped grounds and neatly constructed building with steps of stone. But the shrubs and lawn were withered now, the steps coated with a dingy layer. Litter was caught in the hedge and windswept into corners. Inside, the floor hadn't been cleaned in twenty years and grime filled the creases. Every door, bulletin board, window, panel, and counter was falling apart in some way.

In front of the post office stood a pay phone, and a line of folk waiting to make calls blocked the wide steps leading inside. Being an oddity in this African town, as I walked toward the building a dozen empty stares fixed unapologetically on me, making me feel uncomfortable. Pushing my way through the line, I knew it was a struggle for them to stay clean since most didn't have a bathtub. But after so many months now, I had reached a point where I couldn't ignore the smell any longer.

Once inside, as I stood in line to buy postage I looked with disgust out the window to the neglected yard next door. Rather than make use of the town refuse collection service, in front of the building someone had simply dug a pit and heaped it full of garbage, most of which an impertinent breeze had now scattered about.

Standing there in line, I felt almost smothered, sensing more than usual the fact that Zimbabweans seemed to have little sense of personal space. They often stood so close their bodies pressed against one another, the person behind me breathing against my neck with a year's build-up of morning breath. Nor did it help that my shortness made my nose inconveniently aligned with so many of those unwashed armpits.

On top of this was the strain of it being several months into the sugar cane cutting season. Before a day's cane could be cut the fields had to be burned, sending a thirty foot wall of violent orange flame sweeping over miles of cane. During the day in summer, thermal waves coming off the sun-cooked earth lifted the soot and charred bits into the atmosphere. Then in early evening as the thermals dissipated, these flaky chards floated back to Earth. They called this Chiredzi snow, the black slivers settling over everyone's lawns, the quiet roads, and on resting cars. As the evening cooled, soot then sprinkled over the drowsy town, leaving everything in our home perpetually covered in grit. With the perfect stillness of midnight, the tiniest charred particles were the last to descend, so while we slept we breathed this miniscule grit of burnt cane.

The peasants were also igniting the bush, and if our town happened to be downwind, choking smoke clogged the air. Some days we inhaled an unpleasant, sharp odor of newly burnt vegetation, while on others, musty day-old smog. I could find no mercy since our neighbor regularly burned trash in his yard, sending toxic fumes of rubber and plastic to fill our house. Suffocating road dust was everywhere, stirred up during the day and carried skyward by the thermals, only to settle back to Earth at night. Pollution poured out from behind—to use my mother's words on a visit—"smoke-bomb buses" and trucks. There was no escaping the stifling air, and each morning Darren and I woke with stuffy noses and eyes itchy with grit. My lungs felt heavy and breathing was like sucking through a straw.

I had finally reached my saturation point with the filth, poverty and decay, feeling as though I'd fallen into one of those huge African potholes and could barely peek out. Of course it didn't help that getting a good night's sleep was impossible, even with my ear plugs jammed in, since I couldn't escape all the howling dogs and shrieking roosters. I longed for an untroubled world.

Yet Africa lures a person into enduring beyond what's bearable. Everyday life now featured the water off, phones down, or power cuts. Blackouts lasted several hours and descended upon us in morning or early evening. Darren preferred to take this pain after business hours, because during the day our workshop technicians simply sat on the floor waiting for electricity. But outages after nightfall also sapped our spirits, as we sat in a dark and silent house, only weak candlelight casting shadows and no music to cheer us.

What wore on me the most though, was being relentlessly surrounded by utter poverty. Each rail-thin person in grimy rags I saw, added up to a thousand pin pricks at my heart.

I had never experienced such a weighted cloud over my soul. It wasn't depression, and it wasn't really sadness. I supposed it was emotional fatigue. I felt mentally and emotionally exhausted from the daily struggle of life in Africa and needed to just get away. Nearly two years had passed since I'd been to the States. The time had come for a trip back home.

Chapter Twenty-five

███

felt some guilt about leaving, even for just a month. While everyone else was stuck in Zim, I was free to run off on a whim. But I
needed this chance to restore my sanity.

My flight was booked out of Johannesburg, and Darren and I
were to start early on our all-day trek to get there. Closing my suitcase with a click, my spirits already felt lighter, the combined prospect of seeing family soon and of a well-needed break from Africa.
While I took care of last minute details, outside I heard the trills of
hornbills and kingfishers. As its music mixed with soft sunlight it
seemed Africa was whispering to me, trying to make amends.

The last thing to do was close up my office. I filed a few papers
away and tidied my desk, covering my computer against dust that
would settle in the room even with windows closed. After shutting
the panes tight, for a moment I stood looking out thoughtfully,
whispering back to Africa that in spite of everything I did still love
her. Then standing close to the glass, I stretched my arms wide to
draw the curtains.

With a start, I suddenly glimpsed an unexpected visitor, en-
twined in the lattice window grill just above my head. For a split
second his glossy black eyes and my startled blue ones, only inches
apart, were locked in surprised stare. For my part I was enchanted.
He was one of the most beautiful snakes I'd ever seen, brilliant lime-
green with a hint of yellow, mellowing to tan near his head. His

body was delicate and slender, his glistening scales looking silky smooth, and I guessed he was the fatally poisonous boomslang.

After a moment I recovered from my awe, then carefully reopened the window to watch him slip out and swish easily away. With a smile I couldn't help think that this was just like Africa. To send a captivating messenger, but of the most lethal kind, to wish me a safe journey and certain return.

*   *   *   *   *

I sat poised on the edge of my seat, peering out the window and feeling a tingle of excitement. As the jet swooped down towards Seattle I felt welcomed by a familiar skyline. While we taxied and then parked I was itching to be off the plane, overcome by an impatient desire to see, hear, smell, and be surrounded by my own culture and people, and to have my feet firmly planted on home soil again.

Finally, I pressed my way out of the plane and into the jam-packed baggage area. What a relief to be crowded among my own tribe. Here I knew the unwritten rules of how to go about things, and it felt so stress-free to not have to shove my way to the luggage carousel, or compete for a place in the exit line.

It was intoxicating to be home again, and I wanted to sing out and twirl 'round in sheer delight. So when the unsmiling customs official gruffly asked me questions, I had to hold back a laugh and keep from exclaiming, "Shall we rather dance?" I could have hugged the diligent sniffer dog wandering among the crowd. By the time the fourth customs officer asked me if I was sure I didn't have any *biltong*, being African dried meat like jerky, I couldn't keep from grinning. He looked at me disapprovingly, but let me pass through the open doors to a wide blue American sky beyond.

My body felt feather-light and my feet had a spring to their step. Surely the weight of the world was much less on this part of the globe. I buoyantly made my way to the domestic terminal, delighted at being surrounded by so much cleanliness, and even more, the glorious absence of stench. Yes, that was it, what was most noticeable was all that was missing. No peeling paint and decay, no gurgling coughs and snotty noses, no rail-thin children begging for change, no one with glassy eyes full of pain.

I felt overwhelmed as I walked through the busy concourse to my gate. People rushed about, talking intently on cell phones as they nipped past. Screens flashed long columns of flight data and TVs poured forth with unending chatter. Shops were packed with too many things, and an abundance of food overflowed from busy eateries. Here the pace of humanity clipped along at a startling speed. Is this how I used to live? Had I really managed to keep up with this quickness of life?

I sat down near my gate to wait for my flight to Anchorage, feeling at one time exhilarated and dazed by it all. As I watched the whirl around me, I realized the flurry had purpose and people were at ease. Is this the way the world really is, I thought, or is my life in a sleepy corner of Africa reality?

The pace wasn't all that made me feel like I'd been dropped into a sci-fi movie. Besides the unimaginable tidiness was the Hollywood-like affluence, everyone dressed in what seemed to be chic outfits—no holes, no stains, and no dinginess.

I embraced the comforting familiarity of this environment. Here among my own I felt safe and welcome. And being surrounded by my kind quickly energized me again, renewing my strength that I only now realized had been drained by the struggle of life in Africa.

* * * * *

The city lay cloaked in silky blackness when I arrived in Anchorage. Stepping out from the plane I felt the numbness of unending travel, but my spirits soared. Family and friends had showed up to enthusiastically welcome me back, and I realized how priceless it was to have those who cared so deeply.

The next morning, with a soothing calm I woke in my mother's house, the home she had lived in for thirty years. This wonderful abode had been with me for as long as I could remember, and its constancy was also invaluable. Africa, where my life was now, had changed so much in just a few years. Yet here was this quiet house, my home, that remained fixed. A steady anchor while the variable winds of life had swept me into uncharted waters.

Although my mother had added on over the decades, the house was mostly as it'd been when I grew up and its blueprint was permanently etched in my mind. The stair steps were still too shallow, but without thinking, I shortened my stride. There was something reassuring in climbing those stairs, each familiar short step reminding me of how intricately connected I was to this place. When entering an unlit room, I was surprised at how my fingers instinctively glided to the unseen light switch, as they had done thousands of times before.

I couldn't help thinking that my family and friends seemed to live in luxury, in homes without peeling paint or ceilings water-scarred from leaky roofs. With doors and windows that shut properly, electricity and phones that always worked. Africa had made me appreciate that such things aren't simply a given.

To see my mother in her secure home also comforted me, knowing that she and the rest of my family wasn't at the cruel whims of an unpredictable country and its dictator. My mother would never have to flee, leaving her home behind, nor would she go hungry. Thankfully, I didn't have the burden of worrying how my family would survive.

* * * * *

I was determined not to step back on the plane without having indulged in one coveted pleasure. During my first year in Zimbabwe I'd gone through Mexican food withdrawals, tortured by episodes of incurable craving. Now on the way to the restaurant, my mouth already watered at the thought of this heavenly feast.

Sitting in a booth, while my friends talked and laughed I was impatient for the waiter to bring those frosty margaritas and crisp corn chips with salsa. And when he put that glistening enchilada smothered in melted cheese and luscious red sauce in front of me, I just wanted to stare at it for a moment in all its glory.

When I finally put that much anticipated bite in my mouth, to my surprise, I found it incredibly rich. Wow, I thought, this is actually too rich! Did I really used to eat such sumptuous meals, and often? Rather gloomily, I realized my years of eating bland Zimbabwean fare meant I could no longer feast on spicy meals and heavy sauces. I was exasperated that my body had adapted itself so much to its change of diet, and now I had to eat such great American standards as zesty Mexican and hot-spiced chili in measured portions.

My appetite felt satisfied though, just being surrounded by so much food. The grocery store was an awesome sight, with packed shelves soaring up to the ceiling, my belly feeling full just looking at all that sustenance. There were a hundred kinds of cereal, cake mixes of every variety, and ready-made frozen meals of anything imaginable. The frozen aisle in Chiredzi on the other hand, was mostly plucked chickens and gutted fish. And as far as ready-made cuisine, about as good as it got was a gravy packet.

When it came time for me to leave, my suitcase was crammed full of scrumptious American foodstuff. I stockpiled such delicacies as Swedish meatball packets, A-1 steak sauce, and Quaker Instant Oatmeal. I only wished I could carry a year's supply of Dr. Pepper and Doritos back, too.

* * * * *

On a golden September morning during my stay in Anchorage, I woke to find "termination dust" had settled upon the mountains cradling the city. This first snow of winter lightly blankets the ridge tops, hovering like a halo above treed mountainsides in deep orange and burgundy. It's a sign that snow will fall in the city soon and with it the autumn breeze takes on a chill, and the cushion of fallen leaves crackles underfoot.

September was always my favorite month in Alaska. The mountains swathed in rich-orange and gold, the air crisp, and the angle of the evening sun casting a soft glow to a landscape of spruce and birch. This time of year is always too short and I wanted to absorb into my memory as much as I could before returning to Zim.

My visit was a well-needed therapy, being in Alaska again and especially spending priceless hours with family and close friends. But after a month, I began to miss my home in Africa. In Zimbabwe

I'd bought coffee to give as gifts, and the fragrance of its roasted, oily beans had wafted out of my suitcase and filled my room at my mother's house. Now on the other side of the world, up in the Arctic, I could draw in the rich aroma of my African home. But when that last packet of coffee was given away, the loss of that familiar scent left a noticeable void. I suddenly felt Africa was too far away.

And although the autumn crispness was invigorating, I missed the saturating warmth of the African sun. Alaska's summer had been rainier than usual, with some of the state having record rainfall. By the time I arrived in autumn, everyone seemed obsessed with the weather. "Will it be sunny today?" they'd muse hopefully. And when the sun did make an appearance, each gushing, "How beautiful it is outside!" "What a spectacular day!" "Isn't the weather amazing?!"

Yet in Zimbabwe I never longed for sunny days. In fact, I scarcely gave it a thought. I certainly took sunshine for granted now, although my return to a coastal northwestern town soon had me appreciating it again. I missed my sunlit veranda, the breeze drifting through the house from windows thrown open, while eating breakfast to the finches' song.

I felt a void without Africa and needed to get back. Still, with shifting emotions I drove away from my mother's house. The neighbors' lawns, on the streets I knew so well, lay blanketed in leaves of russet and gold. As we drove to the airport the city was colorfully awash in falling leaves, swirled by the gusty winds of late autumn. This northwest wind seemed miffed I was returning to his stormy southern cousin in Africa. But I had to leave, Africa was like a magnet that pulled me back. It was time to go home once again.

Chapter Twenty-six

|||||||||||||||||||||||||||||||||||||||||||||||||||||||||||||||||||||||||||||||||||||||||||||||||||||

My journey over land and sea back to Africa seemed easy this time, despite the usual thirty-six exhausting hours of travel. But with only two layovers, this trip was less harried than in the past.

As we left the airport with Darren at the wheel, the African sun warmly welcomed me. And as each mile of scrubby bush flashed by on our drive north, I became more impatient to be out of the truck and touching the soil of Africa again.

At the desolate border post near Beitbridge, always a sweltering spot, Darren and I wrested our way through a tangle of red-tape and chaotic crowds. By the time we were released through the last security gate, the evening sun had dipped low in the sky, gilding the land in gold.

After a quick half hour up the highway, Darren turned our pickup onto the sandy track of Kleinbegin, Sam and Janet's tranquil ranch. I felt jubilant at being home again, and Darren and I descended upon them with all our enthusiasm, declaring an urgent need for a douse in the pool, before the last rays of the day slipped behind the horizon.

Sprinting for the crystal water, Darren and I jumped in wearing the sweaty t-shirts and shorts we had on. The water was deliciously warm from the hot day and its buoyancy made my spirits soar.

When I snuggled into bed that night, I lay there for awhile just soaking up Africa again. The silky night had a scent like dried wildflowers, its pungent sweetness breezing softly through the room, stirred by the hypnotic beat of an overhead fan. I could feel the soul of the earth seeping up through the red ground, free-spirited without the shackles of asphalt. That night I slept deep and restful in the peacefulness of the sprawling ranch, waking in the morning ready to take on Africa again.

The next day as we drove the last two hours home to Chiredzi, a snug contentment eased upon me. Even the dusty little town was a welcome sight. There was something reassuring in the slow-motioned pace of its folk, and in the way a languid breeze carried the red dust through our small town. A place where humanity felt so real and uncomplicated in its simplicity of impoverishment. Where much of life was lived at its most basic: in two-roomed houses with no closets packed with clothes and no driveways filled with cars. Far from the hurried rush that makes each day race by before we've realized it's begun.

* * * * *

As I enjoyed being home again, the trees and bush were bursting with the vibrancy of spring. Pulling up to our house, our gate stood flanked by a mantle of fuchsia blossoms, overflowing from the leafy bougainvillea hedge. The frangipani tree sprawled above was a fountain of soft-yellow flowers, its petals cascading down and sprinkling over the drive. Amongst the branches were cooing doves, and to my delight, canaries and sparrows had also made homes in the garden while I'd been away.

But I knew "it" was inescapable, and wished I could just press my hands tightly over my ears forever. Eventually though, the troubles of our once placid country would have to reach me, and my simple pleasures here in paradise inevitably spoiled.

Greeting me was no shortage of bad news. Clashes with War Vets had heated up again, and in the northwestern district of Karoi where Nicky's sister lived, troubles had been especially fierce. When one farmer and his workers began plowing, War Vets soon arrived on the scene. They insisted only half the field could be tilled, since according to them, the other half was now theirs. In the *Farmer* magazine I read what happened next:

"The farm workers, irked by months of beatings, . . . confronted their tormentors, demanding to know what the 'war veterans' would do for them if they lost their jobs on the farm.

"The workers took it upon themselves to continue with the land preparation. A standoff ensued between the farm workers and the 'War Vets' and the situation became increasingly tense. The 'War Vets" leadership accused workers of being 'used' by the white farmer to retaliate against the 'War Vets' [and] said they would press ahead with 'land revolution'.

"The police could not help much, saying the farmer should comply with the demands, . . . [and that he could] only farm with the 'War Vets" blessing on any portion of land the 'War Vets' have claimed.'"

Nearby, Marshall Roper was out in his fields when he looked up to find himself surrounded by a dozen rabid thugs. Brandishing axes and machetes they ordered him to stop planting, then began to push him around. In the agitation, suddenly a machete sliced across Marshall's face, ripping through his nose and cheeks. As he fell to the ground with his face gushing blood, he managed to pull out his gun and fire into the air, startling his attackers who then fortunately dashed away.

This time at least, the War Vets didn't get their way. Because, while Marshall was in the hospital recovering, his neighbors planted his crops for him.

One hostile skirmish after another ensued, compelling farmers to file complaints in court against the illegal squatting. The courts ruled in their favor, but in keeping with the new trend, the Karoi police had no intention of enforcing the evictions.

On a late September day shortly after my return, Karoi's residents gathered outside their police station. Over three thousand farmers, workers, local businessmen and other citizens of this one-horse town assembled, demanding that law and order be restored.

Yet astonishingly, I was told how the police made a point of scarcely acknowledging them, the Member-in-Charge only begrudgingly coming out to address the crowd after they refused to go away. Even then, he gave their problems only the slightest of lip service.

Knowing the police had given them free rein, everywhere War Vets clear cut trees for firewood and to sell. Taking full advantage of their gangster status, they demanded meat and other food from the farmer. If it wasn't given they simply beat up the stockmen and helped themselves from the sheep or cattle herd. I heard appalling stories of livestock and wildlife being put to death by the crudest methods, since squatters had only blunt instruments and hunting dogs. Now a regular feature of farming life was to discover an elegant antelope or one's champion bull mutilated in an agonizing death.

Worse still, farm workers were threatened with a bone-breaking pummeling if they continued to work. Or forced from their homes, personal effects commandeered, women in the villages cruelly raped. Of course farmers themselves were regularly terrorized, one tactic being to hold a *pungwe* outside the homestead all night, beating drums and chanting angrily until dawn. Along with this the death threats, heated confrontations, and even a few abductions still went on.

My anticipation at returning home to Africa, where my senses filled with the things that made me happiest, was ruined. Along with the country, I was being dragged down into this abyss of disintegration. Could the unraveling be stopped?

With so many others feeling as I did, I understood how the next clash erupted. An hour south of Harare in the Featherstone district, farmers and their workers decided to do something about the thugs wrecking havoc in the area. One spring morning a dozen farmers, joined by many of their staff, banded together and in a convoy of vehicles marched from one property to the next, destroying squatters' camps.

The War Vets were, not surprisingly, seething with fury and quickly organized themselves to strike back. As the farmers' convoy traveled between farms, a group of thugs zoomed after in pursuit.

The bandits called for a police vehicle to intercept the farmers, and upon noticing a cop car following them, the farmers compliantly pulled to the side of the road. They certainly didn't consider themselves to be doing anything wrong.

But in a flash, complete mayhem broke out. Enraged War Vets had swelled up behind, and began firing automatic rifles into the convoy. Panicked workers launched themselves out of the backs of pickups and bolted on foot, sprinting in every direction. Drivers put pedal to the floor, careening off-road in a desperate escape across the grasslands, those still in truck beds pressed flat as bullets whizzed past their ears.

When the chaos finally diffused, the War Vets strutted forward to confidently take control from the police, grabbing the stunned farmers and promptly stripping them of their shirts. The farmers were forced to lay face down on the ground, then whipped and beaten, while their adrenaline-pumped captors figured out what they wanted to do. One of the farmers was fluent in Shona and overheard many in the gang demanding they all be shot. But fortune was with the men that day, as one sympathetic bandit who obviously carried some weight, convinced the others to take them to the police station.

The battered farmers were shoved into their pickups and driven off to the Featherstone station. Luckily when the shooting first started, one had called out a quick mayday on his CB to other farmers nearby. After swiftly joining together, the neighbors were also now headed for the police.

When the War Vets arrived at the station with the captured farmers, the cops were clearly pleased. A lively deliberation between thugs and police then ensued, as they argued about what revenge to mete out. In the midst of their squabble, they were surprised to see the other farmers pull up outside, accompanied by the beaten farmers' workers, who had wanted to rid their homes of the War Vets just as much as their employers. As several pickups skidded to a halt in a swirl of dust, the workers jumped out and stormed the station. Angrily, they demanded the release of their bosses, with the debate now between the enraged workers and the fickle police. By the time the wrangling was over and the farmers reluctantly released by the cops, the War Vets had, most conveniently, disappeared.

Law and order were now truly gone. Bandits ruled, leaving me to wonder when this sinister version of a Wild West show would end.

* * * * *

One lazy afternoon not long after this, Darren's mother Georgie was driving into Harare and noticed a policeman walking towards town. This wasn't at all unusual since most Zimbabweans didn't own cars. She stopped to give him a ride and they started up a pleasant chat. Eventually the conversation came around to why the police didn't do more about the crime and illegal squatters.

"Honestly, the police are a disgrace," Georgie, always direct, said without apology. "They don't have any pride in doing a decent job."

The officer only nodded slowly in agreement, as he too felt forlorn about the state of his institution. "The problem is that now, sergeants and higher-ups are all ex War Veterans," he explained, "and if farms are taken, these guys figure they'll get a share of the spoils."

The policeman also lamented that ex-combatants were paid a higher wage, plus given a vehicle and other benefits. But because he was not one, he didn't receive any perks. He was obviously despondent about his job, especially the unfairness of pay, saying he couldn't make ends meet on what he earned. Georgie could see he'd lost all desire to put effort into his work, and was too depressed to care whether he did his duties at all.

Her story brought to mind a haunting revelation that Darren heard, one afternoon when licensing our car at the station in Chiredzi. Having fallen into conversation with a policeman there, he asked why they didn't intervene more with the troubles on farms.

"You know, we are in a dreadful predicament," the cop quietly responded, not wanting his voice to carry. "The intimidation from our superiors is immense. All of us civil servants are pressured to support the ruling party and its agendas. We have a constant threat hanging over our heads that if we are looked upon as supporting the MDC in the slightest way, which includes not going along with government's tactics, our life will be in danger."

Not long after this, Darren took a drive into remote countryside to a small mine, to collect an engine needing repair. There weren't many facilities in the tiny settlement next to the mine, but they did include a few tents serving as a police outpost.

Visitors were rare and Darren easily caught attention, to which a policeman wandered over to say hello. After lending a hand to load the engine, the two sauntered over to a shady tree and sat down together for a break from the noonday sun. While they casually chatted and smoked their cigarettes, Darren asked the policeman what his orders were when it came to handling any War Vet situation. The cop responded that their instructions were to simply stay "cool"—in other words, to stay out of any conflicts involving War Vets.

The officer seemed to need a sympathetic ear, because he went on to tell Darren that the police had become very demoralized. "I've been in the force for more than twenty years now and used to always receive my pay on time, but that doesn't happen anymore. Nor are we given food rations or even new uniforms."

He paused to crush out his cigarette, and then with tension in his eyes, went on. "Look at me now. Look at my ragged outfit. I've patched my boots as best I can. Twenty years ago I always had a good pair of boots and a new uniform. Our police camp used to be tidy and our equipment in good repair. But now, look at the shameful appearance of our camp. How can we be proud of this?"

There wasn't much Darren could say. Here was someone who had taken pride in doing a conscientious job, but now his last flicker of enthusiasm had been snuffed out. Plus, it was hard to be dedicated when the pay barely put food on the plate.

So this was the sorry state of our police force. At the bottom rungs, a rag-tag bunch of dejected and downtrodden men. While climbing to the top was a gang of thugs, many recently promoted War Vets, and encouraged by the government to mete out their own brand of "law" enforcement.

* * * * *

As the spring days slipped away, throughout Zimbabwe beleaguered farmers debated whether to plant crops. Banks were giving few cropping loans, not wanting to risk War Vets chasing a farmer off before it was repaid. So if he didn't have enough cash to carry himself for nine months, a farmer had no choice but to close up shop. As it was, the risks of ruinous weather, crop disease, low yields or slim profits made sinking hard-earned cash into a crop a dicey proposition. It wouldn't take much to lose in this game of chance, and as our friend Jean put it, when it came to farming gambling her bucks on the roulette wheel sometimes looked like a better option. For Darren and me it'd truly been a stroke of good luck that our path had led us away from a farm.

And while food supplies dwindled, each passing week saw the Zimbabwe dollar became more worthless. The price of fuel had to double to keep up, which automatically doubled bus fares. With transport costs often a worker's largest expense, there was bound to be discord.

The eruption that followed was called the Bread Riots, although the mania was surely an outpouring at all which had pushed people's lives to the brink. Even so, the price of bread became the thing upon which Zimbabweans focused their outrage. In Harare, streets surged with waves of rioters. Young men and older boys needed an outlet for their unemployed frustrations and recklessly took to vandalizing bakeries, foolishly blamed for the rise in bread prices. Anyone caught innocently buying a loaf that day was promptly given a thumping by enraged out-of-workers.

Neighbors from Chiredzi had the misfortune of driving through Harare when the riots broke out. They later told Darren and me how, in an instant, the road they traveled on became chaotically alive with crowds. From out of nowhere the street was littered with boulders, making it impossible for cars to move. As they tried to maneuver out of the traffic jam, the crowds became more frenzied, young men trying to pull several drivers from cars. Luckily our friends managed to turn around and dodge any danger. However, members of the press covering the riots weren't so fortunate and several took a beating.

While the populace was rioting in Harare, things were pretty much normal down in Chiredzi. Business went on as usual and Darren was paying for parts at a motor spares counter when the subject of the riots came up. Another customer next to him, speaking with self-assured excitement, said folks in Chiredzi were also talking of a strike to protest bread prices.

With an imperceptible shake of his head, Darren asked, "So where would you have your strike?"

"We would start at the bakeries, because they are making too much money," the man replied confidently. "The government should set the price of bread to keep these bakeries from hurting the people."

"Have you considered if you do that, the bakeries might be forced to shut down. How will you get bread then?" Darren asked, and then tried to explain some basics of supply and demand, inflation, and the problems of Zimbabwe's wheat industry. But to this, Darren was only met with a blank stare.

How, oh how, could paradise ever be saved, I thought. This struggling nation still had a long road ahead before the implosion could be stopped.

Chapter Twenty-seven

||||||||||||||||||||||||||||||||||||||||||||||||||||||||||||||||||||||||||||||||

ts bliss came upon us at that hushed hour of midnight. Snuggled up cozy in bed, deep in slumber, my eyes fluttered briefly open at the blessed sound of the rain's rhythmic tapping. That evening Darren and I had heard the low rumble of distant thunder and lightning, a heavenly sound after seven months without a drop of rain, and hoped it was a telltale sign. And indeed, thankfully it had been. Now the end of October, this first downpour usually signaled the start of the much anticipated rainy season, with these early showers always such a relief. Helping to calm the scorching heat and rescue droopy crops waiting for their parchedness to be eased.

Feeling soothed by the rain's gentle tempo, I nestled into my pillow and once again fell fast asleep. I had a beautiful few hours of rest, so hypnotic that I didn't wake when the rain eventually stopped and the tapping from the gutter slowed to quiet drips.

But then from out of nowhere came the earsplitting pulse of a siren. Well, that's what it sounded like anyway and I shot upright in bed. What it turned out to be was the celebratory rapture of thousands of frogs, crickets, grasshoppers and whomever else that had just hatched, sprung, popped and burst into life with the first deluge of the season.

Not much wakes Darren, but even this was so piercing as to pull him out of oblivion. He reluctantly pushed himself up on an elbow to blink drowsily, although the vibrating shriek was too loud to even attempt conversation. Instead, we just lay there in the throbbing darkness wondering if our sleep was finished for the night. Then in a flash came a breathless silence, with only the muffled yaps of a distant dog reassuring us our ear drums hadn't burst. A few minutes later though, just as my heavy lids closed to the peacefulness, the shrill din fired up once again.

This nonsense of the on and off clamor raged several more times, annoyingly more on than off, leaving me completely exasperated. Okay, I thought to myself as I lay in my comfy bed, let's all either be awake for the night or let's sleep. But it must be one or the other. And exactly why is it, I wondered, are there moments when the masses go instantly quiet? I was desperate to know the secret and was surprised to realize that, incredibly, it was the occasional barks of the mutt which silenced the millions. Yet of all the times our neighborhood hounds wanted to let loose for an entire night, this didn't happen to be one.

I was worried the insects' boisterous concert might continue for, well, who knows how many nights. Surely it couldn't last all summer. Quite luckily though, it turned out to be a one night performance.

* * * * *

When it comes to rain, people in Africa are a lot like Alaskans and their sunshine. After the first showers appear, every phone call begins with an eager, "Have you had any rain? How much have you had?" Even the radio announcer rattles off with glee the millimeters bestowed upon each part of the country.

For my part, I was hoping the rainfall meant our water rationing would lighten up. Although our town still had plenty of stored dam water, the treatment system had never been expanded over the years along with the town's sprawl, and now it couldn't keep up. Most of the water was used to keep lawns alive through the hot and cloudless days of early summer, to which the town council continued its annual tradition of sending out notices to fine anyone caught watering his lawn. It seemed all of us in this little hamlet, whether we liked it or not, were going to have yards fashioned in the peasants' minimalist-style of bare red dirt.

The rationing meant the council only turned the water on for brief spells—a few hours in the morning, a stingy couple at lunch, and three hours in early evening. Visits to the toilet had to be planned accordingly. Often in the evening I'd suddenly realize the time was five minutes to eight, when the water was shut off, and I hadn't yet showered. I'd literally sprint down the hall tearing my clothes off as I went, to throw open the tap and dive under the spray. The thought of going to bed covered in a hot day's worth of sticky sweat, coated with a layer of dust, was a loathsome prospect.

The thing was, I never realized how much we all depend upon this precious liquid, until one day when the town council turned the taps on and off, on and off—in the morning and at lunch as usual. Still we noticed nothing out of the ordinary when in the afternoon, as always, we had only hot water from our tank for washing hands, cleaning up dishes, and fixing dinner. Then for some reason that day, they just never switched it on in the evening.

To not be allowed any water at the end of a sweltering, dusty African day was a cruel trick to play. By the time I realized they weren't going to turn it on, half our hot water tank was already used up. All I could do was put a scrap of piping hot dampness in the tub, then add all the ice cubes from the freezer, which scarcely made a difference. At a time when I wanted a cool shower more than anything, I had to settle for a steaming splash in the bathtub.

The next day the water still wasn't on, and by the following morning we were down to a measly quart, kept strictly for drinking. Our hot water tank was now completely empty, so there was no doing dishes or any kind of cleanup. I'd left the plug in the bathroom sink and we were using the same brown puddle to wash our hands. There was no flushing the toilet. All we could do was make offerings to the Water God, praying the town council would get its act together and have the system repaired soon.

At the end of the third day, after fifty hours without water, I was finally alerted by a magical sound—the trickling of the toilet as it refilled. By Africa standards, I could say the council had fixed the system in record time.

So whenever that first downpour came upon us, its bounty brought a celebratory mood to the atmosphere. Having that splendid nectar pouring freely from the sky seemed an amazing gift from heaven. When the rain started, I found it hard to concentrate on work and would stand at the window staring out at the beautiful shower, mesmerized by its soothing rhythm, certain I saw the brown lawn bursting into green shoots before my eyes.

A couple days after our first deluge, Darren and I were invited to a get-together at Hammond Ranch. I suspected that Warren and Carrie, Hammond's American owners, didn't realize they'd been subconsciously influenced to throw a bash by the festive spirit of the first rain which grips everyone. Certainly their timing couldn't have been better and they always gave a great party. And like everyone in the country, Darren and I needed a dose of enjoyment with friends.

I was also anxious to check in on our dog, the lab-ridgeback cross which had joined me on my horse ride with Tore. While Darren and I had been away, Roger the dog had gone to stay on Hammond. It had started simply as Spike dogsitting for us. But then Spike had rescued a young cheetah caught in a snare, and soon our lanky black dog was drafted as part of the feline's rehabilitation.

The adolescent male cheetah, whom Nicky christened Hobbs, had injured a "wrist" in the snare and until it healed couldn't return to the wilds. Hobbs was too young to fend for himself, and Spike was hoping to persuade him to accept our big dog as a link to the world of humans. His idea was for the cat to attach himself to Roger, then Spike could take the cheetah out and teach him to hunt.

The shrubby and ample front garden of the main house on Hammond was set aside as Hobbs' recuperation quarters. Things got off to a disappointing start, however, when Roger was ushered into the garden for their first meeting. Upon the sight and smell of this wild feline he turned heel at a flat-out run, yelping at full volume all the way back to the house. In the days that followed, despite every enticement by Spike, Roger was dead set against letting a toe slip from the protection of the veranda.

After a couple weeks of cautiously eyeing things from a distance, suddenly one day Roger became courageous. Spike was in the garden, bending down and snaking a hosepipe across the lawn, playing with Hobbs who pounced after it. A loyal Roger took the cheetah's darting lunges as a threat to Spike, and vaulting off the veranda, flew towards Hobbs in as much of a rage as the kind-hearted dog could muster.

To Roger's surprise, the cheetah made a quick dash for cover. From then on, although he kept up his guard around Hobbs, they did begin a daily interaction of sorts.

When Darren and I pulled up in front of Hammond's lodge, I was glad to see Roger bounding across the lawn towards us in a tongue-wagging hello. I half-expected to see his velvet ears shredded, or an eye mangled by Hobbs. Instead, living the ranch life obviously suited him.

The day was dimming to evening smokiness as we walked to the open-air lodge, built of sturdy timbers and with a thatched roof, and sporting walls on only two sides. As usual Warren and Carrie were generous with the wine, while several times the vivacious Carrie came bustling out from the kitchen balancing platters of delicious hors d'oeuvres. I always found it a treat when she returned to Zim from the States, bringing luggage packed with wonderful American foodstuff.

Some of the guests had brought their dogs, and along with Scruff a half dozen ankle-biters exuberantly mixed underfoot. Roger was overjoyed to have canine company for a change and easily joined in the fun, despite the other mutts only coming to his knees.

Everyone mingled, laughing and chatting while music played peppy and light, the soaring hearth with its smoldering fire an anchor to the room. The open lodge sat as a golden glow amidst miles of now infinite blackness, and out on dark lawn at the edge of its topaz gleam, above an open fire Spike tended a roasting warthog. As it turned slowly on the spit, glistening tender and crackling to the lick of flames, I could hardly wait to savor it. Not only was pork my favorite meat, but a warthog grown old on the rich wildness of the Africa bush acquires a heavenly tastiness. An hour later, served up with Carrie's scrumptious dishes we had a mouthwatering feast, the more delicious for eating it amidst the sensuous night air. All the while from the riverbed below, a hamlet of frogs croaked deep and melodious.

Darren and I slept the night at Hammond, and upon waking the next morning scurried out of bed with anticipation. Spike had invited us along to feed a herd of Cape buffalo, recently bought by the Conservancy. Gazing upon a herd in plain view was a rare treat, which for veterinary purposes had to be confined to a large bush paddock for a period of time. Because there wasn't enough grazing in this enclosed area, Spike fed them pellets until they could roam free again.

We managed a hurried few sips of coffee before clamoring into the open Land Rover, zipping up jackets to the coolness of an overcast morning, made especially breezy in the open truck. As we weaved along a dirt track through the bush, a heavy mist began to dampen the air, sending every creature to vanish under cover. Hunkering into our seats, for a quarter of an hour we drove through bush weighted and motionless with the gray morning. When we drew up to the feeding area the buffalo were nowhere to be seen, although we spied a few wily baboons perched in trees, waiting to descend for an easy meal. To this Darren asked Spike if it better to wait for the herd to show up before putting feed in the troughs, as otherwise the pot-bellied baboons would raid them. "No, the buffalo should be here soon," Spike replied. "They'll have started wandering this way when they heard the truck."

I kept myself safely in the Land Rover while Darren and Spike went off to make the rounds to each small trough. Carrying bags of pellets, they started near the truck and worked their way to the outer reaches of the feeding area. By this time a lone buffalo appeared and ambled steadily towards them, a handsome brute, with a smooth coat of deep brown and glossy black horns curving down. Noticing the brawny beast walking a beeline for them, Darren furrowed his brow. To this Spike reassured him with, "Don't worry, this guy is rather tame. He always comes near at feeding time."

From the open truck, I watched nervously as the imposing fellow casually followed at their heels. At each trough he had a sniff inside, thinking those pellets surely better than the last. All the while, Darren kept giving wary glances over his shoulder.

"Away now! Stop bothering us," Spike eventually called out with indifference and waved a feed sack towards the wild buffalo. I was a little surprised by Spike's casualness, as these powerful brutes are known for their cocky boldness, and without a second thought will trample a person. This burly fellow certainly looked intimidating enough, and I for one was glad to be a distance away and seated in the sturdy truck.

But the guys soon made it back to the Land Rover without the slightest scuffle. As we started to drive away, the nimble baboons all scampered down from the branches to stuff themselves with pellets. They had only a chance to grab a few handfuls, however, because as we crept beyond the feeding area, from out of the mist-shrouded bush loomed the buffalo. They silently emerged like shadowy ghosts, and I realized that all this time they must have been watching us, waiting for us to leave.

Spike stopped the Land Rover and whispered to us, "Stay perfectly quiet."

Slowly one by one, the mighty buffalo stepped hesitantly out, hovering at the fringe of the meadow with its scattering of feed tubs. Longingly they looked toward their breakfast, and eventually hunger won over caution. I was awed by their magnificence—at one time daunting and formidable, yet with a timid wariness to their large brown eyes.

After watching breathless for some time, we finally left them in peace and puttered off back to Hammond. A rain shower began to stream down with purpose, quickly soaking us to the skin. The three of us welcomed its freshness after weeks of choking dust and heat, even if we were now chilled to the bone. I was still amazed at how suddenly temperatures could become sharply cold in the midst of summer, the sun now lost under a heavy pillow of clouds. In the open truck my hair plastered to my temples while droplets pelted my cheeks, Spike wasting no time in steering us back to the coziness of the lodge.

We all jumped out of the Land Rover and rushed to the warmth inside, to clutch mugs of hot coffee and settle next to the hearth with its roaring fire. It didn't have to be said—life couldn't get much better. For a moment we could ignore our imperiled future, and let Africa's potion of vibrant nature work its therapeutic powers on us once again.

Chapter Twenty-eight

||||||||||||||||||||||||||||||||||||||||||||||||||||||||||||||||||||||||||||||||||||||||||||

My computer had been coughing and sputtering for months, then finally decided to pack it in all together. For me this was no small problem, since I lived five hundred miles from where I'd bought it in Johannesburg. The one good thing, I wryly mused, was at least it had the decency to crash before my one year warranty was up.

Also lucky was that Darren and I hadn't made our planned expedition to Joburg. Darren had one of his workshop machines being fixed there, which was supposed to have been ready weeks ago. Diligently each Monday he phoned the repairman, who assured him it would be finished in seven days time, only to be given the same weary story the following week.

But now, being at an utter loss without my computer, I insisted we head off to Joburg as soon as possible. To this Darren immediately phoned the repairman. No problem, he was told, the machine would definitely be ready next week.

A few days later we climbed into our pickup and set off on our trek down South. Ten minutes out of Chiredzi the quiet highway streamed alongside the barbed wire fence of Buffalo Range ranch, where the scene was not a pretty sight. Everyone around had been joining in the frenzy of "free" wood, leaving areas now chopped void of any large trees. Then the War Vets, above the usual zeal of the locals, had further set match to the bush. The blackened acres of

Buffalo Range were truly depressing, a rank smell of charred grass, wood and earth stinging in my nostrils even with the windows rolled up. Charcoaled stumps stood starkly in vacant abysses, only a scattering of leafless shrubbery that had been spared the ax, but not the flames.

I felt grateful when the burnt acres were eventually behind us, and could relax as we pushed on through airy countryside of un-molested thorn trees and scrub. To break up our long drive we were staying a night with Brian and Melissa, who ranched cattle along with Brian's parents Sam and Janet. In the past, the beef industry had sent quality product to Europe. But with Zim's decline Brian now simply sold meat to locals from a roadside butchery. I shook my head in dismay at another example of the country unraveling out of the modern and back into the archaic.

Their ranch sat an easy half hour off the highway through rest-ful wilderness, the road looking as if it'd been tidily graveled, al-though its loose stones and dirt was no different from the ground it cut through. Soon the road splintered off into tracks of beige sand, the landscape looking sparser than around Chiredzi but with the wildlife doing well. Lively herds of wildebeest cantered through the lean bush in their rocking-horse gait, impudently flicking their tufted tails. Nearby, stately giraffe peered down at us from towering heights. Stocky, pot-bellied zebra, with heads up and ears perked forward in curiosity, stood confidently in the road watching us ap-proach. Then with a playful capriole each bounded back into the shrubbery, their black and white stripes vanishing in an instant.

The long shadows of evening had begun to creep out when we arrived at the ranch, and before the black of night descended, after a quick welcome Melissa took us to visit the most unusual mem-ber of their household. Several years earlier Brian had adopted an orphaned male cheetah, naming the cub Dindingwe, simply mean-ing cheetah in Shona. We found the big cat lounging in his roomy pen out the back of the house. Looking in at him from outside the chain-link, as always I was captivated by the handsome arrogance of these felines. Yet at the same time, I could not convince myself to relax around them. Although Dindingwe had been raised as a pet from his early days, his eyes still sparked with the bold indifference of a hunter. He cast us contemptuous glances, as he casually raised himself up and strolled off. Without a doubt, there was something unsettling in the way his well-muscled shoulders swung with cocky haughtiness.

And in my case, I certainly had good reason to be wary. Two years earlier my close encounter with another cheetah nearly had a tragic end. During a midwinter stay with friends in Kwekwe, the evening we arrived I first made my acquaintance with their "pet" cheetah. Wandering across the dark lawn I found Dindee curled up in front of her cheetah house, her face nestled into her paws. I knelt down and gently stroked her spotted coat, my fingers lost in its luxuriant denseness. Not stirring a muscle or opening her eyes, she acknowledged me with muffled purrs, gravelly and deep. She seemed like an oversized kitten, all snuggled up peacefully in a ball.

The next morning Darren and the others went off with things to do, while I passed the time at the house. It was winter when the air could be bitingly chilly, and I stood up wringing my hands against the cold. Lured by a bright mid-morning sun, I wandered over to the open French doors. The lawn directly in front of the house was still dark in shade, but across the gravel drive and down some stone steps, was an inviting patch of garden awash in warm sunshine.

I decided not to wrestle a lawn chair down to the lower terrace, where a gardener worked not far away. He didn't take much notice of me as I happily nestled down on the grass, to soak up the sun's soothing warmth.

Scarcely had I found my magazine page when I sensed a presence approaching from behind. Soundlessly, in the next instant my page was cast in shadow and from the corner of my eye I glimpsed a slender spotted leg. I had only a moment to think— "Dindee!" In a flash, from behind she locked her strong jaws about my neck, her teeth sinking in. In another instant her sinewy front legs were wrapped around my torso with a crush like a giant python. She slammed me to the ground with the overpowering grip of her jaws, since to her I was no more than the weight of a rag doll. My face crushed into the ground, imbedding my teeth in the flesh of my mouth, and I thought surely the next thing I'd hear was the crunch of shattered bone.

Then suddenly, for a split second her grip eased. Shakily I tried to push myself up, while shouting, "Dindee—No!!", as if I were dealing with an oversized Rottweiler. But each time I tried to raise up, she thrashed me to the ground even harder. Her teeth raked across my face and I felt sure my skin was being shredded, while her foul smell stung sharp inside my nostrils.

Although only minutes had passed, it seemed I'd been fighting for an eternity. With a sense of panic, my mind raced. Where was everyone? Couldn't they hear me shouting? Just minutes before the gardener had been in view, where had he gone? How, oh how, was I going to save myself? The cheetah's strength was a hundred times greater than mine.

Then I remembered a survival tactic from Alaska. If attacked by a bear, sometimes it's best to be absolutely still—to play dead. So as a last desperate effort I yelled "Help! Help!" at the top of my lungs, then became limp and silent. At once the violence stopped. I was lying face down on the ground, hardly daring to breathe. The assault had all been from behind and I hadn't seen even a fleeting view of my attacker. But I could still hear her excited breathing, quickened by the thrill of the scuffle, and cringed at the sinisterness hovering over me.

Those seconds seemed like ages, when I hazily heard screaming shouts and the rush of bare feet across the lawn. Two maids came sprinting from the house, and as they raced up, I guessed the cheetah had probably moved off. But I didn't dare stir until the reassurance of a human touch told me for sure. Soon the younger housegirl was kneeling beside me, her small hand on my arm. She gently urged me up with a whispered, "Madam, it's all right now."

I cautiously arose, looking warily round. The older housemaid was quietly sobbing, her face buried in her hands. She and the other workers lived in constant fear, wondering when they might become the next to be stalked and attacked.

Stunned, I stood for a few moments, still afraid to make any real move. I noticed my earrings had been ripped from my ears, and the two maids and I awkwardly searched for them in the grass. They explained that all the workers had been on their morning tea break, on the other side of the house. The two maids had been chatting outside the kitchen door, when they realized the murmur in the background was actually my distant shouts. With sudden horror they grasped what was happening, and swiftly grabbing their brooms, raced through the house and out the front door. Letting forth with a warrior's cry they flew across the front lawn, swinging their brooms like the mighty spears of their ancestors. At this the vile feline, cowed by their bravery, darted away to the cover of bushes.

I was moved by their courage and daring, knowing they were terrified of the wild cat, yet still took her on with only brooms to defend themselves.

Shuffling back to the house, I apprehensively headed for the bathroom mirror. I didn't want to see what I looked like, expecting my face to be in shreds. As I switched on the light, I saw that my face—amazingly—had been saved. Across my cheeks and jaw were bright red striations where the cheetah's teeth had raked over my skin, yet it was not broken. Nonetheless, the rest of me was a disheveled, bloody mess. I now understood why the older housemaid had broken into sobs at the sight of me.

Had Dindee only been "playing"? It all seemed too menacing, although I supposed if she'd been serious about her attack I might have been killed. Or perhaps her predator instincts had been dulled by her years in captivity, leaving her assault milder than her intentions.

Months later, Dindee had her own tragic end. Found poisoned, her death probably came at the hand of one of the fretful staff, tired of going to work each day wondering if this time they wouldn't make it home alive.

Now at Brian and Melissa's, Dindingwe and I eyed each other suspiciously. Ever since my bloody encounter with Dindee, my brain went into survival mode. Automatically, my movements became fluid and measured. Adrenaline quickened my heart and kept my muscles strained for split-second action. My eyes caught the slightest rustle of leaves, my hearing became finely tuned, and even smells seemed to tingle stronger in my nostrils. Yet still, I couldn't help but be drawn to the commanding presence of these majestic beings.

Brian told us how Dindingwe's situation was a sad one. Like most cheetahs rescued by people, there was no way he could go back to the wild. Not only had he been declawed, but even more because his familiarity with humans would soon get him into trouble. Too dangerous to roam about like the family dogs, he was sentenced to a life behind a fence. As a motherless cub he would never have survived in the wilderness, but his alternative fate didn't seem much better.

The four of us wandered back to the front of the house and settled into garden chairs, sipping cold beers as a well-needed tonic. While the scorching day softened into warm night, our conversation was the usual "how's work", "how's the family", and "what's your plans". But in Zim the answers weren't "okay", "just fine", and "nothing new". For us the crystal ball wasn't just cloudy, the darn thing had downright disappeared.

"You know, Darren," Brian mused, "I honestly can't see past Christmas, less than two months away. I suppose though, we have only two choices: either assume things will get worse, or they'll get better. If all improves and we haven't gone forward with our businesses and lives, then we lose out. On the other hand if everyone has to hightail it, all is lost anyway. So it's best to just stick to business as usual as best we can."

I could certainly see Brian's point, although since everyone's business was suffering there wasn't much money floating around for so-called "going forward". Plus now, any extra cash people did have was quickly stashed away. Before, a Zimbabwean's best return on his money had been to expand his business or farming operation. But now everyone hid their scrap of savings under the mattress, rather than putting it towards expanding industry and commerce. For the country, this was a devastating reversal of habits.

We did take heart in some good news, however. The tobacco selling season had ended with the highest volume ever sold, and while prices weren't terrific, at least this sector had managed to keep chugging along. Another ruling had come out of the courts, once again declaring the farm invasions illegal. Many people were optimistic that War Vets would be off properties by year end, since the rainy season had started and surely they would want to go back to the communal lands to plant their crops. In any case, they couldn't just squat on the farms forever, could they?

Chapter Twenty-nine

||||||||||||||||||||||||||||||||||||||||||||||||||||||||||||||||||||||||||||||||||||||||||||||||||||||||||||||||||||||||||||||||

D arren slotted our pickup into the rush of Johannesburg's freeways and buzz, as we made a beeline to where I'd bought my computer. Warranty repairs had to be done within forty-eight hours, meaning we'd be able to leave by Saturday, in order to be back at work on Monday morning. Next, Darren phoned the technician fixing his machine and was assured it would also be ready by Friday. Other than a few errands, we had nothing else pressing to do.

Through the grapevine we'd heard that Willem, our Dutch adventurer friend, had recently moved to Joburg looking for flying work. But Darren and I hadn't a clue how to contact him. Driving along through the city's bustle, Darren commented thoughtfully, "Supposedly Willem is living here now. I wonder what he's up to; I wish there was a way to track him down."

Suddenly, Darren slammed on the brakes and made a sharp u-turn back.

"What are you doing? What's wrong?" I demanded, wide-eyed and gripping the dashboard.

"You'll see!" he answered, glancing over at me with a big grin.

Whipping up through traffic, he quickly turned into the parking lot of a shopping complex. In the next instant he was impatiently honking his horn at a green Land Rover creeping along in front of us. Why is Darren being so rude, I thought uneasily, as he could simply drive around if he wanted. Then when the vehicle pulled to one side, Darren steered up close behind.

Uh oh, what's Darren up to now, I wondered, as the driver of the Land Rover jumped out of his car in agitation.

"Hah!" I then exclaimed, when the driver turned towards us. "It's Willem!"

Upon seeing Darren striding towards him, Willem flashed a wide smile. His shoulders relaxed and he threw up his hands.

"Darren, how the heck are you? How'd you ever find me?"

This truly was an unbelievable coincidence that our paths crossed while lost in a frenzied metropolis.

We happened to be standing next to a café and tumbled in to catch up over coffee. Darren and I discovered that for several months Willem had been working as a flight instructor in Port Elizabeth, on South Africa's coast. But he said it wasn't for him and was looking for other piloting work. One of his prospects was to fly freight in west Africa, where his fluency in French would be an advantage. After several pleasant hours, only with reluctance did we part ways.

The next day was Thursday and in the afternoon Darren decided to go see how the repairs to his machine were coming along. I stayed behind, and soon after he pulled out the drive, Willem unexpectedly stopped by.

"What a wonderful surprise," I greeted him. "I can use some company." We took ourselves out to the patio, where we could soak up a bit of warmth from the sun. To me Joburg always seemed too cold, even in summer, and homes had no such luxury as central heat. Not to mention, temperatures hovered in the nineties when we left Chiredzi and I hadn't thought to bring enough warm clothes.

When Darren arrived back a few hours later I could see he was distracted, and he came out to the patio not looking happy at all. Wearily, he sat down beside us.

"So how's it going with the machine?" I asked, suspecting the answer wouldn't be good news.

"Actually, the guy hasn't even started working on it," a dismayed Darren said with a hint of disgust. "He took off a few covers and had a peek inside, but that's about it. This is so infuriating because for

the last eight weeks he's been assuring me the work was nearly finished. Even yesterday he said the machine would be ready tomorrow, yet there's no way he could have finished it in two days. Why
couldn't he just be honest with me?"

"Well, is he working on it now? How long will it take?"

"I don't know, several days at least. But it certainly doesn't make
sense to drive back to Chiredzi without it. We'll have to stay until
it's finished."

Although Darren was ready to tear his hair out, it scarcely occurred to me that the repairman was being unprofessional. I'd been
in Africa long enough now that I was used to the fact that companies worked on their terms, doing the job when and how it suited
them.

"The problem is lack of competition," Willem commented,
leaning back in his chair and folding his arms. "Businesses in Africa
often don't have to provide good service because they have no opposition to fend off."

Well, I certainly knew that to be true, as I often felt lucky to have
one person around who could accomplish what I needed done. For
instance, if there had been someone to fix my computer in Chiredzi,
I would have gone to him regardless of service or price. And most
were also blissfully ignorant of that most important aspect of doing business: customer service. I remembered when trying to buy
a farm, the real estate agent told me to keep calling back now and
then, since he considered it up to me to find out when new properties came on the market.

"When I worked in the Middle East, we used to say we had to
consider the pi factor into every project," Willem remarked with
a cynical edge. "That is, everything took more than three times as
long as it should. I've noticed in Africa though, it's the pi squared
factor—everything takes ten times as long." To this Darren and I
could only sigh, unable to disagree.

The next day a well-rested Darren woke feeling impatient. Taking quick puffs on his cigarette he paced with his morning coffee,
downing it in a few gulps. I'd never known him to be good at waiting around.

"Today I've decided to plant myself in that guy's workshop until the repairs are finished," Darren soon announced. "If I don't sit there, it will never get done. And I don't have an alternative since he's the third person I've taken it to and I've run out of options."

I also thought the best thing was for him to go there, as even just staring at the man would make Darren less tense. Certainly better than sitting with nothing to do. After he went off, I called Willem on his cell phone and asked what he had planned for the day.

"Nothing much. Just killing time until I hear back on these jobs. Why? What's up?"

"Darren's spending the day where his machine is being repaired. Can I tag along with you?"

As it ended up, Darren spent the next six days at that workshop, sometimes into evening. While this did get the repairman going, it was a big job even with Darren pitching in. Now that our plans had been sent into a tailspin I was glad I had Willem to chill with, mostly spending our time hanging out in coffee shops and restaurants.

One afternoon we headed to the office and shopping complex called Sandton City, where Willem could check his e-mail. Sandton was an exclusive area of Joburg and the modern center with its twin tall buildings certainly looked impressive. Even the underground parking garage was bigger than the whole of Chiredzi town.

After slipping into a parking spot, Willem and I walked into an elegant lobby, its walls of marble and shiny gold elevators leaving me blinking and dazed. Arriving on a shopping level we stepped out to a profusion of white tiles. Polished handrails glinted in gold as I paused to gaze up to high ceilings of cathedral opulence, luminous light floating down soothingly in only the way luxury can.

While Willem went off to do his e-mailing I took myself on a stroll amongst the exclusive shops. The plush scent of perfume was everywhere, as I envied satin gowns glinting with sequins and sumptuous velvet pillows to lean back on and dream. I found it unreal being amidst all this luxury, a world of affluence that gave me a sense of relief. Reminding me that everyplace wasn't like the dust-coated, pealing and pot-holed, litter-strewn town of Chiredzi. Still, it seemed only a magician's illusion that would disappear if I blinked.

Willem and I rendezvoused at the Japanese restaurant, open to a spacious corridor of more crisp white tiles. Coming from offices, men and women in tailored suits carrying briefcases walked past at a steady clip, their purposeful steps tapping out a beat of sharp echoes.

I thought how such an environment should have a familiarity from my accounting days, but instead I felt awkward and out of place. I seemed to belong to the other side of Africa now. And I did look a bit of the ruffian in old Levi's and hiking shoes, and wearing three shirts because I hadn't brought enough warm clothes. Willem wore scuffed leather boots, and from a black cord about his neck hung a leopard's tooth. Dressed in sturdy khaki cotton from head to toe, he looked every part the African explorer.

Willem sat relaxed and completely at ease, unlike me who felt we'd crashed a party. I didn't let my discomfort keep me from savoring the delicious meal though. Willem finished his lunch before me, and as he leaned back reflectively in his chair, began to expound on the dining perils to be met in Africa.

South Africa, it had to be said, was unique on the continent, with its miles of well-kept freeways and other modernity. Most of Africa on the other hand, was sparsely connected by potholed two-lane roads, or more likely, bumpy donkey cart trails and narrow footpaths. Towns where supplies can be bought for a hard-earned dollar were often hundreds of miles apart, making the logistics of creating a restaurant meal an admirable feat. Willem mused about what it took to have the simple privilege of a cold beer in some rustic African town.

"First of all, someone has to be able to grow the barley. Which also means there can't be drought, floods, or some scourge of barley disease," he began in seriousness. "Then at the brewery, spare parts to fix the many breakdowns need to be bought from some distant country. Assuming, that is, the foreign currency can be found to buy them. Next, the crates of beer are transported from the factory to the distribution warehouse and on to the restaurant. Sixty percent get broken on the pot-holed roads in the process. What's left finally reaches the restaurant, but then the electricity is out. Luckily there is a generator, which amazingly still works, and there's even fuel to run the thing. So at least the fridge can stay cold. In the end, it's a downright miracle that the frosty bottle of brew makes it to the table at the restaurant! No wonder it's triple the price.

"Of course, the more rundown a country is," he continued, "the more that pint of ale costs. With this job I've applied for I might end up in Gabon, which Lonely Planet lists as one of the most expensive places in Africa," Willem concluded with a wry smile.

On our way home, we stopped by the liquor store to buy drinks for the evening. As I was paying I saw Willem walking towards the register, his arms precariously loaded with a half dozen kinds of beer. I had to grin—you never know, one of those many steps for the beer to reach that restaurant in Gabon might not happen, and better to indulge while you can. Some days more than others we seemed to be sailing on a ship headed for the shoals, doomed to imminent shipwreck.

* * * * *

Back home, as soon as Darren and I pulled up to our doorstep I rushed inside to fire up my computer. A few minutes later I leaned back with a big sigh, as to my immense relief it worked fine. I had several weeks of bookkeeping piled up, plus was anxious to get my e-mail going. In Joburg I had bought the cord needed for connecting the cell phone to the PC. Now sitting at my desk, I excitedly dashed off an e-mail as a test.

Sending messages through cyberspace was pure luxury, so the next morning I was up early to quickly make a cup of coffee and head to my office. But to my horror, when I tried to turn my computer on there wasn't even a bleep. The tiny green light lit up, but that's as far as it went.

"This cannot be happening—*again*," I raged in disbelief. My PC had worked for a mere day. Worst of all, we had just made the nine-hour journey to Johannesburg and back, including the stress of the sweltering border and its usual hassles with customs and immigration. The expense of such a trip, plus valuable time away from work, meant going back was out of the question.

It was still early in the morning and I had to wait until the computer store in Joburg opened before I could call them. Then they simply instructed me to phone the manufacturer. When I did this, I was told someone there would phone me back. Not surprisingly though, I was the one to eventually make the call again. I couldn't believe my good luck when I was then informed they had a subcontractor in Harare who did warranty work.

While this may sound simple enough, each phone call I tried to make took several attempts. There were far too few phone lines going out of Chiredzi, so often during the day I couldn't get a dial tone to call out. Also in Zim, it was rare for a company to have a single phone number with multiple lines. Instead, the company might have ten numbers. If nine of those happened to be in use, the caller may have to phone all ten before hopefully discovering the one line not busy. But if all ten were tied up, the only thing to do was phone every single number again. Added to this, the phone system in Chiredzi was strictly rotary dial. So all of those many numbers I called took time to slowly tick, tick, tick out.

When I finally got through to Harare, I was tiresomely passed from one person to the next. Eventually I managed to get the guy on the line who handled the warranty work. With his address now in hand I jumped in my car, dashing off to the Swift depot in Chiredzi so my computer could get to the city on the next truck out.

I was told my machine would take only a day to repair, so with transport time I should have it back in three days. The warranty manager also said he'd call me when it was fixed and let me know what was wrong. But of course, once again I did all the phoning.

Finally on Friday, after yet another round of trying to get a call through, the manager told me my PC was now working. He would send it on Swift that afternoon to arrive in Chiredzi by Saturday morning. He couldn't tell me what had been wrong, so I asked him to send a report along with it.

Saturday morning came, but no computer. I wanted to scream in frustration. Yet in Africa time it would have been a miracle anyway, to have received it back in just a few days. Nothing could be done but wait until Monday. When I then called the manager he explained that Swift hadn't picked up on Friday. On Tuesday my PC finally arrived, but of course there was no scrap of paper to say what had been done.

Although I felt relief when the computer fired up perfectly, the whole long exercise had left me exhausted. I felt as though for the last four weeks I'd been beating my head against a brick wall. I'd often felt like saying, "Just forget it!", but my PC was the most expensive thing I owned after my pickup.

With my computer finally working, I should have been motivated to dig in and get caught up with my work. But despite actually having solved my problem in the end, the whole process left me suffering from Beaten Down By Africa Syndrome. The Syndrome can completely snuff out your ambition, when after so many of the tasks you're trying to accomplish are turned into Herculean feats—and still you get nowhere—it builds up to an unbearable frustration. Rather than explode with it, the mind simply convinces the will that the thing wasn't so important after all. A person's drive flickers out to the slightest of embers.

Darren was also showing symptoms. We just had such a tangle of problems wearing us down. Ironically, however, the very best cure for Beaten Down by Africa Syndrome, was a healthy dose of the continent itself. To which we conjured up just such a remedy.

Chapter Thirty

||||||||||||||||||||||||||||||||||||||||||||||||||||||||||||||||||||||||||||||||

A few gleaming rays darted over the horizon, as we kicked back covers and eagerly pulled ourselves out of bed. Clutching travel mugs, Darren and I jumped into the pickup before five on a Saturday morning and headed off. Our exciting destination: the national park named Gonarezhou. Or translated into English, The Place of the Elephant.

Meeting us were Spike and Nicky, along with Spike's friend Jerry, who worked at the Malilangwe Trust Wildlife Conservancy. Years earlier the trust had bought private ranchland adjoining Gonarezhou, then launched into the formidable and costly undertaking of converting it into a wildlife sanctuary. A Noah's Ark of game had been purchased and reintroduced. Their efforts meant that rhinoceros, lion, elephant and other game were once again romping about in this corner of paradise.

We met up at Jerry's house in the conservancy, then wasted no time in setting out in his double cab pickup. The early morning was still pleasantly cool, the grass heavy with dew, our open windows inviting a sweet moistness through. Following a smooth track we made our way across Malilangwe's sprawling acres, where I was surprised at the variety of terrain. We first passed through open grasslands dotted with stubby regrowth, where years before crops had been tried without success. Our path then cut through a shady forest, twinkling with shafts of light. Leaving the woods, we next motored on through the typical Zimbabwe bushland of semi-dense shrubbery and smallish trees.

We wanted to be early at the fishing grounds, but couldn't resist stopping now and then to gaze upon the incredible wildlife. Leggy, honey-colored giraffe peered down at us with large eyes rimmed in long lashes. Brawny buffalo gave low snorts as they paused to watch us, steam wafting from their nostrils in the early morning air. Numerous plump and stout-legged zebra checked us out too, with big ears, bristly manes, and velvet black muzzles. Behind them fine-boned impala, colored in fawn, glided through the scattered bushes in delicate leaps.

Soon however, we entered the park, where we weren't expecting to see much game. In privately-owned conservancies anti-poaching efforts had helped to protect the wildlife. But in the underfunded national parks the game were pretty much on their own. Ten years earlier, Darren had flown over Gonarezhou and looked down upon magnificent herds of Cape buffalo streaming over the landscape. But if there were any in the park now no one ever saw them. So it was with some surprise that I spied a couple of alert, shadowy-colored kudu. But they stayed well hidden amongst the bushes and kept a watchful eye on us.

The five of us were chatting away, puttering slowly along, when out of nowhere a thunderous bellow shattered the quiet morning. We all jumped and nearly hit our heads on the roof at the bone-jar-ring scream. Although we couldn't see a hint of the beast, we knew it to be the warning roar of a highly agitated elephant. He must be in the bushes nearby and Spike wanted to stop and try to catch a glimpse of him.

"No way!" Jerry, who was driving, stated adamantly. "I've been charged by one of those brutes on this corner before and I'm not stopping!"

My guess was the defensive elephant was simply trying to keep his herd safe, having learned that, after decades of persecution by poachers, humans often brought suffering and a terrible death.

Twice more we came across elephants before reaching our fish-ing spot, but they were very people-shy and scrambled into thick bush at first sight of us. To see them so easily panicked was disturbing, as usually animals in parks become less wary of their stream of visitors. Yet I also knew that in the normal course of things park animals aren't relentlessly hunted down by poachers, and here in Gonarezhou, the harassment made them skittish and reclusive.

Twenty minutes on a flat track brought us to our first river crossing. Here Jerry had to creep the truck across a makeshift causeway of boulders and rocks. As we traversed our way, he pointed to the old bridge not far downstream. It was a startling sight, seeing how mangled the bridge had been by Cyclone Eline a year earlier. While visitors in cars could not enjoy the park, for us anyway, forging the river in four-wheel drive was in the spirit of wandering into wild Africa.

Before reaching our spot, Jerry negotiated us through two more shallow riverbeds. The last, stretching ten times as wide, was the life-giving Runde River. Half our crossing here was not through water but over white-beige sand. The loose grains instantly fell away under the tires, and we held our breaths as the pickup groaned against its pull, losing speed with each turn of the wheels. But finally we made it to the middle where clear water flowed, and now bumping over large rocks seemed easy going after the heavy sand.

Easing up the bank on the other side, Jerry parked in a spaciously treed spot. A high embankment looked down to the broad Runde, and on the opposite shore the beautiful Chilojo Cliffs soared up majestically. Stretching for miles, the towering sandstone face stood scored with vertical stripes of reddish-brown and ocher, to tones of pink and cream. From where we stood the colors blended into a ruddiness of peachy-orange, the soft hues giving the cliffs a hazy, unearthly look, like something from an imaginary world.

Nicky and I wandered over to the edge of the high bank, almost like a cliff itself, and gazed down to the lazy river. From this vantage we could make out the cloudy gray forms of an astonishing number of crocodiles, lying motionless under the water. We wondered if this profusion was due to the law requiring crocodile breeders to release young back into the wild each year. This was supposed to make up for the original harvesting of crocodile eggs from rivers, but the outcome was now a dangerous overabundance of wild crocs.

The five of us pitched in to rustle up a breakfast of eggs and bacon on the gas cooker, and once fortified, headed off in search of a way down to the water's edge.

As we hiked down to the river, I gazed in astonishment at the spectacle about us. Littered amongst the greenery lay car-size bundles of skeletal shrubs and limbless dead trees, starkly gray with twisted roots frozen lifeless. Once again, the aftermath of Cyclone Eline's ferocity. I was stunned at how the river had raged to such heights, flicking these mighty trees about like spent matches.

After negotiating our steep hike down to the river, we settled upon a spot that looked appealing. A strip of rough sand, only a few feet wide, the vertical hillside pressing close behind. There wasn't much space and before long Spike and Jerry were edging their way around a bend, hunting for the ultimate fishing hole. In front of me, Nicky and Darren cast their lines into the water's mysterious depths. I wasn't fishing and sat down to lean gently back against the sandy slope, letting out a comfortable sigh.

Just sitting there, with the dreamy cliffs hovering to my left and the placid river easing past ahead, I could feel my stresses melting away. The cliffs looked calm but watchful, as if keeping a protective eye over its territory. The day was warming and the still shaded sand felt cool under my palms. Rugged trees grew out of the packed sand of the hill, letting through only a dappling of the sun's vigor. The river's edge lay trimmed in vibrant yellow wildflowers. Not far in front of us a Pied Kingfisher flew past, its checker of black and white feathers streaking along just above the water, close to the shore. I watched as she made a sharp turn towards the bank, and in that instant a delicate chatter erupted from the flowers. The next moment she darted into the swathe of yellow, lost from view, and I imagined the hearty homecoming that greeted her there.

As I sat relaxing against the bank, I tried to make out any crocs that might be eyeing us. But it was a nearly impossible task. What looked to be the rim of a submerged rock could instead be a pair of croc eyes. It was hard to tell, as the many trees along the river cast long shadows, mixing confusingly with dark patches of water, and I wondered which might actually be from flat bodies lying underneath.

Nicky and Darren were trying for tiger fish, managing to catch a few small ones, the size of large trout. This fascinating fellow must have been given his name because of his glistening scales, dark orange upon white edged round with black, just like a tiger's spots. And with shark-like teeth, intimidatingly large for his head. Darren also hooked a squeaker fish, so nicknamed because of the desperate squeaking noise it makes when taken out of the water. Being a dull gray color with a broad mouth, they are small, but can hold their own with a half dozen spikes, the size of darning needles and sticking out dangerously straight from their bodies. A wiggling squeaker can pierce clear through a person's hand before he's even realized it's happened.

Squeakers aren't the best eating, one of those which a fisherman doesn't want to take his line. Plus amidst all those spikes and desperate squiggling, Darren was having trouble getting the hook out of its mouth. All the while, the panicked fish squeaked frantically.

"Darren, hurry up with that poor thing!" Nicky ordered. "You're going to kill it from suffocation before it makes it back into the water."

It didn't help matters there was no flat surface on which to lay it. Eventually though, Darren managed to remove the hook, while also avoiding lancing his hands with a spike. When he slipped the squeaker back into the river, the small fish quickly swam away.

Even so, Nicky and I ganged up on Darren. "That fish was out of the water too long, it's going to die," Nicky declared.

"I think Nicky's right," I chimed in. "It did seem quite weak."

Only a half hour later, when we had all forgotten about the harassed little fish, our jaws dropped at an amazing sight. Before us a large tiger fish swam purposefully by in clear view, just under the water near the shore. He was an impressive brute, sleek and powerful, with the sun glinting off his polished scales. A rare marvel indeed, since usually the water was too murky, or the fish too far under the surface, to be seen. But added to our awe was horror. In its mouth, between its razor-sharp teeth, it proudly held a squeaker, flaunting the smaller fish as if showing off its prowess as a hunter. Of course this smaller one looked suspiciously like the one Darren had caught. Nicky and I knew we couldn't blame him, but surely his weakened squeaker hadn't stood a chance against a cocky tiger like this one, who had found himself an easy lunch.

Becoming bored with the fishing, Nicky decided to return to the pickup. I walked along with her, and when we saw Spike and Jerry making their way back from another direction, I thought I'd better go call Darren.

Down at the river's edge, I found Darren still enjoying his fishing. He liked his spot, standing on a flat rock only big enough for his feet and level with the water. The rock rested just in the river and behind him pressed a vertical bank as tall as himself, where I now stood looking down. While I tried to convince him it was time to go, he suddenly interrupted me.

"Cinz, do you see that tiny bump, just out a ways?" he asked, studying the water's calm surface. "Do you think it's a croc?"

I immediately scanned the tranquil, dark expanse of the river. It looked completely smooth, until I spied two knobby bumps barely showing above the surface. It could have been an edge of a log or rock, but no, the bulges were two eyeballs intently focused upon us, or on Darren anyway.

"That decides it," I pronounced. "I won't let you stay here fishing, and certainly not by yourself."

But Darren had already started to reel in his line and pack up the tackle box. As he gathered his things he said to me, "Can you still see him? Has he moved? Or is he staying in the same spot?"

I kept my eyes glued on those two little knots, which didn't seem to be moving. But it was hard to tell. The deep, slow-moving river played tricks on my eyes, while I stared hard with concentration. At least if I could see those eyes Darren was probably safe. Usually when a croc decides to attack he swims completely submerged, plowing a straight line to his victim, to burst from the water out of nowhere.

Darren was in a precarious position, standing on the small rock level with the water and with nowhere to move. Quickly gathering up his fishing gear, he handed it to me on the sandy ledge above. While it'd been easy enough for him to slip down to the river, crawling back up the vertical of packed sand was more complicated. Darren felt uneasy as he struggled to negotiate his way up, knowing the croc would see him looking away and not on his guard, plus the struggling movement would be an added attraction to the beast.

"Can you still see the croc?" Darren asked with a nervous voice.

When I had reached down to grab his fishing gear I had, of necessity, looked away for an instant. Now as I scanned the calm water, it was like gazing across an empty ocean. I couldn't find the eyes again, but luckily, in another minute Darren was standing next to me. A shiver ran through my core, and we wasted no time in climbing higher, far out of the croc's reach.

Back safely at the pickup we all piled in, to drive off to another of Jerry's favorite fishing spots. When nearly there, he negotiated the truck across land thick with tall grass, hiding a surface of tire-size holes and jagged humps. Now midday, the sun scorched down, and he jostled the pickup across the rugged meadow to park under a big shade tree. The river lay a fair walk away, to which we all felt suddenly ravenous and swarmed to the back of the truck to hunt for lunch. Our breakfast leftovers of cold greasy bacon and sausage tasted delicious when eaten out of the tailgate and washed down with frosty beer.

The guys soon strode off towards the open river, a fifteen minute walk under the full force of a noonday sun. Nicky and I opted for the shaded pickup, where the view was hypnotically relaxing. The openness around us lay carpeted in swaying yellow grass, the wide river just visible off in front as a meandering swath of purple-gray. Behind it towered the soft-orange Chilojo Cliffs, while at our backs the trees and shrubs grew steadily fuller, until becoming thick bush once again.

The two of us munched on salty bacon as we chatted about Russian history, the breeding habits of birds, and our favorite Broadway plays. After awhile we draped ourselves inside the truck with the doors open, the dry heat saturating us like a soothing sauna therapy, and coaxing us into peaceful sleep.

By the time the guys returned, Nicky and I were now peering through binoculars at all the busy birdlife. Most numerous were the bee-eaters, beautifully feathered in soft turquoise, mauve, and clean white. I had forgotten my bird book, but with the expert Nicky there I didn't need it anyway.

Heading back, we set about retracing the route we'd come in on, again negotiating the wide Runde not far from our first fishing spot. Upon reaching the other side we were greeted with a handsome surprise. Standing with heads proudly high, appeared several knightly waterbuck. Amazingly they didn't run off as we crept past, and their soft-gray coats looked thick and healthy. I imagined the park to harbor only struggling wildlife and was glad to see some hearty characters still about. The intrepid buck, whose ribbed horns curved slightly in, kept a watchful eye upon us as we motored by. With their shaggy hair and tufted beards they looked more suited to a wintry place, while each donned a circle of white on his rump, flicking a tail at bull's-eye center.

Once back in the Malilangwe conservancy Jerry drove us slowly along, stretching out our wonderful day while we kept the laughter going. In an instant, we were silenced by a privileged sight. Before us loomed an awesome male rhinoceros, walking purposely through the open bush and obviously with a mission on his mind. Every ten yards he stopped, turned his rear to a bush, and let forth with a spray having the force and volume of a fire hose. Jerry explained there must be another male in the area and this chap was marking his territory. We watched enthralled. The dark gray rhino was stunning—full of vigor, strong, stocky, and intimidating even from the safety of the pickup. His large horn curved upward, and by rubbing on trees was honed to a sharp tip, now pointed defiantly skyward.

With all eyes fixed upon him, the big guy pretty much ignored us, even unhesitantly jogging in front of our truck on the dirt road. His gait was airy and light, surprisingly so with such stubby legs and ungainly bulk. As he trotted along, he wove smoothly from one side of the road to the other, glancing over his shoulder at us and brazenly waving his mighty horn towards the truck with powerful shakes of that massive head.

We arrived back at Jerry's house with the sun hovering low to the horizon, drenching the Earth in a golden glow. In seemingly one motion, we all piled out of the truck and into his crystal blue pool. The day was gently fading, and that brief time between afternoon and evening was restful. I stayed in the water longest, floating on my back and looking up to a tall sky of soft, rich blue. All around lay green lawn and gardens, while palms fringed the pool's edge. A dozen emerald nests of the weaver birds hung precariously from palm leaves, looking in danger of plunking down into the water around me. The pool rested on a small plateau and the view looked out to an expanse of unspoiled bushland. An intoxicating spot, which I found difficult to leave as the last of the day faded.

I now felt rejuvenated again, ready to return to life on the other side of the African coin. For me, the price of enduring Africa's struggles was still worth the reward of these irreplaceable times.

Chapter Thirty-one

||||||||||||||||||||||||||||||||||||||||||||||||||||||||||||||||||||||||||||||||||||||

The summer heat blazed with force, the rickety old air con in my office doing double time. Even late in the evening, when I laid my hand on the plastered walls inside our house, they radiated like an oven. Although now mid-December, the expected rains hadn't followed those first few showers in late October, intensifying the heat to an unbearable degree.

Our workshop was shutting its doors for two weeks over Christmas and New Year, and since we were going away, I decided to leave our TV and VCR with Tore. Usually he didn't like to be corrupted by such instruments of frivolity, but I thought he could use a good dose of distraction. Throughout the country the War Vets continued their campaign of harassment and Tore had more than his share on his ranch. A large encampment of women and children, along with War Vet men, were taking a steady toll on the trees for firewood, and on his cattle and game for the dinner pot.

Nor had the confrontations ceased. Tore was visited by ZANU-PF officials, who said if he paid money to the party War Vets on his ranch would be moved off. The reps, accompanied by a couple of policemen, also informed him they knew his staff were MDC supporters. To this Tore responded that he didn't know if they were or not, although from what he could tell, nobody seemed supportive of ZANU-PF and its policies. He was then firmly told it was his responsibility to instruct his workers to be loyal to the party.

On one of my weekly veggie collection visits I found Tore busy in his office, organizing a Christmas party for children of War Vets camped on his property.

"You know, they have so little," Tore said to me. "They are very poor, these people. I'm simply putting together a few treats for the kids." I thought how this was just like Tore, who didn't have extra bucks himself, going out of his way to do something for the very ones causing him problems.

Tore also told me his church was throwing a Christmas party for orphans whose parents had died of AIDS.

"Why don't you come?" he asked. "It'll be nice. We're having a service with singing, followed by snacks and a movie for the kids. Each year we also put together packages for the orphans, which we hand out at the party."

I was certainly curious about how a bunch of orphans might be managing, and the next week decided to drop in at the little church. Once there I discovered it wasn't just the small group I'd expected, and my heart tugged at the sight of a hundred orphans of every age. Yet they were all cleanly dressed in decent clothes, much better than the tatters of most children I'd seen in town and along country roads. Tore then explained that many orphans lived with a relative, although quite a number simply managed their own household without an adult, the older ones looking after the younger. With respectful poise they all sat cross-legged on the floor facing the podium, and after the short sermon and prayer, it was time for song.

I watched enrapt as the children began their singing in a lilting reverence. With each new hymn they became more enlivened, and by the third song were standing, arms held high and softly waving, faces lit with broad smiles and voices ringing with joy. What a wonderful surprise to see these orphans so happy and healthy, and ironically, they appeared to be getting a better start in life than many other children in Zimbabwe. FACT—Family AIDS Caring Trust—made sure they went to school and were provided with their basic needs.

After the stirring service, a table of snacks was laid. The children all filed politely past, each holding a bag that was filled with popcorn, cookies and candy. With barely a murmur they once again assembled on the floor for a movie. When the film ended each were then given a large sack, filled mostly with basic food items—cooking oil, sugar, powdered milk, a bag of dried sardine-like fish called capenta, laundry soap, a cooking pot and other small necessities.

When I left to make my way home, I was lost in thoughtful reflection. Feeling both inspired by the sight of the well-cared for orphans, yet sobered by their numbers. The fact was, the enormity of the AIDS epidemic in southern Africa was beyond comprehension. Beyond what I could even begin to imagine.

At the time of the orphans' Christmas party, one of four adults in Zim was HIV positive. How frightening to imagine if in the States, a quarter of my neighbors, co-workers, and even more chilling, my family, suffered from HIV.

Adding to the crisis, Zimbabwe had a million orphans, from a country of just twelve million people, the numbers swelling daily. No one could guess what this generation of youngsters, half growing up without parents, would mean to society. What if in the United States half of the children in every classroom were orphans? Humanity had never experienced such a horrific phenomenon.

Not long after moving to Africa, I noticed that while Zimbabweans didn't like it when their spouses cheated, this didn't seem to be considered contemptible. I knew both Zimbabwean men and women whose spouses had not been faithful, and while they had not been happy about it, they simply shook their heads with sadness, not treating it as an unacceptable tragedy in their marriage. Actually, from what I could see, there seemed to be a startling degree of tolerance to adultery. This may have been the same forbearance with which they approached most of their troubles, but in this case, it had deadly consequences.

Of course in this male-dominated society, women were the ones more often expected to tolerate adultery. If a husband had a mistress there wasn't much the wife could say. Men had the power and influence, and a woman must simply accept the cards she's dealt.

And this may have been the biggest factor to the AIDS crisis in Africa. Women had so few choices. They could not tell a husband to stop messing around, whether with mistresses or prostitutes. They could not tell him to wear a condom and they could not deny him sex. It was just not done. This may slowly change, but in the meantime they bore the overpowering weight of customs that trapped them as victims of a lethal disease.

Then too, I realized another factor was that many women were not educated. If a woman found herself in a desperate situation—her husband had died or abandoned his family—government programs were virtually nonexistent. So how then could an uneducated woman feed her children? Possibly as a laborer, though the foreman might only give her a job if she had sex with him. And I supposed to keep the job, she had to pay this fee on an ongoing basis.

Well, if she had to trade sex for work, what was it to be a prostitute and feed her children better than as a laborer? Maybe at least then she could send them to school, so they'd have more choices in life than she did. Sadly, that was an uneducated woman's options—laborer or prostitute. And when working the street corner, plenty of other women offered the same service, so she must give a man what he wants. Meaning sex without a condom. A prostitute who tried to make a man wear a condom was a very hungry woman indeed. Africa's trucking routes were notorious as a link in the spread of HIV, where the relatively well-paid, rarely-at-home-with-the-wife drivers, and the rural women far from other opportunities for work, fatefully met.

While a fortunate few may be saved from AIDS by drugs, she might instead wither away from malnutrition, still not having the means to feed herself and her children.

What an outsider usually sees is only the last stage of an AIDS sufferer's life—the emaciated body, the pain, and the entreaty in her eyes. Not glimpsed are the many years, days, and hours of enfeebling struggle, which a life of poverty had already crushed upon her before the illness. Drugs might give some relief to her last days, yet the entreaty in her eyes does not simply reflect the AIDS but the pain of the entire cruel life.

What I wished for my friend Africa was more empowerment of women, education, and job creation for all. If more of these things came about, AIDS drugs might not be needed. Without improving the human condition paradise could never be saved. As I strained to look at what the future held, all I could see was a further spiraling into the abyss.

Chapter Thirty-two

||||||||||||||||||||||||||||||||||||||||||||||||||||||||||||||||||||||||||||

I pulled down the blind, switched off the light, and locked the door behind me. Like all businesses in Zimbabwe we were joining in the annual ritual of everyone going off for the two weeks over Christmas and New Year. Virtually the entire country shut down and our workshop was to follow the flock. Losing out on an income for those couple of weeks was certainly a painful hit, but since few companies would be open, there wouldn't be much work anyway. Plus, closing up shop for awhile was a good way for our workers to take their leave. Since each machinist did a different job in an assembly line type of set-up, we found it easier when everyone downed tools at the same time.

Darren and I on the other hand, didn't feel in need of a two week vacation. But in Africa-time a person mustn't be in a hurry to make money or get things done. Africa insists we all take time to smell the daisies whether we think we need to or not. So while Darren and I were forced to cool our heels, we decided to go stay with our good friend Roy near Victoria Falls.

As we set out, the day beckoned in a flood of yellow sunshine. We cruised along through gently heaving lands, content under their blanket of scrubby bush and squat, wide-limbed trees. After driving all morning and into afternoon, Darren pulled to the side of the road so I could takeover at the wheel. Stepping out of the pickup, as I stretched my legs I scanned each side of the highway, where sitting casually amidst the airy shrubbery was a troop of baboons. They seemed to be just hanging out, as though this was their home and a main road happened to pass through it. As Darren and I strolled to opposite sides of the truck, the baboons continued to chat away, wholly relaxed and unconcerned about us being amongst them. I'd always known them to scamper off when people came near, so was surprised and honored by their trust. Being in the midst of their private world was a rare pleasure, if only for a fleeting pause.

Settled comfortably back in our seats, I let the pickup gently roll forward. At that moment two baboon youngsters playfully chased each other into the highway. Right on the center line they joined in an impromptu wrestling match, their tangle of thin arms, legs and tails looking like a bouncing ball of loosely wrapped twine. With our pickup already moving, the troop leapt up in animated distress, the females excitedly waving their arms, shrieking at the males and demanding they do something. At this, two large fellows eased down from their comfortable perches. Without much concern they jogged over to each scoop up a little one, holding him loosely to his chest as they hustled off the road.

The day was just turning amber as we coasted into Matetsi River Ranch. The heat here could be as relentless as in Chiredzi, but soon after we pulled into Roy's drive, dense gray clouds boiled up. Booms of thunder ricocheted over the land and lightning crackled through a darkening sky. The next thing a fierce wind plunged sideways, rain rushing down in a windswept deluge as blinding as a snowstorm. I thought how our timing had been perfect. Not only had we arrived in the last moments of daylight, but the heavens had waited until we were safely off the road before unleashing their enthusiasm.

As I stepped out of the truck, Roy swept me up in a big bear hug. I adored this gentle soul, perpetually upbeat and always thinking of others. His tousled red hair and unbuttoned shirt cuffs, along with a continual state of disorganization, gave him a scattered appearance. This made a curious combination with Roy's analytical mind and sportiness, plus strapping physique like an uncle who'd been a wrestling champion. This brawny man also had a fondness for cats, and one of his gray felines was often scooped up in his arms. Roy and I shared an enjoyment in the ritual of dining. Unlike Darren who, ever practical, considered eating more of a chore like brushing his teeth. Something to be done quickly and efficiently.

Managing the ranch and its upscale lodge along with Roy were Mark and Kate. Kate had jaunted off to Portugal for Christmas, but had kindly offered Darren and me her cozy chalet, invitingly perched on a steep hill above the lodge. A little farther away the two bachelors lived in the main house, which I was thrilled to find splendidly decorated for Christmas. The guys had decked out a gangly evergreen-like tree with silken balls, crystal ornaments and little Santas. Wreaths dotted with red berries, and ropes of sparkling tinsel, hung festively about the doorway arches. When the Christmas tree was lit, its rainbow of pixie lights filled the room with the same twinkling shadows I remembered from Christmases past, stirring within me a childlike joy.

The next morning we awakened to Christmas Eve, a pleasant summer day with a cooling shower in mid afternoon. Evening came clear and golden.

"To celebrate tonight, I have a special spot I want to take you," Roy announced to Darren and me. Ten minutes later we motored out the drive in anticipation.

"I know this is a bumpy ride, but it'll be worth it," Roy apologized, even though Darren and I were enjoying our ramble through rugged bush. After twenty minutes Roy parked the Jeep and we all climbed out.

"Come, this way," Roy beckoned, and with curiosity we trekked after him through the long grass. Next we pushed our way through a web of thorny shrubs to discover we stood on a high ledge, hypnotically suspended above a meandering swath of the Matetsi River. The view from so far up was stunning. We looked out to an infinite scape of woodsy bush, dry and stony, yet with a burgeoning healthiness. Elbowing our way through thorny branches, we found seats on some craggy boulders.

"I like this place because of its commanding view of the sunset," Roy explained, his gaze peaceful. Indeed we now looked out to a glowing sphere, hung low in the sky and churning in molten orange. Wisps of clouds fringed the wide horizon below, while to our left cumulous billows floated like fluffy meringue. Within it slivers of lightning occasionally sparked, yet an absence of thunder left the mood tranquil.

As I gazed far out, I didn't want to blink and risk missing a moment of nature's shifting canvas. As the smoldering orb began to sink to our right, the horizon there first burned liquid-gold, then deep velvet orange, and finally ruby red. At the same time on our left, farther from the setting sun, the meringue's colors were more mellow, easing from soft-yellow, to creamy peach, to sienna.

Soon we were set afloat in sapphire darkness, surrounded by a warm hush, the elements calm and serene. Only when lightning bolts now and then ricocheted through the boiling clouds hidden to our left, was I reminded of the intensity still out there.

Already feeling awed, the next thing Venus came out brighter than ever, casting a delicate sparkle across the rippling purple river. Fireflies then slowly appeared, twinkling amongst the cloaked bushes around us. Eventually the trillions of stars lay suspended above, so clear out here in the sweeping wilderness, a silken veil over the heavens. Nature's display was more spectacular than the most impressive fireworks show could be, and without a doubt, this reigned as my best Christmas Eve celebration ever.

* * * * *

On Christmas morning we woke to no electricity. This regular nuisance caused little stir amongst us, and was one reason I always made sure to bring a flashlight. And even more important, my gas-fired curling iron, as no matter where I was on Christmas I liked to be able to fix my hair.

Darren and I climbed into the open Jeep to follow a track from Kate's chalet over to the main house. As usual, the wildlife peeked at us from the bush. I first spied a timid bushbuck doe, the size of a small deer, her russet coat delicately flecked with white. A few minutes later I caught sight of several cautious waterbuck, whose shaggy beards hung down under velvet-gray muzzles. We also passed stocky eland, with smooth hides of light beige and looking to be cousins of the proud Brahman bull, but with stout horns spiraling up to strong tips.

When we arrived at the house, Mark and Roy walked out to greet us in a festive mood. We all strolled round to the back garden, where we could settle into chairs under a densely leaved tree, making an umbrella of lushness above us. As we relaxed with our coffees, above our heads finches hopped exuberantly about in the branches, chirping along with the Christmas tunes floating out from the house. In two bird baths close by bulbuls, sparrows, doves and a half dozen others competed for time in the water, splashing vigorously in the morning sun. Nearby, a miniature waterfall skipped down over its rocks and into the swimming pool, where larger birds like the iridescent starlings took their refreshment at this less crowded place.

By noon the day had worked itself up to a fervent warmth, enticing Darren and Roy to shed their t-shirts and dive into the pool. The merriment of Christmas was in the air, and soon the two of them had a contest going to see who could jump in and make the biggest splash. As I watched amused, their enjoyment seemed to further rouse the energetic birds in their baths, wanting to add all the more to the spray.

Just beyond the garden, on the edge of the bush, Mark had created a pond-size watering hole. While we sat with frosty drinks at the pool's edge, dangling our legs into its shimmering blueness and looking beyond, from out of the wood's shadows appeared a troop of baboons. Cautiously, they scampered the few yards to the hole's still water, then paused to drink with eyes watchful upon us. Their boldness gave a dozen graceful impala antelope the confidence to shyly follow. At the pond's rim they lingered and took delicate sips for some time. Eventually though Scruff could contain herself no longer, and made a few yapping bounds in their direction. In a soundless flash, the baboons and impala glided back into the bush and out of sight.

In late afternoon we headed inside for Christmas dinner, where the bachelors, Roy and Mark, revealed a marvelous spread. With the festive tree all aglitter, we feasted on ham as delicious as I'd had in Alaska, and along with the music, candles and champagne, the only thing at odds with the holiday atmosphere was the warm summer air. But summer Christmases seemed natural now, and I was happy to trade those snowy white landscapes for this unbridled African wonderland.

* * * * *

On New Year's Eve I decided to make enchiladas, which from the guys' point of view was a foreign and unusual dish. To be sure, I had bought the tortillas and other ingredients in Johannesburg months earlier, and by the time these delicacies had arrived at Matetsi, they had traveled in our pickup for over a thousand miles.

Half way through fixing the enchiladas, the power was snuffed out again. All I could do was sigh, this being an inevitable frustration that came with the rainstorms. While a storm might last for an hour though, the power could be lost for days. As a predictable state of affairs, the lodge was equipped with a gas stove and oven, so we decided to abandon the main house and instead have dinner there.

The mellow warmth of evening had taken over from the force of afternoon, and the four of us settled into canvas chairs at the edge of the high hill in front of the lodge. Stretched boldly before us, the wide horizon glowed gold from end to end. On our right hovered the setting sun, while to our left far below, lay a shallow manmade watering hole. The place always drew a wealth of wildlife to what was a rather marshy spot.

As we sat soaking up the last rays of the day, this was also the time when the animals quenched their thirst. We watched as a small herd of wildebeest casually made their way to the water. Then not unexpectedly a half dozen zebra soon appeared, the striped equines known for their fondness of hanging out with wildebeest. Also the ever present baboons, and through binoculars I watched them preening at the water's edge, enjoying the last hours of daylight before disappearing into trees for the night.

After our open-air dinner we all went to get cleaned up. We planned to celebrate New Year by venturing into Victoria Falls for a party. From the chalet Darren and I drove to the main house to meet up with Mark and Roy. Along the way I felt in the company of friends, as next to the track numerous glowing green eyes watched us from out of the blackness.

An evening shower had once again washed the heat from the air. As we set out on the highway, a dampness misted up from the warm tarmac in thick swirls, creating a mysterious, lightly churning fog around the car. Half way to town we passed a triangular yellow caution sign, the standard type which usually sports an image of a deer, or in Alaska, a moose. This one however, had an elephant on it. As we whizzed past in the darkness, Mark commented that, of the numerous times he had traveled this stretch of road, he'd seen virtually no wild animals, and certainly never an elephant. In decades past these mighty pachyderms had freely roamed this territory, but we had a good chuckle at the absurdity of the Elephant Crossing sign now.

Only a few minutes later, our talk faded out. Distracted, we all strained to focus on a ghostly wavering in the darkness ahead, at the farthest reach of our headlights through the mist. As Roy slowed the car, we could finally make out the towering shadowy forms of— elephants!

Roy pulled over at once and we peered in awe down the headlights' beam. A group of young bull elephants was slowly crossing the highway in single file, then one by one vanishing into the blackness next to it. Their sloping gray forms swayed forward in a floating motion, as though hovering above us, as we sat looking out at the level of their knees. There in the misty dark night, they looked to be spirits from an era long past.

When we finally drove on, we quietly talked about the noble beasts we had just seen. Where had they come from? Probably the national park nearby. But where were they going? We could think of no sanctuary in the direction they traveled. Elephants need a vast area to roam and have become lost souls in this world of human sprawl. We couldn't guess how their destinies would play out in the years ahead when, after all, nearly every rhino had disappeared.

And as it was, none of us could even picture our own futures. We didn't know how long we'd be living in our homes; let alone what country we might land in. None of our jobs were secure with every industry collapsing. A year from now would we find ourselves, suitcase in hand, on another shore?

Every person in Zimbabwe was saying the coming year would be more trying than the last. And those of us still here couldn't blame the ones who'd left, nor those who continued to leave in a steady stream.

I thought back to New Year's twelve months before. Everyone had been positive then, certain the year ahead would be better. We would make it so with the very force of our determined optimism. But now, everyone said times to come would be worse than already seen. Actually, it gave us relief to acknowledge it. Helping to lessen our burdens in a way, by not struggling against them but instead spending our energies carrying them compliantly. There would be no expectations, so no disappointments.

In the *Economist* magazine, I read that average income in Africa was now less than it was in 1971, a tragedy of "political ineptitude" at a time when the rest of the world had enjoyed thirty years of unparalleled prosperity. The writer went on to say that while Zimbabwe was a "corrupt, inefficient and disintegrating country", its ability to bring about democratic change put it in a better position than most African nations.

This last note gave me both a feeling of optimism, and of sadness. Surely it was a positive point that we lived in a country better off than most of Africa. Yet mostly I felt sad. To think that, of the fifty-four nations on the continent, only a few existed at the dismal state found in Zim. It was a sobering thought.

* * * * *

A few days after Darren and I arrived at Matetsi River Ranch, a group of War Vets started camping out there. They immediately began to stump trees and crudely clear areas of bush. A couple days later, employees of the government's District Development Fund showed up to start plowing with their brand new, bright orange Renault tractors, a gift from the French. I liked to think the French hadn't intended for their tractors to be used to tear up virgin bushland, in a wasteful attempt at growing crops in an area impossible for such ventures. But then, the French government was still hosting Mugabe and patting him on the back, while other democratic countries were instead taking punitive action. So maybe they didn't mind their tractors being used for his political agenda.

Mark tried to talk to the War Vets, this particular group of a lethargic nature, but they were simply carrying out what they'd been paid to do. He also went to see the Member of Parliament for the area, the equivalent of a senator in the States. While the MP did make an effort to help with the situation, he had no power to change it.

During our stay, Darren and I watched as War Vets chopped and ripped and dug out a bit more each day. I supposed that, in the whole scheme of things, it was still a minor dent in the wilderness. But since they carried out their destruction along the roads to the lodge, the advance of each day's damage was glaring. We had to edge our pickup around the shiny French tractors, quickly rutting the tracks Mark had so carefully maintained. He had sloped them in such a way, and with the right mix of sand and gravel, to keep erosion at bay. His contour ditches, which angled away from the track and into the bush in order to drain off water, were soon mangled by the tractors. But of course the War Vets didn't take such elements as erosion into consideration, or they wouldn't have been planting cornfields in a climate akin to west Texas in the first place.

Some months later they decided it even easier to plow around the game watering hole below the lodge, since the area was sparsely treed. Their crops never did well in the murk of this sometimes swampy spot, and with the wildlife all scared away from their drinking place—not to mention the sight of scraggly cornstalks trying to pop up in this now unpristine wilderness—the property could no longer be an attraction to tourists and stay viable.

"Madam, excuse me, but may I ask a favor of you?" a maid working for the lodge said to me one morning during our visit.

"Yes of course, what is it?"

"Please madam, if you know of any position open in Chiredzi, can you recommend me?"

"Oh, are you unhappy with your job here?" I asked, surprised at the request.

"Actually, I like it very much," she politely replied. "The problem is, War Vets will be getting this property soon so I need to find work elsewhere."

I laughed and said, "They certainly will not! You needn't worry about your job." Little did I realize I was wrong, since without tourist business to keep the place afloat, eventually she did find herself out of work. And in a manner of speaking, the War Vets did wind up with the property in the end.

Another anxious worker at Matetsi asked Darren if he could overhaul his car engine for him.

"And as soon as possible, because I might need to get off the ranch at a moment's notice, if the War Vets become hostile," the man explained, looking tense.

"If that happens where will you go?" Darren asked with concern.

"I'll head to Humani," the fellow answered, "since I grew up there, and when the land is all parceled out Humani is my best chance for getting a piece."

It was a chilling revelation to hear, having nearly spent my life's savings buying a farm. It'd be the same as if, for instance, I worked at a factory, as had my father before me, and now I thought this meant I was due to own it.

Towards the end of our visit, one afternoon Roy and I sat on the chalet's stone veranda, gazing out over miles of treetops. From the stereo drifted a gentle panpipes melody, and amidst the serenity and beauty, we found ourselves trying to come to an understanding about Zim's situation. How had the country fallen into such a shambles? One major factor, certainly, was Mugabe. As the headlines on one newspaper read, "The Mess One Man Can Make". But how had he managed to stay in power? Of course he used brutal intimidation as one of his tools. But I would have thought the millions would rise up against it, a logical assumption by someone such as me coming from a democracy. Yet the majority of Zimbabweans were simple folk with a culture still dominated by tribal ways.

Roy and I talked about how, in only a matter of decades, the tentacles of the modern world had crept into this harsh land. Roads, bridges and cosmopolitan cities had sprung up, bringing with them the written word, and Western legal and political systems. Tribal society had seemed to take a backseat to the blossoming modernity. But now, we saw the peasant's chosen lifestyle gaining ground again. The roads were disintegrating, electricity was becoming a scarcer resource, and medicines that came in capsules were fewer on the shelf. The idea of a representative government had lost its effectiveness, with parliament no longer a voice for the people but a tool of an omnipotent leader. But did the peasant care, we had to wonder? Standing barefoot next to his mud hut, did he really miss these things?

In sober reflection, Roy and I spoke of how Zimbabwe was slowly going backwards, back to a time before Westerners had made homes here. This wasn't our opinions but fact, since we watched it happening before our eyes. The infrastructure of roads and railways, power stations, availability of clean water, medical care and education, were all collapsing. The people in the cities hadn't chosen this since they did not support Mugabe. Rather it was the rural peasants, eighty percent of the population, who carried the day.

"I suppose Zim will get to the point where everyone other than peasants have left, when it becomes too unbearable to live here," Roy lamented. "Then things will really fall apart. No road will be traversable by car anymore, only by donkey cart. When trucks can't travel throughout the country there'll be no more supplies. Everyone will have to live off the land. Every drop of water will have to be carried in a gourd on a woman's head, from only a half dozen rivers that flow year round.

"But I can leave," Roy continued after a moment. "They can let it collapse and I can go elsewhere, if that's how they want to live. Sadly though, all these trees you and I are now looking upon, in no time will be gone. Every last one chopped down for firewood. The animals have already begun to disappear and soon this wilderness will become a wasteland. Then I don't know how the peasants will survive."

Yes, that was the problem, there was no going back to the way it'd been, the days when everyone just subsisted off the land. In 1900 less than 500,000 people lived in Zimbabwe, while now the population was 12,000,000. There was no possible way for all these people to go back to hunting antelope, growing their patch of grain, and living off the fruits of the forest.

Of course, plenty of Zimbabweans lived in modern houses, enjoyed watching TV and driving their cars, made sure to have regular dental check-ups, wore a suit and wanted a good education for their children. They were people whose grandparents had probably lived a peasant's lifestyle, but who themselves existed in the modern world. Yet even they were a minority in the country. Their fate was determined by the majority, being the peasant living in the mud hut.

I thought back to a conversation earlier in the day, with the cooks in the kitchen at the lodge.

"So it's now the new year! What do you guys think this year will bring?" Roy asked, making polite talk as he hunted a drink from the fridge.

They took his question in all seriousness, and reflecting thoughtfully, one of them responded, "Fuel shortages."

"Yeah, that's probably right," Roy said with a sigh, "And what else?"

With a low smile drifting over his face, the other cook matter-of-factly stated, "Hunger."

He was referring to food shortages, to which Roy looked at him quizzically, asking, "Then what? Will the people be angry with the government?"

"No, after hunger, there will be death," the cook answered with a strained laugh.

"How can you laugh when you say that?" I blurted out, thinking starvation was not to be taken lightly. Yet, even though he had smiled, he'd made this statement with a tone of complete gravity.

"Why should I not laugh? I am not afraid of death," he answered simply.

This was all too similar to conversations Darren sometimes had with the machinists at his workshop. When the talk turned to the roads falling apart, the telephones not working, no fuel or other calamities, they would exclaim with a hearty laugh, "Sure—we are *buggered*!!"

I knew this to be typical of the cheerful Zimbabwean spirit, eternally light-hearted, taking strife and hardship in stride. But to their detriment, this ability to endure a seemingly infinite amount of adversity also contributed to the largely unchallenged decay of their nation.

As Roy and I sat together that quiet afternoon, reflecting on the future, we both seemed powerless to steer our fate. Which I supposed was how each Zimbabwean felt, as they lapsed into a state of acceptance of their condition. Then, trudging through each day as best they could, knowing the burden never lightens, they figured that, well, they might as well bear it with a smile. And how can you argue with that?

Chapter Thirty-three

As Darren and I cruised along, our pickup gliding easily over the highway, the magnificence of the day was uplifting. A powder-blue sky dotted with cottonball clouds, the air luminous with sunshine. The birds flew jubilant as they stretched their wings like sails, catching the buoyant updrafts of summer's warmth. Perched on telephone wires, the vibrant Roller birds—robed in turquoise with mantles of purple—casually scanned their territory like lords in a high castle. Around a bend we coasted past a dell of green reeds, where a flock of crimson-cloaked red bishops burst out in flaming vigor.

Having arrived back in Chiredzi with still a few days of vacation, for an afternoon we decided to drop in on Butch and Jenny, who were looking after Humani Ranch while Jenny's folks were away. Darren now slowed our pickup to cross the Mkwasine River at the conservancy's entrance, where motoring down into the dry riverbed and edging across its concrete causeway, was like descending into the heart of the Earth. Here nature had created a beautiful collage, with a scattering of boulders, strips of sandbar, clusters of river shrubs, and a translucent ribbon of water draped through it.

Making our way on a washboard road through the bush, we were granted the always enjoyable sight of dainty-hoofed impala springing gracefully across in front of us, carefree flashes of fawn with curved delicate horns. Driving along over the road's loose stones, we glimpsed motionless gray kudu in the edge of the bush, watching us with large, watery eyes and oversized ears. With a split-second flinch they dropped back into the shadows.

Upon our arrival at the house, as they came out to greet us Jenny radiated her usual cheerfulness. I was glad to see Butch, too, looking relaxed and in good spirits. The four of us passed a pleasant few hours in the sunny garden catching up on news, before making our way to the airstrip for a late afternoon flight, the time when the heat-soaked air settled into creamy smoothness.

We walked through tall grass along the airstrip, my palms brushing its soft wheat top as it swayed to the breeze. Next to the turf runway and beyond a fence, stocky ranch horses grazed, occasionally throwing us a glance in curiosity. When Butch finished the preflight we all climbed aboard, to zoom over the coarse grass towards a blue horizon.

The plane's wheels left the jarring ground and suddenly we floated through the air. As I looked out the window, close by and standing long-legged in the grass was a flock of brilliant white storks. As Butch swept to the left they reluctantly took to the skies, gliding off to our right with languid waving like a sea of gentle whitecaps.

A few minutes' flight had us coasting over the rugged Turgwe River, and as I peered down at the water rippling along, I glimpsed a dozen baboons gathered at a bend. When we flew overhead, they scampered away across a clean sandbar and disappeared into the maze of bush.

The Turgwe led us to the conservancy's eastern boundary where Butch swung north to now trace the wide Save (Saw-vey) River. Out my window, to the west of the river I looked upon the conservancy's deep green landscape, a healthy wilderness of prime wildlife habitat. But as I turned and looked past the river east, I saw the depressing sight of communal lands, all sallow beige and barren, its patches of cornstalks struggling to come to life in the cruel climate. Alongside huts of red clay, too many goats rummaged for flecks of green, and I wondered how long the flexed, brown arm of the river could hold back this tide of human sprawl.

As we pressed northward for several minutes, the mighty waterway led us to an agricultural scheme. Upon the once spartan plains of the Middle Save district lay square farms of five hundred acres, all connected by concrete canals fed by the vitality of the year-round flowing Save River. Within many fields lay large circles of bright green, crops grown by circular irrigation systems. In this un-forgiving climate of limited options, Butch's brother-in-law Steve grew cotton in summer on his Middle Save farm, while irrigated wheat could be managed in winter when the heat wasn't so intense.

We glimpsed Butch's sister's house ahead, and he eased down to tightly orbit their home. The farmhouse sat in the middle of a little Eden with shady trees, colorful flowers, green lawn and crystal blue pool. Theirs was an alluring spot, but I knew it'd been paid for with a terrible price. In the midst of Zimbabwe's civil war, while doing his rounds on the farm, Steve's father had been coldly shot dead by guerillas.

Butch turned the plane westward to once again fly over miles of thick bush. As I scanned the unbounded expanse below the game was hard to spot, well camouflaged under a canopy of deep green. Only the blond giraffe, whose heads poked above the treetops, stood out now and then. There were just a few open areas, where man-made watering holes lured the wildlife out of the cool shadows. As we flew over one, a group of elephants looked up at us with trunks raised and large ears flapping, perturbed by the noisy bird buzzing overhead. At another waterhole, a mixed herd of wildebeest and ze-bra drank cautiously. When we zipped past above, the jittery zebra glanced skyward, then nervously swung round and made for the edge of the trees.

Approaching the churning Turgwe again, Butch eased us down to a lower altitude, then over the winding river dropped to below the treetops. While we skimmed the rocky water, I strained to look into the forest-like bush on each side. The turns in the river came quickly with the plane's speed, the water coursing under us in a powerful rush, but I managed to glimpse a herd of amber impala. Then with excitement caught sight of a gray-brown reedbuck, dart-ing through the undergrowth.

Eventually we'd have to come back to Earth and the fading sun hurried us along. Strolling back to the house, Jenny's golden-orange curls glowed like a candle amongst the creeping shadows. At the last snuff of twilight we passed the outline of a handsome brute, a warthog which we might not have seen if his glinting ivory tusks hadn't shown so brightly. I admired how those large tusks, curving out and up, looked both daunting and brilliant, like Africa herself.

Darkness had descended by the time Darren and I got on the road home. As always in late evening, every few yards we came across a sedate nightjar bird lounging in the middle of the track. Looking like something between a quail and sparrow, only at the last possible second did they flap awkwardly up into our headlight beam and out of our path.

At Humani's boundary Darren eased our truck down an embankment and then carefully steered through a trickling stream hidden in blackness. I knew its clear water weaved through thick bush on our left, like a babbling brook through an enchanted forest, and when I peered into the darkness I saw a blinking colony of fireflies hovering above it. They formed a curvy twinkling through the undergrowth like fairies on parade, and I felt blessed to have been given one more amazing day in this changing, and surely disappearing, land.

* * * * *

I still couldn't believe my good luck. Just a couple days after visiting Butch and Jenny, an extraordinary event was to happen and I would get to watch it. Right there above our little town in the middle of nowhere, the rare showing of a lunar eclipse was to be put on just for us.

There was one catch, however, it being the plumb middle of the rainy season. But fortune held out, and evening arrived blue-black and cloudless. For the occasion Darren and I were dropping in on his aunt and uncle who lived not far from Chiredzi, where his uncle managed a farm that bred ostrich and crocodile. I listened intrigued as he told how the valuable croc eggs were carefully looked after in incubators, the hatched youngsters then raised with a watchful eye. Finally at the appropriate age, they were sent off to the farm's immaculate butchery.

He explained how there is an art to raising crocodiles. The leather market demands the pattern on the skin be perfectly symmetrical, and many things can spoil the pelt such as fungus or small wounds. So the growing crocs were looked after meticulously. Their meat was also prized, mainly exported to Asia where even the crocs' feet were considered a delicacy. As Darren and I toured the sterile butchery we saw the final product. Neat Styrofoam packages covered in clear plastic displayed the clean reptilian feet, long round toenails and all.

After dinner the warm summer air drew us outside to relax on the lawn. We had a perfect view, looking up between trees in the garden to the northeast, where amid the thickly scattered stars the moon rose large, full, and brightly white. As we sat talking, waiting for a lumbering Earth to ease between sun and moon, a revelry of squeaking bats flashed past our ears, dodging back and forth under the roof eaves behind us. Their lively commotion brought to mind one evening when I lived on Rungudzi, and unworried, noticed several bats fly into the house. After an hour when I hadn't seen them leave, I suspiciously went to see what they were up to. The last room I checked was the bathroom, and when I flicked on the light I spied them comfortably tucked in for the night, hanging motionless in the shower. They looked like gray-brown mice with too big ears, and with of course, black hairless wings folded neatly at their sides. They met my gaze with brazen stares, as if to say, "Really, this house is big enough for all of us."

Slowly the Earth's shadow crept over the alabaster moon. First as a smoky rim, then gradually covering more of the shimmering disk. After an hour the resplendent moon was completely veiled by our Earth, although it still hovered high in the night sky, transformed into a russet, sultry glow. As the Earth moved slowly forward, a sparkling white fringe reappeared on the orb of smoldering embers. Truly an unreal sight, in what sometimes seemed my unreal existence here.

* * * * *

Life was good, and the next weekend Darren and I were off on a favorite outing, visiting Spike and Nicky at Hammond Ranch. As we pulled up to the main house, I was delighted to see several fawns in the clan of impala does living there. The demure ladies made this bit of manicured grounds their home, along with its border of rough bush. Unbelievably, Spike told me how, in fact, fawns are usually born in the first few weeks of November. But the does had done the improbable, actually waiting until after the cheetah was gone in late December to drop their fawns.

Hobbs the cheetah and our dog Roger, the big lab-ridgeback, had certainly formed a relationship over their several months together. Unfortunately it ended up more of a rivalry than a companionship. Then a couple weeks earlier, Spike was to go away for Christmas and knew it wouldn't be practical to leave Hobbs in the care of others. Once he'd been gone for several days and left Nicky to look after the big cat. She had found herself with a mini battle on her hands, trying to persuade Hobbs to return to the front garden after sneaking out yet again. He'd decided he preferred to hang about at the back where everyone came and went, and where the impala stayed.

Nicky finally tried to lure Hobbs back to his assigned quarters with a nicely tender, still furred and hoofed antelope leg. This prize certainly got his attention, but as he licked his chops, he reckoned he didn't need to be tricked back into the garden to have it. Why not simply grab it from Nicky? But she too could be tenacious and it ended up a tug-of-war around the yard, before Nicky was able to wrangle the cheetah back into his digs.

After losing that skirmish, Hobbs held a grudge against Nicky. Whenever she watched TV in the living room at the main house, he would sit on the veranda and glare at her through the glass doors, giving her a piece of his mind with low growls. And when she went for a dip in the garden's pool one day, which Hobbs considered to be in his territory, he came charging at her with menacing snarls. To this she splashed at him, then Hobbs hissed back, and the chip on his shoulder grew a little bigger. Eventually, whenever she had to walk in the garden Nicky made sure to carry a piece of rubber hose, just in case she needed to give him a good slap to protect herself.

So with Spike going away over Christmas, before he left he knew the best thing for all concerned was to release the cheetah back into the wilds. Hobbs' ankle injured in the snare was now healed, and we could only hope his instincts would keep him alive, since he'd lost his mother before his survival training was finished.

One sunny day in mid December, Darren and I dropped in at Hammond to find Spike busily preparing to fit Hobbs with a radio collar. First the cat was darted to put him to sleep for a few minutes. Then while the young cheetah lay silent on the lawn, Spike hurriedly adjusted the collar upon him. I kneeled down and stroked Hobbs' amazingly dense coat, the color of yellow grass tinged with gold. As he lay on his side softly breathing and peaceful, I thought how his sinewy wildness gave him a ferocity, yet at the same time he seemed so vulnerable.

What a relief it must have been for the dainty impala, living nervously in the back garden, when the foreboding presence and smell of this ruthless predator vanished from over the fence. Within a week of Hobbs' departure the pregnant does gave birth to their fawns, after remarkably having held back the event for a month.

Now early January, when we pulled up to Hammond Spike was heading out to shoot an antelope for the staff's meat rations. Nicky decided to join us and we all climbed into the bush-kitted Land Cruiser with Darren at the wheel. A dewy fragrance of morning still hung over the ranch, carried softly in the breeze as we eased along in the open truck. Motoring down through a dip in the road we splashed through a trickling stream. To our left under shady trees lay a pool of dark purple water, its lily pads floating undisturbed, each with a lavender flower. I found the serenity catching. Now and then the bush smoothly opened, revealing grassy areas where wildebeest, zebra, impala and eland grazed, content in the morning's yellow rays. Stocky warthogs trotted away from us in quick snaps, pushing themselves into tall grass. Ever watchful, Spike pointed out an occasional shrike or goshawk looking down from high branches.

As we rocked gently along, curving our way through hardy bush, I fleetingly wondered at something lying across the track far in front. The object looked like a thick piece of black rubber hose, tapered at each end. Darren knew to drive around anything suspicious rather than over it, and without even thinking, steered the truck slightly into the bush.

But the tire must have just clipped it, as in a flash a massive snake spiraled up, his large hood unfurled, only inches from Darren in the driver's seat and without even a door between them. Completely enraged, the cobra spun round in fury, his eyes level with Darren's. By the time the beast calmed his agitation enough to look for the culprit who'd disturbed him, our truck was yards down the track.

Darren stopped the Land Cruiser and we all looked back in awe at the magnificent creature. The chillingly deep black cobra stood tall and angrily alert, his wide hood stretched taunt. He was enormous, even Spike saying he'd never seen one so big. He fiercely scanned the area around him, particularly eyeing the bush on each side, although for some reason never focusing on our noisily idling truck a few yards ahead. Finally, he warily eased down to the ground, and still looking around with suspicion, soundlessly swished off into the bush. Without a doubt, he was one of the kings of our thorny jungle.

A couple hours later Spike had successfully bagged an impala ram for the workers' dinner pots, and we headed back to the lodge for lunch. Nicky made pizzas and a pitcher of Pimm's, an interesting alcoholic concoction discovered during her years in London. With the heat of midday beating down the swimming pool drew us like a magnet, where we alternately sprawled and dipped ourselves waiting for the afternoon sun to lose some of its punch. For evening's entertainment Nicky and Spike planned to take us up a smooth rock *gomo*, or "hill", to watch the sunset. They tried to describe it as we lounged about the pool, but Darren and I just couldn't picture this unearthly feature, leaving us all the more intrigued.

Trekking off again in the Land Cruiser, the narrow track was now shaded with evening's approach, the bush next to it filled with creeping shadows. As the day cooled it was the time when the wildlife ventured out and our eyes carefully searched the undergrowth.

Mostly it was Spike who picked out the occasional gray kudu or red-brown duiker, peering at us through the thistles. But then suddenly Nicky leapt up, the first to spy several buffalo, up ahead on the edge of the track. Upon reaching the spot a minute later we were thrilled to discover more than thirty. The beasts eyed us warily, a muffled snort to be heard here and there. Under our stares their dark forms shifted nervously amongst the low trees, yet they did not run off.

"This is truly amazing," Nicky exclaimed. "I honestly never thought such a day would come, when I'd regularly see buffalo, elephant and rhino all here on Hammond. Only earlier this week I came across the other two." The event certainly was remarkable, as it'd only been five years since Hammond became part of the Save Valley Wildlife Conservancy. Before that it'd been a cattle ranch and host to little game, and definitely none of these rarer beings.

Eventually we dragged ourselves away and left the buffalo in peace. Still making tracks for the rock *gomo*, after awhile Spike turned off the dirt trail to follow two barely visible tire tracks, overgrown with tall grass. We made several stops and turnarounds, as we weaved and ducked through the thorny bush. But with Nicky standing and helping to direct Spike, it wasn't long before we popped out of the low trees. There it stood, looming before of us. An impressive and surreal sight, this rounded rock several stories high, looking like a half-buried asteroid.

After a short discussion between Spike and Nicky about the best way to the top, I nervously realized Spike intended to simply drive up. The steep rock was cut with crevices, some a foot or more wide. But he didn't hesitate to put the Land Cruiser in low gear, and the next thing we were inching up a near vertical face. The view before us was only clear blue sky, and I felt sure the tires would lose their grip and send us careening backwards.

But we made it safely to the top, and what an awesome spot it turned out to be. The land around sprawled for miles, with only a patch of low hills in a distant corner. We seemed to be looking out to the edge of the world, while below lay a dark green Earth blanketed in rounded treetops, dusted with haze. A soft blue sky was easing to muted gray, as behind us the sun dropped below the horizon.

Spike had brought along a portable antenna, trying to catch a signal from Hobbs' radio collar. Since returning after Christmas he hadn't been able to receive a signal from Hobbs at all, nor had the cheetah been seen. Now still without success, Spike repeatedly swept the antenna out to the countryside before us, hoping for a hint that Hobbs was out there. Alas, it seemed he was truly on his own.

With the end of day, low whistles and coos from countless birds floated up to us from out of the trees. Then somewhere a leopard barked croaky and deep, each of his grunts fading out like mist through a forest. As the last rays of daylight were snuffed out, we leaned back against the warm stone, peering up at an expansive cosmos coming to life with the darkness. A shooting star swept over the night sky as Spike was giving us an astronomy lesson, rounding it off by saying our sun is really just an average star, nothing special. It made us realize how insignificant our small world was, and our own little problems upon it, so trivial in the whole scheme of time and the universe.

"At least we can say that a chapter of our brief lives has been spent in the magnificence of Africa," Nicky declared, continuing with, "And when a person leaves the continent, they are never the same again." Yes, we all nodded, every place we may live hereafter will seem less soulful than when our home was in this peerless land.

Chapter Thirty-four

||||||||||||||||||||||||||||||||||||||||||||||||||||||||||||||||||||||||||||||||||||||

Over the summer I hadn't stopped by my buddy Tore's as much. This wasn't a conscious change, and in fact when I thought about it, Darren and I were visiting many of our friends less. Conversation just wasn't what it used to be. There was always an overwhelming amount of bad news these days, and any sprinkling of good was only smothered by it. All of society seemed to have taken on a dreary lethargy.

When I did finally drop in at Tore's workshop one day, I found him looking strained, his shoulders sagging and noticeably dispirited. This was so unlike him and I felt a stab at having to see him this way. I realized this was partly why I hadn't come sooner. It was unbearable to watch a friend suffer.

While Tore and I sat in his office, he matter-of-factly told me that, chillingly, he and his foreman had received death threats from War Vets. Was it worth holding on to a property when your life could be in danger, I thought to myself. I didn't have to say so to Tore, as by now most people had reconciled themselves to losing everything they'd proudly built up with sweat and sacrifice. Harder to come to terms with though, was the financial loss of their farms. It could mean an entire life's savings vanishing into the deep, along with this sinking ship of a country. Tore talked distractedly about how he had nothing for retirement, his ranch having been his security for the future.

Tore was also struggling to find the foreign currency needed to pay for his daughter's college tuition in South Africa. While I listened and searched for a few encouraging words, he said he had decided to sell his transport business. It was then I realized why something seemed different about his workshop. I now noticed he'd tidied up a bit, and removed a heavy layer of dust and grease. I cast a glance up to the tall ceiling, and sure enough, the colony of spider webs was gone. Somehow the loss of this community of beings left his office somber and desolate. Seeming, too, a reflection of Tore's own spirit.

Like everyone, he had to find a way to reconcile in his mind the hopeless circumstance he and his country were in. Fate couldn't just be random, there had to be a means to arrest the spiraling freefall.

"Politics is a struggle between good and evil," Tore said to me in earnest. "Once the aggression starts, it is a curse that continues from one generation to the next until it is stopped in its tracks. It's the same as when a person is slapped on the cheek. If he turns the other cheek rather than hitting back, the cycle of violence will end."

As Tore paused, I was sure I saw some of his strength returning. "Our country is poised on the edge," he added, pulling himself up. "The opposition must stay resolute, resisting violence in order to halt the cycle. And," he concluded, "it takes a very brave person indeed, when the only weapon he fights with is peace."

As I listened without any wisdom of my own, I hoped Tore's noble convictions would ring true, for the sake of everyone here in paradise.

* * * * *

I was wrested from peaceful slumber by the tinny chime of the cell phone. Drowsily eyeing the bedside clock I saw it to be the unsettling hour of midnight. Next to me, Darren was barely awake as he now held the phone to his ear, and I could just make out a murmured voice saying there was some kind of trouble on Humani. Everyone was having to flee and Jenny's sister Sarah would be arriving at our house soon.

It was late February and this was very disturbing news, because not long before Butch had only just scraped out of a close call on the ranch. He'd been looking after the place while Roger was in the States, and one afternoon the Humani game scouts sent a garbled call on the shortwave radio, asking Butch to come to the cattle dip for some sketchy reason. Something didn't seem right and he drove up to the dip with caution, stopping the Land Rover where he could easily dash away. Butch cast a slow glance round as he reached to turn off the key, at the last moment spying a figure crouching behind a bush. Before he could wonder at this, at the instant when the engine cut forty barbarous War Vets sprang out of nowhere, flying towards him swinging broad-bladed pangas, knives and clubs.

Several lunged at the cab of the truck, intent on dragging him out. One tried to snatch the key from the ignition, while the rest of the mob rushed about the truck shouting in frenzied confusion. Some were glassy eyed, surely high on *imbanje,* the local marijuana. They began to rock the Land Rover in an attempt to roll it over. Despite the many arms pulling at him Butch managed to rev up the truck, and with wheels spinning in the dust, speed safely away.

Understandably rattled, and feeling fortunate to have made off without injury, Butch promptly phoned the police. Only the next day did they decide to mosey on out to the ranch, calling a meeting with the War Vets. While Butch stood next to the cops, the leader of the thugs angrily told him he was lucky to have gotten away, that they would have killed him if he hadn't escaped.

"What have you got against me?" an astonished Butch asked in bewilderment.

"It was agreed there'd be no game scouts in the area around the dip," the leader shouted. "Scouts have been patrolling that part of the ranch which is off limits to all except us."

"But I didn't know anything about this," Butch explained, keeping his composure despite such a deal sounding dubious. "Why didn't you come talk to me? We could have worked through the mix-up without fighting."

The police, taking the side of the War Vets as usual, then chastised Butch for allowing scouts in the area. And that was the end of it.

Butch's close call was all the more unnerving because it happened only weeks after another farmer had been killed. Henry Elsworth and his twenty-year-old son had just pulled up to the main gate of their farm, when armed men sprang from the bushes and opened fire. The son, who was driving, leapt from the truck to take cover, only to collapse to the ground when both legs were shattered by bullets. As his seventy-year-old father made a move to go to him, he was also sprayed with rounds, his dying words imploring, "Please, just leave us alone. We'll leave the country tomorrow."

Darren and I were naturally distressed when we met Sarah as she pulled into our drive. Her pretty brown eyes were wide with her midnight flight, her Jackie O hair ruffled. Her flustered state wasn't helped by our barrage of questions, since all we knew was that everyone living on Humani—other than the hundreds of workers who simply couldn't get away—had been forced to flee their homes. Sarah's pickup was loaded with chests of her mother's keepsakes, photos, important documents and other valuables. While we carried everything into the house, we pressed Sarah for more details.

She recounted how that evening, a dozen of them had stayed on the banks of the Turgwe until well after dark. Sarah's dad Roger was one of the first to make his way home, and upon walking through his front door the phone promptly rang. In broken English the caller exclaimed, "Where have you been? I've been trying to contact you. Get out now—there's going to be trouble!" Roger didn't know the caller and was not the type to become rattled. But not wanting to take chances, quickly returned to the river to tell everyone they must disappear from the ranch. To this they all scrambled home and loaded up what they could, twenty pickups then speeding off in every direction.

What kind of trouble did the person mean? And who did Roger think the caller might be? Did everyone make it safely away? Sarah couldn't answer our questions, and was tired and unnerved. The three of us went uneasily off to bed, saying a little prayer that their exodus would end up being a needless exercise.

The following evening, when the three of us settled onto our veranda in the warmth of late day, the dogs lying contently at our feet,

Sarah calmly told us more. The latest troubles began a couple weeks earlier, when War Vets on Humani had coyly asked the ranch's game scouts to have a meeting. When the too-trusting scouts showed up, they were immediately jumped on and overpowered. In the tussle their small guns and bush knives were wrested from them, and they were shackled with their own handcuffs meant for poachers. The War Vets then proceeded to beat the scouts so mercilessly, that afterwards they had to be carted off to the hospital.

A week later, when most of the battered game scouts were back at work, the War Vets had the audacity to ask for another "meeting". Naturally the memory of the last painful and degrading encounter was still fresh in the scouts' minds. "Yeah, all right," they said, "let's have us another 'meeting.'"

The scouts' shotguns were loaded with birdshot as a minimal defense against animal attacks, although the pellets were pretty useless against a charging elephant or angry lion. At this second encounter, when the thugs made a lunge towards them the scouts unhesitantly opened fire. At close range even the mild birdshot was potent, with one of the attackers hit in the face and another in the stomach, although none were killed.

This time the police speedily appeared at the ranch, confiscating every gun on the place, and demanding to know who was responsible for sending scouts into that area. Whoever it was, would be arrested on a charge of inciting violence. This had happened to another rancher we knew when some of his workers had clashed with War Vets. The police had purposefully arrested him at the beginning of the weekend, so he'd have to spend a few days in jail, waiting until Monday when a magistrate could issue bail.

Even though the scouts had acted on their own, Roger told the police, "I sent them there. I'm the one responsible." But the cops were not happy with this answer. What they really wanted was to arrest one or two of the young white chaps who worked under him, knowing they couldn't intimidate Roger by acting against him directly. For one thing, despite being a man of few words, his forceful character unnerved them. Roger's Shona nickname was Shumba, or lion, because of his sometimes fierce disposition. Not to mention, years earlier he'd survived hand to claw combat with an enraged, wounded lion. During the many years the local police had been involved with various incidents on Humani, they had never gained the psychological upper hand when dealing with Roger.

The other thing on the policemen's minds, was when trying to intimidate someone, they knew it more effective to harass that person's family or those close to him, rather than simply roughing up the person himself. The cops thought they would have more leverage against Roger if they held a couple of his young safari guides in custody, rather than Roger himself. But without a stitch of evidence against any of them, the police had to satisfy themselves with the arrest of four game scouts.

The night of that shooting, "the Humani crowd"—as Roger's family and those working for him were known—had slept in the bush. Sarah had been among them, and now told us how a convoy of twenty vehicles had crossed the rushing Turgwe, half going east, half west, to spend the night hidden away from the incensed and unpredictable War Vets. Sarah said her aunt, who lived on Humani with her husband, was the most upset about being uprooted from her home. I remembered Sarah's aunt sitting on the sandy bank of the Turgwe, carefully unpacking her china tea set, her flowered dress blowing softly in the breeze. She was a gentle lady who desired only to live a quiet, simple life on the ranch where she was born. But her home was on African soil and its shifting sands had no sympathy for such "selfish" longings.

The week after scouts had shot at War Vets, Roger received the anonymous phone call. He insisted everyone leave Humani who could. That way if there was a clash, the police could not then blame and harass one of them as a means of putting pressure on Roger. As everyone fled that night Sarah came to stay with us, while Roger and his son drove into remote bush to pass the hours until dawn.

In the ranch village, five hundred workers and families were at the mercy of the War Vets. The beatings and intimidation had continued without let up, and a shroud of fear continuously hung over their lives. On this particular night, many of them also fled to hide in the wilderness.

While Darren, Sarah and I sat talking on our veranda, comforted by an evening breeze and surrounded by flowers and lilting birdsong, such dreadful events seemed incomprehensible.

Then as the sun touched the horizon, Darren's cell phone rang.

"Hi Darren, this is Guy. I'm trying to track down my sister Sarah. Is she there with you?"

"Wow, Guy, how are you doing? Yeah, Sarah's here, but exactly where are you?"

"My dad and I are still out in the bush. Luckily we can get a cell phone signal with the antenna on the truck. But we're fine, other than being eaten alive by mosquitoes last night!"

"Well, at least they're all right," Sarah said, after talking to her brother and dad for a few minutes. "The police have asked Roger to meet with them at his house. So he'll probably be going there soon and hopefully this can all be straightened out."

"Does your dad know who might be at the house?" Darren said warily. "If a bunch of angry War Vets are there and things get out of control, the police will be outnumbered and not able to protect him."

"Humm, that's a good point. My dad probably doesn't know what the situation is there," Sarah said thoughtfully. "Maybe I should suggest he not go."

Then Darren came up with a good idea. "You know, why don't I call your dad's place and see if anyone picks up the phone. If the cook is there he can tell us what's happening."

We didn't think anyone would actually be hanging around the house at this tense hour, so were surprised when the phone was promptly answered, although it turned out to be a stranger. Playing it cool, Darren simply asked if he could speak to Roger. To this he was told, "Sorry, he's not here. But can I take a message for him?"

Darren's friendly inquiring soon revealed he was talking to a policeman. The helpful fellow then informed him they were expecting Roger to arrive anytime.

After Darren politely said good-bye, our conversation turned into an only half-joking debate about which "visitors" might be sleeping in Roger's bed that night, and what prized possessions might "disappear". At least Ann's most cherished memorabilia was safely tucked away with us. "Can you imagine when these overseas safari clients call the house and the cops answer the phone?" Sarah laughed, trying to stay light-hearted about it all.

The next day, we were relieved to hear that Roger hadn't come to any harm at "the meeting", the gist of it being the War Vets insisted he hand over a large portion of the ranch. They'd graciously let him keep a part of his property, so he'd stay and maintain the boreholes for water and pay the electricity bills. The situation was still volatile and Roger told Sarah he didn't want anyone coming back to Humani just yet. He and his son were to pass another night in the woods.

By her second evening with us, and after sitting around for many more anxious hours, Sarah was losing the last of her patience, now completely fed up with the harassment her family had to endure.

"I don't understand it," she vented in frustration. "How can a country with the most peaceful people in Africa become like this?"

"But Sarah, it isn't most of the people causing the problems," Darren answered as soothingly as he could. "It's these twenty thousand so-called War Vets, really just government-paid thugs, running rampant and creating all this havoc."

"You'd think though, the other twelve million would do something about it," I commented casually. But I knew why that hadn't happened, as we'd had these conversations plenty of times before. I remembered one evening when sweet-faced Courtney, a just-out-of-college Peace Corp volunteer from California, had visited with Darren and me. She was telling us about her difficulties when it came to accomplishing almost anything in Zim.

"How can I say it?" she had said, searching for the right word. "It's that Zimbabweans are, well, such *passive* people." And another visitor had once thoughtfully observed, "Zimbabweans give the impression of being very laid back. On the whole, quite unassertive."

As a friend said to me, it was because of Zimbabweans' gentle characters we could live in a country with virtually no law enforcement and still crime was low. Most wanted to avoid conflict of any kind, which generally makes for a pleasant society. But this same serene and unconfrontational collective nature, also made it easy for trouble-making elements to run unchecked.

As Sarah dwelled upon her family's situation, she told us how her grandfather Jimmy had warned of this very thing. It was back in the 1920s that a young Jimmy had immigrated to Zimbabwe, when forced to abandon his home in Turkey because of turmoil there. At the time, the undeveloped land that later became Humani ranch was in the middle of an area labeled "Unfit for Habitation". No one had wanted to live there amongst the dangers of malaria and sleeping sickness, marauding lions and devastating livestock diseases, unrelenting heat and little water.

Over the mid twentieth century when Jimmy lived in Zimbabwe, the two societies that existed there, the Western and the tribal, came into conflict more and more. In 1980 after years of civil war, the two merged and a new society intertwining both was born, one of many changes that set the country on a different path than anything before.

"In 1980, my grandfather Jimmy told his children and grandchildren we had only twenty years left in this country and on Humani," Sarah solemnly said to Darren and me. "Well, it's sad to say, but I guess he knew exactly what he was talking about."

That is, he predicted that those who strove for a productive future would be overrun by those such as the Mugabe regime, whose only goal was bleed every last drop from Zimbabwe's land and her people.

Chapter Thirty-five

|||||||||||||||||||||||||||||||||||||||||||||||||||||||||||||||||||||||||||||||||||||||||||||||||||||||||||||||

B y early 2001 Mugabe was intent on wiping out the last institutions standing in his way to total despotic rule: the judiciary and the free press.

In truth, I was surprised he hadn't slapped the leg irons on the judiciary years before. Throughout the ongoing dramas over the question of land and its ownership, they had firmly backed up the legal code, even when going directly against Mugabe's wishes. A judge standing up so bravely for the law could pay dearly for his ethical deeds, with unthinkable harm to himself or his family.

Mugabe was already seething with the judiciary over the land issue, when they further inflamed his anger by ruling against his ZANU-PF party in election disputes. The MDC had filed complaints with the courts saying ZANU-PF had unfairly won parliamentary seats through intimidation and other tactics. In most cases the judges agreed with the MDC and ruled against the president's party.

Steam must have been shooting straight out Mugabe's ears as he heard each new court ruling, putting him near to spontaneous combustion. In a desperate attempt at self preservation, he began to harass and threaten judges, pressing the most "rebellious" into early retirement.

In March 2001, an alarmed group from the International Bar Association came to Zimbabwe to hold discussions with Mugabe. When they put forth their concerns about the land crisis, he instantly cut them off. He informed them the issue was a political matter, and as such did not fall within the domain of the judiciary. They didn't push the point, as this was really one of their lesser worries. Their main concern, as stated in their report, was the "intimidation of judges", particularly the practice of forcing them to resign, along with the "attacks and derogatory remarks against the judiciary and lawyers". They also wanted to be assured there'd be no "manipulation in the selection and appointment of judges" and that the courts' decisions would be enforced. Well, I thought to myself, these were certainly nice thoughts, but only wishful thinking for Zimbabwe's immediate future.

As can be imagined, the free press had plenty to say about Mugabe and his government, which he found utterly intolerable. For most of his reign he'd been spared the agitation of a critical media, because in the past radio stations and papers had all been government-owned. But in the mid '90s when the country was booming, private newspapers were among the businesses to spring up. He soon realized what a thorn in his side the media could be. When an independent radio station tried to set up shop in late 2000, Mugabe promptly had their equipment seized, the owners and commentators threatened, and their operations shut down.

Now, any non-government paper paid a hefty price for its independent voice. *The Daily News* overtook the government's *Herald* in popularity, and as a reward for its success, their offices were bombed. Not stopping there, the News' journalists and editors were violently harassed and charged with criminal defamation, and even worse, occasionally imprisoned for a couple days of horrific torture.

The vibrant '90s also saw international magazines making their way onto store shelves, along with the availability of satellite TV, where before had only been the government station. Now with CNN, BBC, *Time* and *Newsweek* unleashed, Mugabe's control over the news was intolerably hamstrung. His reaction was to expel foreign journalists from the country, particularly those from his hated nemesis, Britain. Some were given only twenty-four hours to leave. Hardly enough time to pack a suitcase, let alone the homes they'd lived in for years.

I read an article by a journalist who'd lived in Zim for ten years when she was suddenly banished by Mugabe. In exile, she sentimentally wrote about first arriving in the country, and her excitement about this land seemingly on the way up. She told friends back home Zimbabwe was an example that Africa could work, with its tidy towns, clean parks, decent roads, railways, hospitals and schools. Children were educated, people had plenty to eat, and she looked forward to her future here.

But the idyllic détente began to disintegrate. With an election upcoming, she described how Mugabe's government went about systematically destroying the judiciary, free press, and rule of law, and with cold-hearted disregard for its citizens, used its private militia to unleash violence, turning Zimbabwe into an uncivilized land.

In poignant words she said it was only her concern for her child's safekeeping that kept her from challenging her deportation. She declared it to be a time to stand up to bullies, before they destroyed a country whose plunge could take with it the last hopes of a continent.

* * * * *

The once prospering drilling ventures of Darren's friend Craig weren't going well. Only a couple years earlier the Aussie had turned a comfortable profit, but now most of his equipment sat idle at his base in Harare. Eventually he ended up with no choice but to tell his workers many would be laid off. Rather than being upset, however, they were excited at the prospect of the lump sum payoff required by law. They weren't concerned about the business going under, probably figuring they'd find a job elsewhere.

While Craig tried to scrape enough cash together for the payouts, the workers became impatient. After a couple weeks, although still on the payroll, they were frustrated at not yet receiving their stack of cash. War Vets caught wind of their dilemma and offered assistance. With a thumbs up from the workers, Craig's equipment in Harare was promptly confiscated and carted off to ZANU-PF headquarters.

This forced Craig into a "negotiation" of sorts, although with War Vets involved it was more a campaign of threats and aggression. In the meantime, a drilling project came up that could have provided cash to pay the workers, but with his equipment all hauled off that wasn't an option.

Meanwhile, another friend of Darren's who owned a transport business also found himself besieged by War Vets. Months earlier he had fired an employee for theft. Although the worker did not deny it, the chap now had War Vets "representing" him, insisting he be paid a healthy payout. The owner was determined to not give in to their bullying, but it was the same as dealing with the mob. These government thugs dropped in at the company's office daily to disrupt operations and harangue the employees. Finally worn down, the owner paid the blackmail just to get the thugs out of his business. The War Vets then took half the bounty for themselves as compensation for their "services".

This seemed to be how Mugabe's latest terrorizing tactic began. War Vets looked for opportunities to "help" disgruntled workers with complaints against employers. Maybe Mugabe thought this was a way to win over the labor constituency, since the opposition MDC was largely labor union backed. Mugabe obviously felt he needed to lure workers over to his side, his supporters having mainly been rural peasants.

This harassment of businesses over labor disputes seemed to be working so well, the ruling party soon expanded it to a general aggression against companies. And then insanely, even to the workers. Employees from a few large corporations were marched to the downtown headquarters of ZANU-PF for political "reeducation".

Finally, the harassment simply became extortion. In one typical case, War Vets descended upon Phillips International and demanded money from the regional manager. When he phoned his boss in Amsterdam he was immediately told to just pay the gangsters, since it wasn't worth risking his life. These early successes of extorting cash from companies only fueled the War Vets' fervor.

Increasingly, a steady stream of business owners and managers were hauled from their offices and marched to ZANU-PF headquarters. There they were slapped around a bit until they willingly wrote out a generous check, not wanting to find out the consequences if they didn't. For some, this was the final blow to an already struggling business, forcing them into liquidation.

Soon the bankrupt owner had War Vets pushing him for payment on behalf of his laid-off employees. By law he had to pay it anyway, but this tactic meant the thugs could demand a fee from the workers. For one person we knew, a couple days after his staff had been happy to receive their payouts, they showed up at the company offices wanting their jobs back, too. The owner patiently explained that his company was in bankruptcy, he was closing down. The workers were upset at this news. Why wasn't he keeping his business going? They couldn't understand why he didn't just carry on.

The painful swelling of unemployment had created a morose and surly populous, and a desperate Mugabe lashed out at businesses. The government made ridiculous statements, saying companies would not be allowed to close or lay off workers, as if money to stay afloat could magically appear. One threat published in the government newspaper read, "The militants have vowed to assault any managers who cause unemployment in Zimbabwe."

Through it all, I sat as peacefully as ever on my veranda in Chiredzi, thinking the bizarre stories I heard from Harare were truly insane. Here Zim's economy was on its dying legs and the government was intent on beating out its last gasps of breath. Even more unbelievable was the terrorizing of the people. We knew Mugabe was doing it to stay in power, which should translate into winning the support of the populous, but his tactics were the logic of a madman.

Soon, what became known as the Company Invasions were expanded to include charitable organizations. A non-profit food bank was "invaded" and its stores carried away. The Zimbabwe director of CARE International, a Canadian, was threatened and taken hostage. Hours later, he was only released when he agreed to pay a "settlement", supposedly on behalf of disgruntled former employees. When the Canadian High Commissioner tried to intervene on the director's behalf, even he was roughed up. Many other aid agencies, including the Red Cross, were harassed and some of their managers held until ransoms were paid.

This extortion campaign was going so well, the leader of the War Vets, Chenjerai Hunzvi, publicly announced that embassies of foreign countries not supporting Mugabe's regime would be the next targets. The Zimbabwe government followed this up with a reckless statement, saying it would not step in to protect these delegations if they were perceived as supporting the political opposition. This raised the eyebrows of more than a few people in high places and foreign officials quickly phoned the presidential palace, looking for immediate reassurance that Mugabe fully understood his obligations under the Vienna Convention, requiring him to protect foreign embassies and their staff in Zimbabwe.

With the Company Invasions dealing a fatal blow to the economy, not to mention Zimbabwe's international reputation and credit rating, the Minister of Industry and International Trade resigned. Frustrated with Mugabe's campaign of lawlessness, he prudently made his announcement while on a trip to South Africa, and from there, he and his family made their way to the safety of the United States.

Then, quite suddenly, although the Farm Invasions pressed on, the Company Invasions simply ceased. There were whispers saying Mugabe's ministers had talked him into it. However it happened, it made one thing clear. What Mugabe had characterized as spontaneous chaos beyond his control, an "uprising" of the populous, was really premeditated mayhem released on the country and its people. And there was certainly someone out there, who had the power to make the violence stop in an instant.

Zimbabwe had enough natural wealth to lift her people and their land from the ashes, if only for the want of a moderately responsible government. Was this simple necessity too much to ask?

Chapter Thirty-six

‖‖‖

No matter how desperate things become in Africa, the pace doesn't change and, well, she still insists we take time to smell those daisies. With the Easter holidays upon us, our workshop, like many businesses, was closing its doors for ten days.

As Mugabe's latest tactics plunged the capital into turmoil, I felt an urgency to spend time with the Africa special to me. I stubbornly wanted to hold on to that beautiful Africa, but as my hand reached out I could feel her slipping away. I was grasping, clinging, trying to keep this friend without whom I'd be lost. I shook my head no, at the thought of facing the road ahead without the rich, poignant, flourishing Africa.

For Easter, Darren and I decided to spend a few days in the Eastern Highlands. The place was sentimental to me, since its southern end was where we'd first tried to buy a farm. I'd also spent enjoyable times in the northernmost district with its fine fishing and golfing, and the rugged Nyanga National Park. The park's high-air mood was restful, its spacious mountains lightly treed, a scattering of charcoal boulders peeking out from a carpet of yellow grass. Beyond the park the mountains became steeper, the winding highway north hypnotic, as it skirted the mountainsides with wild Mozambique on the other side. Places like this is what kept the life flowing in my veins.

Having yet to explore the central Highlands, I booked us a room at the Chimanimani Hotel for our visit. Before heading off, Darren loaded a drum of diesel on the back of our pickup. I couldn't remember when we'd last bought fuel at the pump. Some time the previous year anyway. Darren managed to keep us going by buying from friends who had storage tanks. It was a sign of the times when an exclusive hotel in Harare advertised, "double room, breakfast, newspapers, free downtown parking, tea and coffee, and forty liters of fuel."

April was my favorite time of year, especially in the Lowveld, where the intense heat of summer finally eases to a more gentle warmth. The butterflies all venture out, fanning in soft air no longer oppressive with heat. In vibrant bloom are yellow sunflowers the size of dinner plates, looking as perky in the wide acres of commercial farms, as in the humbler squares dotting communal lands. Although April was early autumn, the flora of the Lowveld celebrated their release from the stress of summer by adorning themselves in bursts of new blossoms.

As Darren and I set out on the highway, I felt a sense of relief seeing the land green and healthy. The rains, thank goodness, had finally showed up in March. After those first few showers in late November there hadn't been any real rain in southern Zimbabwe. But the dams had still been full, and the commercial farmers around Chiredzi growing irrigated sugar cane hadn't been too concerned. Rain isn't reliable in this corner of the world, so its absence now and then was to be expected. With plenty of water in dams, town dwellers like me weren't in danger of running out either. Only the subsistence farmers, trying to grow their patches of corn, suffered from the lack of rain. Even the few around Chiredzi who had access to irrigation didn't seem to use it much, instead relying on rainfall to water their crops. But when the showers finally came in March, it arrived too late to revive the stunted cornstalks planted months earlier.

As we leisurely motored eastward, we saw many folk ambling along the highway and in the surrounding bush, all carrying a bucket or large basket. The women balanced theirs atop their heads, hips gliding side to side in smooth tempo as they walked. Everyone was collecting mopane (moe-paw-nee) worms, from the millions on a slow migration down the tree trunks and over the ground. Even the paved highway was a-squiggle with them. Actually, they weren't worms at all, but pretty orange caterpillars that would turn into Emperor moths. They were called mopane worms because they live in the stout mopane trees. The plump caterpillars, over two inches long, were considered an annual bounty by locals, relied upon to provide a nourishing dose of much needed protein.

The highway made a long sweep round to head north, and we now skirted the western side of the Highlands. Its hills rose up on our right, while spread to our left was the flat farmland of the Middle Save agri-scheme. Moments before we'd crossed the bridge spanning the wide Save River where the aftermath of Cyclone Eline was still to be seen. In an unnerving reminder of nature's brutal strength, house-size wads of tangled brush clung thickly around the bridge's high pillars.

Luckily we weren't in hurry, because when we spied a small pile of rocks in the middle of our lane up ahead, Darren slowed the truck. Usually we simply veered around the various obstacles that regularly dot the highway, not giving it a second thought. As we came close to the rocks, however, we could just see a small and simply-made sign balanced in front of the pile. On it, an arrow pointed to the left. Obviously we were being directed to an alternate route, probably something to do with the bridge up ahead, although we could see no reason for it.

We found ourselves following a crudely made trail down to the riverbed. There we discovered concrete had been roughly poured over a collection of boulders to create a makeshift, and we liked to assume temporary, causeway. As our truck slowly bumped its way over the shallow river, my jaw dropped at a most unbelievable sight. To our right, the mangled remains of the concrete highway bridge towered above us, with several massive chunks scattered in the ravine below. Most terrifying of all, from midway of the span to the high opposite bank, the bridge was missing. Only the cement wall that sealed the bank was still intact. With horror, I realized if we hadn't slowed for that pile of rocks and seen the tiny arrow, we would have continued to fatefully speed along. Only to suddenly vault into open air and dive face-on into the concrete wall.

The sight was a revelation. A reminder that while Africa's essence was in danger of being snuffed out, by tying my fate to hers, in some unexpected instant I, too, could be extinguished.

We weren't as surprised to find the next bridge also damaged by last year's cyclone. We came cruising up to it at a good clip, but Darren slowed to five mph when we saw the asphalt gone. The rough surface of jagged stone was nearly undrivable, sending our pickup into spasms, even at a turtle's crawl. In this case, the bridge had been simply "repaired" by piling numerous large rocks into the gap, then shoveling dirt in between. As we bounced our way over, putting our Isuzu's suspension to the test, I shook my head at the notion that this was actually the main highway. An all too lurid spectacle of the depths to which paradise had crumbled.

We soon turned off and began to curve our way up through mountains eastward. The air below had been saturated with warmth, but as we began to climb it became crisply cool. The difference in temperature after only minutes of driving felt unearthly. Also strange was seeing moss growing on trees in southern Africa, known for being hot and arid. Yet this is what I treasured about her, the joy of always discovery something new and amazing.

As we steadily made our way towards the Chimanimani district, the valleys tightened and the mountains packed in close, becoming steep. The main industry was timber and the mountainsides were either laid with tidy blankets of tree plantations, or left as dense bush. The idea of living on these precipitous slopes did look wholly impractical. Otherwise, I was sure humanity's sprawl would have taken over here, too.

After checking in at the hotel, Darren and I were impatient to begin our vacation by seeing some sights. The park's entrance was not too far, so we decided to head out at once. An easy few minutes down a paved road took us past a sign telling us the park lay only a couple more miles. We forged ahead on a well-maintained dirt road, cutting a path through neat lines of wattle and pine.

But after twenty minutes of unchanging scenery of cloned timber, we wondered if we were off track. Doubling back, at the mileage sign seen earlier we realized we should have turned there, meaning through a farmer's front gate. Really, I thought, is this the gateway to a major national park? A hint of how little pride the government took in a national treasure.

I felt like a trespasser as we now pushed our way between rows of coffee trees, still not believing this rutted path was actually the main road to the popular park. But I should have guessed, now realizing the well-groomed lane we first followed was on land owned by a timber company, who kept their roadways up. But because the park was a government enterprise, a rough track was only to be expected.

Despite this dubious start, when we reached the foothills the woodsy and lush highland terrain was simply awesome. A heavy mist had started to come down, however, and the track was turning into slippery mud. For a brief moment we considered going back, but since we had only just managed to get trekking in the right direction, wanted to creep on. The beauty of the place was too alluring to resist.

As I looked with eagerness ahead, rising before us through the mist were mountainsides of dense bush, healthy in deep green. As the track gently climbed, we crossed several crystal brooks that quickly disappeared underneath the lushness. The terrain soon became tightly packed mountains with narrow valleys like high ravines, the track ahead twisting enticingly along a vertical slope. Forest pressed all around, and next to us the lower parts of the trees were without branches. I peeked through airy undergrowth to the nearby mountains, green valleys curving in between. While I looked on, a misty blanket settled over the hilltops and into the next valley, closing the world in snug around us.

The heavy mist turned to light rain as we gained altitude. The track was holding up surprisingly well, mainly because a bit of gravel had been sprinkled in the more vulnerable spots. But I was still nervous, as there was no way to turn around on the narrow, winding track. Nor did I see a single side barrier to protect a vehicle from pitching over the near vertical edge. Whenever our pickup lost its grip on a slippery patch, I'd envision us sliding perilously backwards, before catapulting over the verge. But inevitably the truck quickly gained traction again, and the path ahead always looked sound enough.

The rain came down heavier the higher we climbed, and every other minute we thought about turning back, if that was even possible. By the tachometer we were only yards from the park's front gates, where at least there should be a parking lot to turn around in safely.

We edged around a ninety degree bend and started up another span of slippery track, expecting the park entry to appear around the corner. As we crept carefully along, we peered before us through the tunnel-like growth. Could it be that the track up ahead was gone? Oh, my gosh—Yes! To our utter disbelief, it looked as if a large washout had come pouring down the mountain, ripping a gully like an earthquake fault line through the road. Stunned, we knew there was absolutely no way to continue forward. Once again, I felt the pang of being cut off from that which sustained me, the heart of Africa.

But now what to do? If we tried to reverse down the slippery track, sooner or later on one of those ninety degree bends, we'd end up launching over the edge. There was no other choice—we had to turn around. To do this Darren first had to back, or rather slide, down to a spot behind us where the path was a measly few inches wider. I kept a white-knuckle grip on the dashboard as he then began to maneuver around. As the pickup turned ever so slightly, it seemed we were hanging dangerously out in space, with only the far drop of the mountain before us.

This was all too nerve-wracking. I had to either escape the truck, or risk heart failure, even though the trees were thick enough that if we did tumble over the brink, we probably wouldn't roll far.

Once standing out in the drumming rain, I felt some relief at seeing two feet of track still in front of the tires. Plus a small lip to help keep them from sliding over. I could hardly watch though, as

Darren maneuvered our two-wheel-drive pickup around, inch by inch. The edge of the track was not packed, and the wheels were more inclined to dig into the soft ground than pull forward. With each turn of the wheel, the truck slid a bit sideways down the steep path of now slimy mud, and in the end, I had to give a few heave-hos at the back to coax it into gripping the loose ground.

Yeah! Thankfully we were now parallel with the road again. Looking at the space in which Darren had turned I couldn't believe he'd actually done it. Even more mind-boggling was the fact we'd been lured into such treacherous situation. With my heart rate still in overdrive, I wanted to shout that if the government wasn't going to keep up the park's safety, then they should simply close it to visitors. No matter where I went I seemed caught in paradise's crumble, scrambling to stay ahead of the implosion before it snatched me up, too.

Darkness swallowed the mountains behind us, as we arrived back at the hotel. Covered in mud and famished, Darren and I hurried to clean up and head downstairs. The hotel had been built in the Fifties and had a distinctly aging colonial look. Although the bedrooms were comfortable enough, the downstairs lounges were musty and deserted, so we passed them by and went directly to the high-ceilinged dining hall. Too brightly lit, the expanse seemed more like a conference room than an inviting restaurant. To us the outside patio, its stones laid on the edge of a hill, looked more appealing for dinner.

The evening was nippy with a saturating mist, so we pushed a table close to the wall under an overhang. The waiters and other guests surely thought us crazy, but we found it relaxing in the fresh air, looking out to a hushed, black night. The gardens below were buried in low clouds, only a few hazy spotlights reminding us we weren't perched on the rim of the world.

Darren smoked a pipe in reflection and its aromatic scent hung in the moist air. I, too, was consumed by my thoughts. How wasteful was this destruction of Zimbabwe? Here was a country gifted with the diversity of resources to provide prosperity for both her people and unparalleled nature, but instead, a rabid government was intent on bleeding every drop of life from the land.

The lights of the hotel carried for only a few feet before us, and I peered ahead into an infinite darkness. The void pressed like a black hole consuming everything. My friend Africa was out there, but part of her was vanishing, the emptiness and loss feeling tangible. She is slipping away, I thought in despair.

The next morning we edged our way through the mountains on the other side of town, headed to the famous Bridal Veil Falls. With such things as the highway turning precarious, the wilderness cut off and Africa withering, every moment felt precious. Rounding each bend I expectantly gazed ahead, anxious to arrive. Finally, tucked at the end of a secluded hollow, I was granted a riveting sight. One hundred and sixty-five feet of crystal water tumbling down a natural sculpture of polished rock, before settling into a shadowy pool.

I stepped out of the truck and into a magical scene. This was her, the Africa I knew, and my heart skipped a beat at seeing her again. Before me, the falls throbbed with ceaseless power. Standing at the edge of a green glen, I looked towards the falls and its clear pool, a brook drifting out. Strong msasa trees along the stony creek shaded its twinkling water, as it curved through an enchanting hollow. Underfoot, a multitude of fuzzy white caterpillars squiggled in the emerald grass, looking enticingly soft to touch. Nature had created a hypnotic mix, with this rhythmic beat and filtered sun, perfumed air and dewy lushness.

I felt swept up in the serenity, where Africa talked to me like she used to, when she was strong, healthy, full of promise. Regaining a lightness to my step, I followed a footpath to the base of the falls. At the pool's rim the spray was pleasantly cool, the cascade's vigor pulsing in my ears. With this natural altar towering before me, I bent down to touch the mirrored water. Here in nature's cathedral, I could hear Africa's voice again. My mind spoke back: Yes, whatever happens, I will always remember you this way. And I needed to believe, for my own peace of mind, that after all she had done for me, in small ways, and in hidden spots, her spirit would keep going. That what was beautiful and good about her would not be lost forever. One day, surely, the puzzle of how to create prosperity for all would be solved. Whatever the future held, she had made me, and for that I was eternally grateful. Thank you my friend, Africa, for making me whole. For completing my soul, while giving me the best of yourself, in what could be your last days of splendor.

Epilogue

||||||||||||||||||||||||||||||||||||||||||||||||||||||||||||||||||||||||||||||||||

n the years since this story ends, Zimbabwe continues to decline. As of this writing Robert Mugabe, at age 90, is still president. Zimbabwe's elections have all been tainted with varying degrees of violence, intimidation and foul play. The country's economy languishes, her people living more dismally then when I first visited over twenty years ago.

All of my friends have lost their farms. They cannot say exactly what became of the land previously under their care, since they do not venture there. Most farms in Zimbabwe have either been given to Mugabe insiders, or become dotted with huts and goats, steadily deforested by the struggling poor. While Sam and Janet still live in their house, the fence between them and the communal land is gone. The ranch is now scattered with peasant folk, its arid acres void of birds and animals, the place looking like the desolate land that used to be on "the other side of the fence."

The collective ranches of the Save Valley Wildlife Conservancy, such as Humani and Hammond, have so far managed to hold back a tide of total devastation. It's a touch and go business. At times forces such as politics and human needs have made it harder to protect the wildlife, while at times the pendulum has swung in nature's favor. Still, it is a tenuous existence.

Oh, and as for me . . . well, that's another story.

HOMEBOUND
PUBLICATIONS

At Homebound Publications we recognize the impor-
tance of going home to gather from the stores of old wisdom to help nourish our lives in this modern era. We choose
to lend voice to those individuals who endeavor to translate
the old truths into new context and keep alive through the
written word ways of life that are now endangered. Our titles
introduce insights concerning mankind's present internal,
social and ecological dilemmas.

It is our intention at Homebound Publications to revive
contemplative storytelling. We publish full-length intro-
spective works of: non-fiction, essay collections, epic verse,
short story collections, journals, travel writing, and novels.
In our fiction titles our intention is to introduce new per-
spectives that will directly aid mankind in the trials we face
at present.

It is our belief that the stories humanity lives by give
both context and perspective to our lives. Some older stories, while well-known to the generations, no longer resonate
with the heart of the modern man nor do they address the
present situation we face individually and as a global village.
Homebound chooses titles that balance a reverence for the
old sensibilities; while at the same time presenting new per-
spectives by which to live.

CPSIA information can be obtained at www.ICGtesting.com
Printed in the USA
LVOW05s1755220614

391149LV00001B/227/P